love from

Jeremy

x x x x

the open garden

the open garden

louise earwaker & neil robertson

australian gardens and **their gardeners**

A SUE HINES BOOK   ALLEN & UNWIN

Dedicated to the gardeners who made this book possible, and to all the gardeners of Australia

Gordon Ford beside the main pool at Fülling.

HALF-TITLE: Providing a colourful foreground for the house on Horse Island, prostrate *Callistemon* 'White Anzac' and *Melaleuca* 'Robin Redbreast' surround a birdbath, with kangaroo paws and *Leptospermum* 'Rubrum' behind.

FRONTISPIECE: In the garden of Cooramilla, an engraved tablet by sculptor Ian Marr nestles among brachyscomes and a specie gazania.

First published in 2000

Allen & Unwin
9 Atchison Street
St Leonards NSW 2065
Australia
Phone: (61 2) 8425 0100
Fax: (61 2) 9906 2218
Email: frontdesk@allen-unwin.com.au
Web: http://www.allen-unwin.com.au

National Library of Australia
Cataloguing-in-Publication entry:
Earwaker, Louise.
The open garden.
Includes index.
ISBN 1 86508 142 6.
1. Gardening – Australia. I. Robertson, Neil. II. Title.
635.0994

Designed by Ruth Grüner
Typeset by Ruth Grüner
Indexed by Russell Brooks
Photography by Leigh Clapp, Trisha Dixon, Mike Gillam, John Hay, Merv Hodge, Geoff Lea, Michael McCoy, Alex Makeyev, Annie Mayo, David Sandison, Marg Thornell and Gerry Whitmont
Printed in China by Everbest

10 9 8 7 6 5 4 3 2 1

foreword

This lovely book is the voice of gardeners all over Australia.

It explores the relationship between the owner and his or her garden through their own words.

These many different gardens are the result of idealistic creation and therapeutic hard labour. They encompass everything from dreams for an enchanted place for children, to the chase for a collection of a particular plant. The gardeners tell how they themselves have been influenced by other gardeners, and how they have responded to a seemingly limitless originality of planting combinations and design.

The gardens here have all opened their gates for Australia's Open Garden Scheme, but they have been developed not primarily for public consumption but for personal enjoyment and pleasure, for philosophising, or for putting the heart at ease. They respond to their environment, which in Australia is hugely diverse.

Australia's Open Garden Scheme was established in 1987 to provide for Australia what the National Gardens Scheme and Scotland's Gardens Scheme have given to Britain. Its mission is 'to promote the knowledge and pleasure of gardens and gardening across Australia' by opening our finest private gardens to the public on one or more days a year. The owners are on hand to discuss planning and planting, and to answer any questions by visitors. This access to firsthand information has been so hugely successful that the Scheme has expanded into every state and territory of Australia.

For the public our garden days offer a rare treat and the opportunity to see gardens of a calibre and diversity only found in private hands. We believe the Scheme has been instrumental in stimulating the very strong interest in gardening presently reflected in the many television and radio programmes, magazines and books that are devoted to a celebration of Australia's gardens. In our own case, the continuing increase in the number of people who visit our gardens is ample evidence of this interest.

The Open Garden is just a sample of the beauty and diversity of the thousands of gardens that have opened for the Scheme over the last fourteen years.

The book's beautiful illustrations complement the gardens as described by their creators, and whet the appetite of the 'would be' and 'could be' in us all. The text is an eloquent description of the breadth and depth of knowledge we have beyond our garden gates.

We must all be grateful to Neil Robertson and Louise Earwaker for weaving together this wonderful tapestry of gardeners and gardens for us to enjoy.

Tamie Fraser
PRESIDENT
AUSTRALIA'S OPEN GARDEN SCHEME

In an entrancing spring scene at Pigeon Hill, coral pink and yellow deciduous azaleas grown from seed contrast with a foreground of evergreen 'Blue Diamond' azaleas.

contents

foreword v

introduction ix

building on tradition 1
manar 4
salisbury court 10
woolongoon 15
cherry tree 20
ashfield 25
wallcliffe house 31
wigandia 36

in their element 42
minnie thomas's garden 46
pigeon hill 52
cooramilla 58
michael mccoy's garden 63
tugurium 69
dennis richardson's garden 75

going troppo 80
alba 84
tan jung sari 89
dennis hundscheidt's garden 94
eudlo cycads 99
waterfall cottage 104
illalangi villa 109

a frame for living 114
pat gaffney's garden 118
brinkhurst 122
penny rudduck's garden 127
reverie 132
the mosaic garden 138
domaine du castellet 145

the battlers 150
jenolen 156
the hedges 158
dianne mcclelland's garden 160
russell's camp 165
myrabluan 170
combadello 176
rockdale 180
boolooroo 184
karabine 187
myalla 193
geoff miers' garden 198
bruce and meg simmons' garden 201

return of the native 206
fülling 210
carramar 215
the sorn 220
wyemando 226
dryandra 231
merv hodge's garden 236
horse island 242
windgrove 248

acknowledgements 254

picture credits 255

conversion table 255

index 256

introduction

GARDENS ARE ABOUT PEOPLE. The story of how and why a garden came to be made is as fascinating and idiosyncratic as its planting and design. In this book, forty-five passionate Australian gardeners from every state and territory tell their own garden story and present the garden through their own eyes.

Together, they paint a detailed picture of contemporary Australian gardening in conditions ranging from desert to tropical.

When Australia's Open Garden Scheme first started to expand across Australia from its home base in Victoria, those asked to recruit gardens to open often replied: 'But we don't have any gardens here like yours.' They were expressing a widely held belief that the European-style gardens of the great homesteads and cool hill station areas set the only standard for Australian gardens.

Since then thousands of gardens have opened for the Scheme around Australia, exhibiting an extraordinary range of styles and approaches that reflect their different situations, climates and plant interests.

The eurocentric view is maintained in gardening literature by a predominance of European writers, and has generally been reinforced by Australian garden writers. Observations about our gardens have always been drawn from a very small sample. The experience and insights of Australian gardeners in a large part of the country have rarely been recorded.

Wherever the Scheme opened gardens, it encouraged the gardeners to write their own notes to hand out to visitors. Reading through these notes, we realised we were sitting on the raw material for an exciting book: one where gardeners themselves would draw us into the garden and bring it to life for readers.

As we started our slow crawl across Australia, sending out interviewers and photographers armed with extensive questionnaires and picture briefs, we were unsure what would emerge. But the material that came back surpassed our highest expectations. Our gardeners had not only taken us on an intimate garden tour, pointing out details we would never have seen for ourselves, they had talked about their own gardening journey, bestowed valuable nuggets of information about favourite plants, soils and the effects of climate, and shared with us their visions, insights and philosophies.

If we had been hoping for a recognisable 'Australian Garden' to emerge from the picture, we would have been disappointed. Yet each of these gardens, made by men and women of varied ages, circumstances and experience, is strongly of its time and place and unequivocally Australian for that reason. While Australians borrow freely from the overseas gardening styles they see and read about, all good gardeners adapt such styles to their own unique site and conditions. In addition, the character of the Australian environment, the colour and texture of its vegetation, the diamond clarity of its light and the feeling of space—as much psychological as physical, and expressed by one gardener as a sense of too much sky—infuse even city gardens with an unmistakable mood.

Against the soft yellow wall, the colours of wisteria and oranges at Reverie take on a luminous quality reminiscent of a Chinese wallpaper.

Without too much straining we were also able to identify a definite Australian approach to gardens and gardening that is informal, pragmatic, resourceful and gently ironic. Even formal gardens tend to evolve rather than being rigidly confined within a fixed plan. In the country, many gardens start around the house and ripple outwards with a fluid attitude to boundaries: as the garden grows, the fence moves out. Even suburban gardeners frequently end up buying the block next door or spilling onto the nature strip.

The feeling of transience affects all gardeners. But the truism that gardens are constantly changing has its point sharpened for rural Australians by the context of untameable and unpredictable elements—floods, fires, drought, cyclones, searing summer heat and wind—that shape their lives and regularly destroy plants and even whole gardens. In that perspective, gardeners can never get complacent or take their creations too seriously. One gardener, who puts her garden to bed each summer and replants the greater part of it each year, summed it up by saying that you just learn to live with the elements. When you are losing your stock to drought, the garden's life becomes secondary.

There are few Lost Gardens of Heligan in Australia. Gardens here are impermanent. Even trees are relatively short-lived, and the early gardens were generally not made with substantial structures: plants provided most of the architecture. The fate of abandoned gardens is usually to be burned or eaten by stock.

Gardens have survived in close to original form only with continuous care, and continuity was the main factor we looked for in selecting the historic gardens that are important reference points of Australian gardening and social history. The gardens represented here have been lucky to find in each generation a gardener faithful to the original qualities but creative and sensitive enough to make their own imprint in changes that give the garden a future as well as a past.

The vast range of climates and conditions and a gardening tradition still in its infancy mean Australian gardens continue to be largely experimental. Plants surviving in old gardens provide a valuable starting point for new gardeners of a particular region who are seeking a garden grammar.

But only a fraction of the plant potential for Australian gardens has been realised, even in the cool temperate zones traditionally reliant on the northern hemisphere's lead for the bulk of their plant material. Australian gardeners are still playing with a palette that can be extended to include plants as yet untried in gardens: plants from Central America, South Africa and Southern China, for example, that may prove far more suitable for our conditions than those of Europe and North America.

Australia's cool climate plantsmen can also take advantage of a longer growing season and milder winters to combine plants in fresh ways. Applying a knowledge of plant needs and natural habitats enables exotics to be skilfully blended with interesting local species, to marry the garden harmoniously with its setting.

There is even more exciting potential for tropical gardens, where the plant lexicon is still being compiled. In Queensland, a new breed of plant collectors and designers are working on the threshold of uncharted territory, exploring the use of plants whose textures and sculptural forms are dramatically different. In design, the influences of Asia and Central and South America are strong.

Just as Australian wines are different from those of Champagne and Burgundy, so we need different labels for our gardens. The backlash that followed the perceived horticultural cringe towards cool climate European gardens suggested that Australian gardeners would be better off turning their gaze to the Mediterranean. But for the majority of our gardeners, the 'Mediterranean garden' (in itself an unsatisfactory label that often has more to do with English ideas of the Mediterranean than those of Mediterranean people) is no more appropriate than a northern European woodland. Even in areas most approximating to a Mediterranean climate, Australians need to adapt this sort of garden to suit an intenser heat and a more brilliant light if the garden is to be comfortable. The dense shade of deciduous trees, limited areas of hard landscaping softened by plenty of leafy plants and an avoidance of glary light-reflective surfaces characterise the 'Mediterranean' gardens represented here.

For inland gardeners, the harsh environment prompts a garden where one can escape the sun rather than seek it. The ingredients of the oasis: lush green vegetation, clumps of trees, and frequently a shaded pond or billabong are key elements. And essential to most is the restoring coolness of a stretch of lawn, however small.

Responsible gardening is a concern of most Australian gardeners. Awareness of the fragility of land and resources has been one driving force behind the unusually strong tradition of native plant gardens in Australia. Few gardens elsewhere in the world are made entirely with native plants. The opportunity to use a unique and diverse flora is a great attraction for plantsmen, and as the knowledge of native plant characteristics increases, for designers too. We found that designers of native gardens are among those most firmly grounded in the traditional principles of landscaping and horticulture.

As with tropical plants, there is a vast amount still to be discovered about native plants and their use in gardens. As a result, gardeners must largely do their own research and trialling, actively seeking out or developing for themselves garden-worthy plants. One gardener commented that many non-native gardeners join the Society for Growing Australian Plants because of the high standard of botanical and horticultural knowledge to be found there.

Implicit but rarely expressed directly is the idea of the garden as a spiritual experience. The last gardener in this book offers a vision for the future that relates both to the current movement for natural gardens and the enduring myth of the garden as a place where one may regain Eden.

building on tradition

HISTORIC GARDENS POSE PARTICULAR CHALLENGES FOR THE GARDENERS WHO INHERIT THEM. For the first five gardeners in this chapter, 'marrying the garden' has meant arriving at a balance between preserving the past, accommodating the effects of change, and putting their own creative stamp on the garden.

MANAR is one of the earliest continuous Australian gardens. A landmark decision to remove the formal driveway which cut the main vista has realised Joanna Gordon's aim for a natural flow towards the garden's margins, which now, blurred and softened by time, melt into the pastoral landscape.

The importance of the view out has always been recognised at SALISBURY COURT in New England, where the first gardener built a ha ha for an uninterrupted vista of paddocks and a billabong. Here too the formal front driveway has gone, making the garden more private and intimate, while more relaxed borders have replaced formal beds for annual display.

The garden of WOOLONGOON in Victoria's Western District is remarkable for its strength of continuity in a century of significant changes to the lifestyle of rural Australians. It is protected from radical alteration by a gardener for whom the maintenance once carried out by four full-time staff is an almost single-handed labour of love.

CHERRY TREE in Western Australia had a shorter history when artist Jane O'Halloran inherited it, but in that time the garden had become overcrowded with close-planted enclosing trees. Thinning them out opened the garden up to its surroundings. Garden features and structures with a strong sense of the vernacular tie it to its place and time, and sympathetic perimeter planting allows the garden to blend into its setting.

The garden of ASHFIELD, like many old city gardens, dwindled in size as pieces of land were sold off for development. While aware that no garden can stand still, Barbara Jennings has skilfully made use of the historic bones—old pear trees and box hedges—to shelter and display her collection of cool climate plants.

At WALLCLIFFE, there was a dramatic natural setting, a fine old house and a romantic history, but only vestiges of the original garden. A fortunate meeting between the owners and a gifted stonemason provided the missing link. The house, which had always seemed to 'float' in its setting, was provided with a fitting stage: great terraces and steps of local limestone.

The final garden in the chapter is a new one that picks up on a neglected tradition. At WIGANDIA, William Martin has rekindled the genius for planting of the great nineteenth-century Australian landscape designer William Guilfoyle.

OVERLEAF: A deep pink rose planted in the nineteenth century tumbles into a box hedge of the same vintage at Ashfield in Hobart.

five generations of gardeners

MANAR JOANNA GORDON

Manar is at Braidwood in the Southern Tablelands of New South Wales, 70 km east of Canberra. The land was settled in 1840 by Hugh Gordon who based the design of his Australian garden on the original Manar, his family's property in Scotland. Manar is a 2 hectare (5 acre) garden with alluvial soil, and enjoys a kind climate due to its altitude (600 metres) and relatively assured rainfall. Although the garden is affected by frost in winter, summer temperatures rarely exceed 30°C. Joanna Gordon has gardened at Manar for nearly forty years.

In the courtyard at the back of the house, valerian (*Centranthus ruber*), rosemary and rue against
a background of ornamental grapevine harmonise with pink washed walls and old brick paving.

WHEN I FIRST came here, Manar was a very beautiful, well-kept garden, which had a full-time gardener and a yardman. It changed overnight from being a very well cared for garden to one that really just had to survive because of the lack of help. In our early days I struggled to find somebody to help me a day a week in the garden. At one stage we had a pair of old men called Cyril and Ernie, who were the gravediggers at Braidwood. One day I went out to see what they'd done and they'd dug a rather grave-like bed behind the bed I had wanted them to weed and dig for me.

Initially we tried to keep it all going, except we fenced off the bottom of the garden, which is actually the most romantic part. I quickly filled up the one rather lovely perennial border close to the house with spring-flowering shrubs to make it easier to cope with. All the bones of a marvellous garden were there—a wonderful backdrop of huge old trees, lots of very formal straight paths—but there was a lot that I wasn't happy with.

When the children were quite young, I began a horticulture course. I had a wonderful design teacher, who suggested I do a history of Manar for my final course project. That really focused me in on the garden more than anything else. My husband Forbes' cousins Jock and Janette Mackay lived at Mona [a historic garden at Braidwood], which represented everything that I loved about gardens and is the Australian garden I have been most influenced by. Many of the plants there had become naturalised and just took off. It was like my childhood garden in England. Whenever I dropped in I felt their joy in their garden, and I always went home with an armful of plants.

It wasn't until the children were well into their teens and I had more time that I began to think about what I really wanted to do with the garden. I mulled for a long while over my first step—getting rid of the gravel driveway that cut right across the vista down the garden.

That was the landmark decision and a huge change that made the garden my garden. And it meant that I had to make a whole new border at the bottom and there was suddenly no driveway to walk across, so you flowed right down and had a reason for going there. All there was in the vista at that time were straight paths crossing in every direction.

From then on the garden began to gel for me. I realised it could become a lovely garden one day.

I wanted to make it part of the house, a restful, flowing garden rather than the more formal garden it had been in its Victorian era.

This garden has a great peace and tranquillity about it. You want to just drift from one area to the next, to be drawn down into it, and there are glimpses of the next little bit that invite you on. You don't want to see it in one gaze and you don't want to be bewildered by too many stimuli.

Hugh Gordon's early letters back to his family asked for examples of anything that grew there, such as the aleppo and stone pines that were such a feature of the original garden. It intrigues me that Hugh married a gardener, Mary Macarthur, who came from The Vineyard at Parramatta. She had also grown up in a beautiful garden.

The house here is on a mound created alongside the original cottage. The driveway came up, like the Scottish ones, through huge trees: pines, elms and oaks with shrubs in between. The garden was designed with the straight paths of English and Scottish gardens, with little walkways at the bottom and shrubs in very formal, rounded shapes. There is a very good photographic record of the garden, which is wonderful to have. Then of course they would no more have dreamt of bringing a plant from the bush into the garden than flying to the moon. They were trying to shut out the bush, to create their own little Scotland. I now have quite a few native plants in the garden but when I buy a plant I don't think of it as a native or an exotic. I think of it as fitting in a particular spot.

Manar's garden has been made mainly by five generations of women, all very keen gardeners. Different parts of the garden really mattered to each of them.

Forbes' grandmother, Charlotte Gordon, recognised the better soil at the bottom and she had lovely borders down there, all completely gone now. She had an old rose garden where I have planted a lot of trees. I am making a whole new secret garden around an oak which has grown splendidly right in the middle of the old rose beds.

In contrast to Charlotte's gardens, the things Forbes' mother Mollie did have stayed and I've had to work round them. That has not always been easy but it did give me a backbone to build on. The little spring garden that she planted when she got the tennis court put in looked absolutely superb in the early photographs, just a mass of spring flowering plants. But it was high-maintenance, like nearly everything that she created, and because there were so many trees it had to have the most incredible amount of fertiliser. I have kept it as a little spring garden walk but now it's mainly Christmas roses with a few daphnes and camellias coming through and I am planting a few more rhododendrons at the back.

The bricked sundial garden near the house has always been tricky, with light, sandy soil. Forbes' Aunt Margaret always said she remembered her mother struggling with that area, and there are pictures of different kinds of garden there, so obviously they all struggled with it. Forbes' mother had a wonderful yardman who did all the brickwork.

I found that garden incredibly hard for ages. Nothing would work. But now in a way it has become the garden that I enjoy most as a challenge because it is close to the kitchen and the part of the garden where I can see easily whether things are surviving. It's also a place where self-seeded plants have an absolute holiday. The Italian lavender goes wild and a little euphorbia does brilliantly as well as cistus, phlomis, brooms and iris.

The bottom part of the garden is the area I love most. The little walkways there were Hugh Gordon's original design. I am really fond of small rather than large gardens and I like a romantic, cottage garden feel. I enjoy going through the little gate and seeing the old gardener's cottage and the lavender walk with the roses at the end.

The overgrown walkway takes you down to the bench at the bottom of the garden and the two stone pines. Originally there were enormous trees that dominated the view from the house. We have replaced them with new little ones. Near the bench there is the 'Albertine' rose along the fence and you look out over the paddocks and get a wonderful view to the hills and the willows on the flat.

To me, the essence of an Australian garden isn't Australian plants. An English garden is an English garden and it could be filled with flowers from all over the world. I think an Australian garden should have a view out, extending out of the garden into the bush or the environment. I love the mixture of European trees with the eucalypts. The colours set each other off so superbly.

With a garden of this size, a huge amount of time and energy goes into maintenance, whether it's blackberry control or mulching to get through the summer and keep the weeds down. I have very little help with the actual gardening but our caretaker does all the lawns, so the garden always looks well cared for. I don't think many people looking at this garden would believe it took so little time.

All the water comes from a well that dries up in the drought. Only twice in my thirty-seven years here has it been really drastic, when I've had to hand-water just to keep a few things surviving. We only water the lawn immediately around the house. You could barely call it lawn and from the point where the old driveway was it looks after itself.

I don't really garden in summer—I water! I have only got watering systems in the new border and rose bed at the bottom. From the minute it begins to get hot in early December, I spend the whole time moving hoses around. Without watering systems everywhere so you can turn them on at night, I have to water right through the day just to get round the beds. This is not water-efficient and, considering our water table is dropping, we need to change. Most summers I can use as much water as I want. Well, as much as I have energy to move hoses.

Everything is absolutely a 'let be' garden. I don't touch things until I have to. The plants are fairly hardy if they are well mulched but they are not hardy enough to survive a summer without water. I often think if I made a list of all the plants that have died on me in this garden, Forbes would have a fit and I would too. It's very hard to remember plant treasures in the heat of the summer when you are just happy to keep everything surviving. However much I improve the soil and try to give some of them a special spot, they get down to the real soil after a while and say, 'Oh!' and die on me.

So I end up with plants that I know do well, like viburnums and roses, hebes, catmint and the old lambs' ear, which is a wonderful plant. But I try not to repeat plants from bed to bed. A garden can be very boring if you just see the same plants again and again. The plants I cherish most are huge old-fashioned roses, which grow into great big overflowing bushes. One species that I collect is viburnum because I know it does well here.

The garden looking out to the northwest has hardly been touched for over twelve months. When we were first married, it was full of lupins and other perennials and looked superb but it was too much to cope with. It needed to change to suit a different time and scale. I planted shrubs and trees to fill it in and make it a non-work garden, which a great deal of this garden really has to be. You have to fill it up with things that will mind themselves, give you interest and colour at the right times of year, but essentially survive.

The top of the bed is dominated by an enormous Manchurian pear (*Pyrus ussuriensis*). They do brilliantly here and together with crab apples are one of the best things you can plant. 'Iceberg' roses go all through, with the most wonderful pink rose 'Canterbury' on either side. In the middle is a large weeping silver pear, *Pyrus salicifolia* 'Pendula'. There is also weigela, deutzia and kolkwitzia, several huge *Viburnum opulus*, a camellia that flowers at the end of winter and as a backdrop *Phillyrea latifolia*, which is an old Victorian-era hedge plant. Mixed in are miniature agapanthus, a pinky red penstemon that spreads wonderfully, phlox and Japanese anemones.

Someone said to me that they were interested in the way I had used shrubs in my borders. They obviously expected me to have either a totally herbaceous border or a shrubbery, as if those were the rules. They hadn't expected the two to blend.

I have lots of problems with wildlife. The cockatoos move onto Manar at the beginning of December. You see them slowly working their way up the front paddock and they are usually into the garden by Christmas. My English son-in-law says it is noisier here in the early morning than it is in the heart of London. We have photos of the orchards in the 1930s with overflowing bags of apples. We don't get one bit of fruit now. Wombats are my worst problem. They move in and out of the garden freely and ringbark the trees.

I love working in the garden, particularly in spring. In summer it's a bit of a burden but I like walking around with my secateurs and saw, making the picture a little better. I love creating vistas and snippets of view, and juxtaposing plants. What I am trying to create is a lot of little pictures. That is what is satisfying in making a garden to me.

Gardens have to change with each generation and I often feel I should start planting for the future and begin to put all the lower garden into roses or shrubs to simplify it. The trickiest thing about this garden is that it's difficult to cut part of it off to make it more manageable.

You have to let a garden dictate to you. It is very easy to come into a garden and say, 'I'm going to have my laburnum walk there and my rose garden there and my herb garden there.' But a garden has its own soul and anyone moving into a landscape or garden should get a feel for what they have there first. And slowly that landscape, that little bit of earth, will dictate to you as much as you do to it.

Gardens can get very over-designed and busy and spoilt. A lot of gardens I have been to are just too thought out. It is like walking into a shopping mall rather than into a street of shops. I could be putting in little walks of this and that and little arbours and statues. But I think you have to be terribly careful not to just fill it up.

I am happy with what I have achieved. Because of the size of Manar, what you can achieve each year is limited. The main effort goes into small changes. Any plans I have I mull over slowly, which is perhaps a great blessing because it probably stops me making mistakes. I might put a tree in and then I move it and I might move it again. And I still wonder about things like the long, straight path, which I keep really for historical memory and for Forbes' sister, Anne. She said that path epitomised for her the memories of childhood, and running down it in the heat of a summer's day.

Views of wide borders and lawns unfold from this favoured spot in the shade of an oak. Stately trees planted by Hugh Gordon in the 1840s frame each part of the garden.

Joanna Gordon and 'Minnie'.

A serene pastoral landscape stretches out beyond the billabong, framed by the garden's old elms.

the view beyond

SALISBURY COURT SALLY CROFT

Salisbury Court is at Uralla in the New England region of New South Wales, 500 km north of Sydney. The garden was begun in 1844 by the Crofts' forebears and faces north to unbroken views of the distant hills. With an elevation of 1100 metres, winter is cold with temperatures frequently dropping to −14°C. Summers are mild and average rainfall, which is summer dominant, is 735 mm. Sally Croft has maintained and developed the 0.8 hectare (2 acre) garden for the past seventeen years.

A simple expanse of lawn replaces the formal carriage drive of earlier times.
The old side gate leads into the paddock formerly used to lead horses to pasture.

I THINK THIS is a very Australian garden, even though it has a lot of exotic trees, just because of the landscape. The garden slopes down to a true Australian billabong with low undulating hills behind it. Everyone who has lived here has been aware of the landscape beyond the front garden, the view from the front verandah.

Owen's great-great-grandmother Eliza Marsh started the garden in 1844 after she married Matthew Marsh and came to Australia. In one of her letters back to her sister she mentions that the vines and the trees have travelled well, and we are certain that the great big oak tree on the western side—there were two others but they blew down—and the old Isabella grapevine over the pergola on the back lawn are some of those original plants.

Eliza Marsh was a knowledgeable and enthusiastic gardener, and must have liked the landscape design that was fashionable in England at the time, because in the early 1850s she established the ha ha. It is very effective and the lawn seems to flow into the paddock. It was originally faced with timber but that rotted away, so they replaced it with the granite stone that is all over the property, which was also used for the house and the garden walls.

The walls around the garden were built by Owen and his father about forty years ago, to keep the stock out. Owen gradually rebuilt them and made them a bit higher.

There was no water supply in the garden originally, so gardening must have been a great challenge. The vegetable garden and the orchard were right down on the creek and there was an old wood-fuelled steam engine that pumped the water. Even my mother-in-law didn't have water here at first. There were some tanks but that was all they had.

But in the early years they had gardeners and so they could manage much bigger gardens. The garden in the nineteenth century extended another fifty feet to the northeast at the front.

Owen's parents were here for forty-five years and made significant changes to the garden. They planted the crab apples, the flowering plums and many more shrubs. The garden had become a bit of a disaster at the front because it was full of elm suckers. They removed them and established the little path that winds around through the shrubs to the gate. But the biggest change they made was taking out the front driveway. My father-in-law got tired of chipping the drive and every time there was a big fall of rain, half the gravel disappeared down into the paddock. He also took up the brick edging and used it for the vegetable garden paths. Taking out the driveway took away the Victorian feel of the garden, with its gravel entrance coming up to the front door, and made it more private.

My mother-in-law used to tell me she didn't really like gardening but that she felt that the house needed a nice garden. She used to grow pansies and poppies and stocks and all sorts of annuals from seed, so she usually had a pretty spectacular show in narrow beds along the front of the house.

Owen widened those beds and I changed the plantings. Because it gets so hot I have planted cistuses and helianthemums, which enjoy the hot dry situation, and plumbago (*Ceratostigma willmottianum*). I love hebes and had quite a lot but I lost them with the frost. The perennials include penstemons, valerian, verbena, and pink and blue forms of veronica, the little groundcover speedwell. And in spring self-sown larkspurs and love-in-a-mist come up. There are also lots of euphorbias and a sisyrinchium (*S. striatum*), which is a stunning plant.

There is an evergreen background of sacred bamboo and laurustinus, and two red maples. Along the little path we established an extra bit of garden which has viburnums, camellias and Persian lilac with some conifers.

We changed very little here at first. We cut down some huge elms that were dangerous and removed a few shrubs and a crab apple from the front lawn so we could open it up. I have done a lot of underplanting around the deciduous trees. I have established *Cyclamen hederifolium*, hellebores, Japanese anemones and columbines. And the giant ajuga with big leaves that go a lovely bronze in winter.

When I first moved up here, I thought I would grow only the things that grew before 1913, like the National Trust. Then I found that catmint, which had always been right along the front of the garden, wasn't on the list, so I changed my mind. But I do love the old shrubs and trees, the old simple flowers, not the modern hybrids. I like the older roses too—like the China rose 'Old Blush' growing near the gate among the woodbine.

We extended the front garden by about fifteen feet and made it wider at the gate. And we extended it behind the tall rhaphiolepis (Indian hawthorn) and japonica hedges to the area west of the house. The rhaphiolepis hedge is a very old-fashioned one. We didn't know what it was, so we sent some leaves and flowers down to the Botanic Gardens and they identified it. It was often found in very old gardens because people collected plants in India on their way out here in the nineteenth century.

Ten years ago, we extended the garden out to where the stables had been, with the big old oaks and elms. This created a shady woodland and it seemed a shame that the stock were the ones to enjoy it. But then we had a willy-willy that blew down two of the old oaks. We are quite enjoying replanting it, putting new trees in. I wanted an understorey of groundcovers and shrubs that like the shade. I have planted several mahonias, which are very hardy evergreens that don't need watering. I like to have various textures and colours in the foliage, especially for the winter.

Between the hedge and the house there is an inner garden with a big clump of black bamboo that is probably more than a hundred years old, two old laburnums and a very aged pear tree. And the old-fashioned jasmine (*Jasminum mesnyi*), which was planted to go over the shed in 1913. I have shrubs for coolness and there is a secret garden feeling, with the little path winding up to the birdbath and the shrubs against the house.

I was very lucky to inherit such an established garden with all the shade of the mature trees. At times I feel this is my garden and then other times I feel as if I am just looking after it, because there is so much history. I would like to think of the tradition going on, of it continuing to be loved and cared for.

good grooming

WOOLONGOON LUKI WEATHERLY

In 1968 Luki Weatherly took over from her mother-in-law the management of the 2.4 hectare (6 acre) garden at Woolongoon, near Mortlake in Victoria's Western District. Established in the early 1900s, the garden is set on a small hill between a natural lake and a dam, and enjoys deep rich soil and good drainage, ideal for the establishment of trees. Old trees are not always an easy legacy and Luki has had to make the tough decision to remove some specimens to reduce competition. Her approach to her inherited garden is gentle and respectful.

LEFT: White geraniums border the perfectly raked gravel driveway at the entrance to Woolongoon. The elegant simplicity of the garden is underpinned by painstaking attention to detail.
RIGHT: Delphiniums give height to a deep herbaceous border, while an arch in the hedge offers an enticing glimpse of another part of the garden.

MY MOTHER-IN-LAW, Patricia Weatherly, was a formidable gardener. She was a great thinker too and she made significant changes to the garden. With four gardeners she had a lot more time to read—her library of gardening books was phenomenal.

So taking over Woolongoon from Mrs Weatherly was a tremendous responsibility. I rather tragically thought that if I worked hard enough nobody would notice she'd gone! I thought I'd do absolutely everything she did and if I made minimal changes nobody would notice. I wanted the garden to look like it had been to a very good hairdresser's, I wanted to make it look neat and tidy and happy and not radically changed.

It took a long time before I realised that I did have to make changes, that I actually had to make up my own mind about things, because the microclimate had changed, trees fell over, and all sorts of other things happened.

When we first came to live in the cottage at Woolongoon, there were several full-time gardeners. But when I took over the garden, I had to manage with only a bit of part-time help a couple of days a week, and the gardener didn't like flowers. He didn't like anything I did, he kept saying the old lady wouldn't have done that. I'd say, well, what would she have done? And he'd say he didn't know, but she didn't do it like that.

In the beginning I said I didn't know how I was going to manage it, and James suggested letting the sheep graze right up to the door. But that didn't seem a choice to me. I saw it as my job to look after it. I still do but I really love it, so it's a total luxury. When I am looking for help in the garden, I really want a maintenance man, because I am the gardener.

James' great-grandfather bought Woolongoon in 1895 at a mortgagee sale. But nobody lived here permanently until James' grandfather got married in 1911 and the big house was built.

There was a bit of garden around the early house but the garden as we know it was planted by James' grandmother. Some of the early pictures show the layout of the rose garden. We don't know where in the garden it was but it shows the roses in a very Victorian design of little swirls and squiggles.

In the 1920s they put in all the great big cypress windbreaks and a lot of very strong Victorian planting that didn't need much water, such as the laurustinus and photinias which are still here.

When James' mother came in the 1940s, hers was a big change because she planted all the exotics. Mrs Weatherly's mother was a friend of Edna Walling [the Australian garden designer and writer] and the family gave her one of her first great commissions. So she brought with her some influences of Edna Walling whom she loved. She said as a child she used to follow Edna round, and the reason she used Latin names was that Edna said that if the child was old enough to garden it was old enough to learn Latin.

During the 1950s a huge number of plants were established, a lot of the stone walls were put in and the paths were laid.

When I started gardening, I thought it was just something else you had to learn, like cooking. It wasn't until I actually started growing things that I found I really did love it. In my first garden at the cottage, I had a mass of colour, terribly tasteless but very strong and healthy.

I still love annuals and use them to fill in gaps. A lot of annuals self-seed, which is another nice thing about them. When I first started, things had died off in the winter and I put in annuals everywhere. They hate it here because they don't get enough sun. Petunias cover three feet without a flower. You have to be realistic trying to plant them in a very shady garden.

The vegetable garden used to be as big as the front lawn. It covered a good acre going right down to the cypresses. It had a huge orchard, all Mrs Weatherly's cutting beds and the asparagus patch, which had been there since the year dot. Then there was the glasshouse, which was formerly the conservatory on the side of the house and was moved in the 1950s. Mrs Weatherly's vegetable gardener grew enormous squashes, carrots and pumpkins for the men—there were still four of them living in the single men's quarters. I'd see him trudging down with the wheelbarrow, and sometimes he'd trudge over to me and I'd nearly have a nervous breakdown at the sight of these huge vegetable marrows, which the children hated.

We halved the vegetable garden straight away and made part of it into lawn. It has become smaller and smaller because we don't need as many vegetables. The vegetable garden was hidden behind a huge cypress hedge. Originally probably it was wonderful for getting things growing on the inside.

It took two gardeners three weeks to do the hedge. They did it three times over two years because that was the policy, and they did it by hand. They went up on trestles and cut the outside, then they did the inside, cutting from the top down.

When the hedge came out about fifteen years ago it became more important that what you saw looked pretty, and that's why I planted trees. Dealing with root competition is a big part of managing Woolongoon.

I see the changes in the garden where trees have gone as opportunities. Mostly they fall over because things have changed, a wind tunnel appears because something else has grown. When they've gone, it's probably for a good reason.

I once asked our tree surgeon Alex Bicknell to trim the broken branches off the row of oaks at the front gate. When I came down about an hour later, he'd taken out every other tree, which was quite a lot more than trimming a couple of branches. He said he knew I wouldn't have let him do it, and I wouldn't have. He said in 200 years you'll be able to see these oaks from the moon. And he's right.

The watering system has been an enormous change in the garden. Watering used to be such a scary job—moving the hoses 125 times. When the old watering system gave up, we knew we were going to have to do something, and the new system has been a huge improvement for doing the lawns. But watering things when they need it is much better than putting on the cannons every time one thing in a bed looks sick. If I had to do it again I'd probably only put watering systems on the lawns.

I do notice untidiness in gardens. I find it very hard to look at plants separately, mostly it's the overall picture. I like plants to look healthy and happy and neat and comfy. I'm not at all fussed about not having things that don't grow here well. I don't feel as though I must have azaleas because azaleas are the plant to have; I'd much rather have something jolly and common like *Sedum spectabile*.

I like my raked gravel very much, especially when it's wet and clean. I think sometimes if you rake the gravel and do the edges, nobody notices anything else. The gardens I like best are very simple, with beautiful trees and spaces out to the trees.

Herbaceous borders are fun. Although you quite often use the same things, you are changing them around, and learning what will look nice with what.

I use a lot more colour than Mrs Weatherly. I like bright colours and I think the Australian sunlight is strong enough to take them.

There are fewer flowers now. The big white borders had a lot in them, wonderful rare and interesting things. They were inside the hedge on the bottom of the lawn and they were very beautiful. Although my herbaceous borders are wilder with not such tasteful colours, they do grow quite well because they get a reasonable amount of sun. The old white borders were shaded, so they put up very long leggy growth. An enormous amount of staking went on.

The only time my mother-in-law ever criticised my gardening was when she said that dot planting is not the answer. Instead of putting things in big amounts, I was inclined to put in one plant, and that's not a good idea. Now I put plants that grow well all over the place, instead of having, say, one clump of cliveas or one clump of sedums.

You shouldn't be afraid of gardening. I was frightened at first and thought the changes I made might look funny. Of course they don't always work, and sometimes there are places where you feel like putting a bag over it and saying, 'don't look here'. I used to be quite apologetic to the plants, saying I'm terribly sorry, I'm sure I've given you the wrong treatment, and apologising, apologising, apologising for hydrangeas which I learnt to prune on the job. But plants are very forgiving. You go down the path and suddenly realise they've pulled themselves together, put their roots down and are looking good.

Luki Weatherly.

lifting the barriers

CHERRY TREE   JANE O'HALLORAN

Cherry Tree is in the rolling, lightly timbered farmland of the Great Southern district, 250 km southeast of Perth. The farm has been in the O'Halloran family for nearly 100 years but it is only since the Second World War that the 0.4 hectare (1 acre) garden has been developed. The soil is red loam and annual rainfall is 450 mm, falling mainly in winter. Frosts are rare and maximum winter temperatures average around 20°C. In contrast, during the long dry summer when days average between 30°C and 35°C, the country is brown, dry and harsh. Growing up in Perth, artist Jane O'Halloran married and came to Cherry Tree in 1986.

Rock-edged beds of drought-defying plants including red poppies, sisyrinchiums, daisies, artichokes and cardoons line the path leading to a folly in the paddock.

In a clever colour composition, repeated planting of grey santolina and golden marjoram, and a background of *Robinia pseudoacacia* 'Frisia' serve to intensify the blueness of the succulent *Senecio serpens*. Roses complete the picture: 'Albertine' rambles over the tank, the yellow noisette 'Céline Forestier' climbs into a tree, and in the foreground is David Austin's 'Yellow Button'.

WHEN WE MOVED here, the garden was all trees. There were more than 130 altogether. I decided to take most of them out at the front to open it up. Lottie, my mother-in-law, had planted a sort of barrage on the west side but some of the trees were really close in. I took them out and I also put a hole in one of the fences. It was a hard decision to take out some of the big shade trees but they were in so close that I couldn't grow anything.

The O'Halloran family came to the property in 1906, to a little wooden house on the river. Then they built a house higher up but that one burned down. The brothers all went off to the war and when Denis, my father-in-law, came back, he bought a farm nearby and then Cherry Tree became vacant and he bought that.

Lottie had a big family and gardening was her escape. She was a really good gardener, who did everything the hard way because there wasn't a spare penny for gardening. She didn't buy plants, she used to grow them from seed. She was a real nurturer.

I studied art at university and that influenced my gardening, particularly in combining plants. What I really enjoy are plant associations and the history of plants.

When I came here, I first of all put down some stones and made little terraces because I couldn't cope with large unstructured areas. I am very much a structure person, so I had to do quite a bit of that.

One of the first jobs was to define the driveway, which was huge to accommodate all the vehicles. I've gradually encroached on it and pinched triangles of garden here and there and planted cistus, yuccas and agaves to connect the garden with the eucalypts beyond.

I've done an experimental low-water garden which is three years old, so it's really starting to fill out now. It has yuccas, cordylines, nice big clumping succulents, and some tea roses that get a hammering from the parrots, but I like to see the roses with those big things. I've gone off them in the past few years but it's nice to put them with what would normally be considered unsympathetic plants. They hold their own and look good.

There are some granite outcrops as you come into the main part of the garden, and I've planted lavenders a very similar colour to the lichen on the granite to lead you into the rocks. I've used unstructured bushy roses and borders of lambs' ears and valerian.

I really love traditional stone garden ornaments but they just don't go in my garden. I go to nurseries and touch them and wish I could have them at home, but they don't go with a pink brick house. I have made my own ornaments and structures that seem to fit the place. The ram's head sculptures with the magnificent horns are called Tom, Dick and Harry. My husband Robert was appalled to find out that the horns weren't from our rams but had come from a friend's farm and that I had paid five dollars each for them! The cog wheel and compass point in the stone paving were just a bit of fun. They are all different coloured stones from the farm, with a drive wheel from a piece of machinery.

The big stone pergola on the east side of the house took a lot of plotting and scheming to get done. The stone for the columns came from the paddocks. There was some huge bridge timber lying by the shed and I used it with the ratty end of the wood facing forward. I wanted it to look like it had been here forever.

West of the driveway there is an area that was started about five years ago when we put the walks in. I wanted to have two paths at right angles but I couldn't because Robert walked across to the shed and then down to feed the dogs. I mulled over it for a long time and finally decided I could have these slightly askew paths. I got around to accepting that and put all the paths in. And then Robert moved the dogs! That is why I had to build that little pergola and folly. There was a path leading nowhere.

I said I wanted to have an Australian dunny and my nephew said he had a roof of one I could have. When Robert lifted the roof up onto those four posts, it fitted perfectly. An old stepladder made a perfect support for a little 'Canary Bird' rose. It has enamel yellow flowers and it lasts for two months.

I've built up the beds with granite rocks. I've used a lot of rock around the garden because it helps to relate it to the landscape. I've used all the plants that I love and can't put in my rose garden proper at the back, which is all pink roses. I've used colours and shapes and plants that I wouldn't use in a bigger garden—melianthus, artichokes, great clumps of dietes. The *Strelitzia nicolai* is going to be a big fan one day. And there are cannas and sisyrinchiums (*S. striatum*), gorgeous juicy grey clumps.

The blue garden is about four years old and has lots of tough, hardy plants like cardoons, plectranthus and succulents making a border around the vegetables. It was inside the garden boundary but it was just a ratty area with a few sick orchard trees, which I took out.

I replaced the old wire boundary fence with a new one, using pickets from an old house, old telegraph poles and planks from the old sheep yards. Then I put in some old gates that were over at the sheds.

The old shed next to the blue garden was originally only half its size and the roof was quite low. We raised the roof and made the shed twice as big. When we moved here, we had a drought and all the lawns and everything died. It was awful and this was the only place we could water. I dug up all the plants that I liked and put them in there. It was our one little green area and it's become a shade house. We have birthday parties there and Easter-egg hunts. Lottie used it as a fernery.

The garden was much more spartan then. I've made it bigger in every direction. I haven't gone outside the garden boundaries but I've made the 'civilised' part of the garden almost join up.

The new area from the tank to the steps is planted in blue and lime green, with a little orange tree in the centre. It was doing very badly in the orchard, so it was looking for a new home. If I had chosen a tree specially, I would have got a cumquat because I want it to stay a low garden. There is a blue succulent *Senecio serpens*, and santolina alternating with golden marjoram. In the background are the shiny dark green leaves of acanthus and then clumps of euphorbia. I am putting in more and more of the tough strong things—I hate plants that die on me.

On the south side of the house are a lot of trees that Lottie planted, including jacaranda, camphor laurel and macadamia. The metrosideros have made big, lush green bushes and create a wonderful archway. You should be able to do everything with plants, shouldn't you—use them as architecture.

Through the arch, near the golden rain tree (*Kolreuteria paniculata*) and a pistachio (*P. chinensis*), is an open area under an Indian coral tree and what I call my proper rose garden. I've planted a pattern of box around it with little box pyramids leading off on the stone path. I've used plants that go with roses. To make this little terrace garden work, the two terraces have to be low and it's a challenge to find plants that stay low in spring.

My favourite roses here are 'Comte de Chambord', 'La Ville de Bruxelles' and 'Duchesse d'Angoulême'. I've got a few gorgeous classic old roses up the back that perform well if the weather's right and I've given them enough water; and a few deep-red ones. I never put in light pink roses now—they just look like used sports socks after a day. I put in something gutsy and bright, lolly pink and red.

What I've done I don't want to change but if I came here now I would do it totally differently. I would have a grand vista of trees right down to the road, a great big driveway, and I would have it all really formal.

What we tend to do in Australia is surround the house with a barrier of trees to sort of close it in from what's outside. What's outside is really hostile, flat bare paddocks with nothing on them, all dry in summer. We want to stop the wind coming in. But you can work out ways of using native trees to link the outer areas to the garden and buildings.

Compared to England, everything seems so alien, so different, so dry and so unsymmetrical, and the trees are so ratty and untidy and everything is so prickly and horrid. Of course you want to put all those other more definite things in. Like trees that are shaped like lollipops.

The garden designer who has really influenced me is Russell Page [English landscape architect, 1906–85]. I've read *The Education of a Gardener* and I've consumed his book on design. His understanding of place really shows in the variety of plants he used in his gardens. He was also very clever with water. But in Australia we don't need these flat levels of water reflecting the sky—it is just too glary.

In Australia we definitely love our little oases and it's a challenge not to try to make the garden English and perfect. The spiky untidiness of the trees here doesn't go with perfect little things. It is good to relate it to what's around you. So the challenge is to use plants that you like but to find appropriate kinds.

the creative steward

ASHFIELD BARBARA JENNINGS

Thirty-five years ago Barbara Jennings came to the historic but neglected garden of Ashfield overlooking the Derwent River in Hobart's Sandy Bay. The climate is mild—in winter temperatures rarely fall below zero and in summer 34°C is exceptional—and the rich black alluvial soil is deep. Over a period of 170 years, Ashfield has shrunk from its original 4.9 hectares (12 acres) to the present 0.4 hectares (1 acre), but original trees and hedges still remain to frame a garden that reflects Barbara's individual style and plantsmanship.

I HAVE SPENT my time at Ashfield putting a little bit of me into the garden. It has been a real challenge but great fun. I have always been a city gardener. My parents' garden in South Hobart, like Ashfield, was an old established garden, with beds within box hedges and a very formal parterre. I am used to working within the constraints of an old garden with hedges and big trees to work around. I have never really designed a garden as such, and I have found it hard blocking out things I don't like looking at.

My husband Roger said there was no way I was ever going to tame this garden. I needed to look at the broader picture and not worry too much. And I had young children and not much time. I didn't begin gardening in earnest until twenty years ago, and then it got more and more intense. Every now and then I wish it wasn't so intense but I can't stop myself. I am addicted.

Ashfield was part of a large land grant covering the esplanade and was originally a twelve-acre market garden bought by David Lambe in 1834. He planted a lot of the trees, including the pears, which are the only major survivors of the original garden. From the 1890s to 1950 it was owned by the Butler family. My husband bought it back for his first wife, who was a Butler. I also knew the family, so I gradually learned the history through the Butler eyes. There are quite a few photos and records about the garden and the plants from that era.

The garden had been let go for many years when I married Roger in 1965. But I could see its potential and gradually started to pull it back into shape. The old box hedges were quite out of control, very large and floppy, and the kids loved falling into them. I stopped them doing that and they thought I was dreadful. I used to tell them I could get a child more easily than I could get a new box hedge. In those days I hand-clipped the hedges, which took weeks. I am sorry I didn't cut them back harder earlier.

It used to be a rambling garden, a wilderness, with the walnut trees that the children swung in and the old grass tennis court where they played football. They had cubby houses in the pine trees where they and their friends learned to smoke and drink. They reckon I've ruined the garden by making it all neat and tidy.

The turning point for me was going to England with a friend in 1988 to look at gardens. We saw plants we'd never seen that weren't available in Australia. When we came back, we started buying in seed and planted a perennial garden.

I started in the top corner overlooking the esplanade. The boys had left home by then but have never forgiven me for destroying their cricket pitch. I'd had a bit of a rose garden in that corner for some years and every time Roger went away I used to spade it out another foot or so. He didn't notice it getting larger and larger. I had to do it without his knowledge because he didn't like anything to change. He didn't understand that a garden can never stand still.

The top corner is sunny and dry and now has quite a Mediterranean feel. The wonderful *Elaeagnus angustifolia* (Russian olive) is better than a silver pear and drought tolerant, though unfortunately it suckers. Cistus grows well and I've got a nice shrubby blue salvia from South America that flowers all year and an interesting echium with a pale blue-pink flower.

The *Euphorbia cyparissias* comes up to a good height and flowers twice but is a bit of a thug. And *Euphorbia rigida* has bracts that go red and orange as they age. That grows over a metre wide and gets very loose, so it's better on a wall. And *Melianthus major* is a splendid plant but it runs so I should take it out.

In the background is *Buddleia alternifolia*, which I prune viciously as soon as it has flowered, and the white trunks of a gum and a birch. The birch was here before I was, so I have learned to live with it, and the two do look good together.

I am sorry now I have roses in here but I've got them and I am not taking them out. Otherwise I would have more Mediterranean plants. I do like the rugosas as a background.

I taught myself to espalier and espaliered a 'Golden Hornet' crab apple to screen a corner of the garden off. Around the pear tree in a shady area I brought the garden out with cyclamens around a bird bath. Part of the garden had been there since 1974 but I gradually made it bigger, doing my secret thing of spading it out a bit further whenever Roger was away.

Hosta fortunei var. *albopicta* (foreground) and *H. sieboldiana* combine with rodgersias, solomon's seal, trilliums and white-flowered tricyrtis around an antique bird bath.

Then I got into my bricklaying period and did brick paths and moved stones. And I moved down the 'Dingle Dell', the garden's only sloping piece of land. It was terraced with railway sleepers because that was all we could afford. I poddled around there a few years without much success. It is so steep, and so dry even in winter because of all the trees. But I have finally put in reticulation and I hope at last it will work.

Large old trees are the hardest things to garden with but I would never be without them. I would rather have no garden, just rough grass, than lose the trees. I am lucky with the pears because they are deep-rooted and you can grow things around them. You have to watch out during the summer when they are taking up a lot of moisture.

After seeing English gardens like Sissinghurst, Hidcote and Kiftsgate, I decided to make rooms, which is a good way of making different areas in a flat garden. I didn't have stone or brick walls, which I would have loved. But within the box hedges I had the old formal gardens that had been allowed to get out of control. I wanted to grow smaller things and more perennials, so the only thing I could do was to break into these gardens and put paths through and create my rooms within them.

It was all a learning curve but I have gradually cleared and planted a series of gardens with winding paths. The dappled shade and moisture suit many plants. I have let the hellebores seed and there are lilies, pulmonarias and white-flowering brunnera, ground-covering vancouveria and epimediums, clumps of galanthus and double primroses. I let all the leaves rot down and use pea straw mulch, which improves the very heavy clay.

What I have done, of course, is historically wrong. But I refuse to be historically correct about gardening and I can't stand formal rose gardens, which is probably what was here originally. A garden moves on and you have to work with different styles at different times. Trying to recreate a period is stupid. They talked about bringing the Government House garden here back to what it was and a friend pointed out that they'd have to remove almost every tree. You can't freeze a garden. I know one day my old pears will die. I hope I die first—it would break my heart. But you have to accept that that's nature, and you move on and redesign the area.

The material they had to work with in the early days was limited. And they weren't going to plant natives because they were intimidated by the bush. I find native plants very difficult to place in this garden because of the trees that exist here but if I started again I would enjoy using them. I would never have an exclusively native garden but I would certainly grow more.

I don't think I would like gardening outside a temperate climate. I have no desire to have a tropical garden. But a Mexican or dry Mediterranean garden would be interesting. There is a little bit of Mediterranean in the top corner and I am becoming fonder of succulents and agaves. But a lot of plants are hard to grow here at sea level because they come from severe climates—high desert, where you get extremes of hot and cold.

I am becoming more and more interested in textures and in tiny things. I have just started some beds of alpines near the house and I think this is a natural progression. Lots of garden writers talk of going through phases. When you start gardening, you go for the bright rather gaudy stuff, whether it's annuals or big rhodos with lolly pink flowers— it's colour, colour, colour and flowers, flowers, flowers. Then you progress with gardening experience to learn that flowers don't make a garden—texture and vistas and other things do. Flowers are lovely but they are fleeting and foliage is always going to be more important.

In the past few years I have tried to simplify my planting. Having played with my perennials, I still want to grow some but it is very hard work. You've really got to be digging clumps up every second year and dividing and replanting, and some will seed about. So I am changing to a certain extent and planting more shrubs. The other thing I am doing is getting away from planting one of this and one of that, which is a period I went through when I was growing lots of stuff from seed. I would now like to concentrate on the plants I know grow well in this garden and have much bigger drifts of a few plants.

That is what I *want* to do but I can't resist anything that is rare and different. I am still the collector and I have to slap my hand every now and then and tell myself I can't do that. For instance, I won't allow myself to grow meconopsis any more, as much as I love them, because just as they come into flower they get battered by the hot north winds

Old box hedges that contain and shelter a large collection of rare and desirable plants impose structure on a series of gardens at Ashfield. In the foreground, a good form of *Geranium pratense* is planted with *Centaurea montana* 'Alba'.

and look awful. My attitude now is that if I want to see them, I'll go up to Fern Tree and enjoy them in a friend's mountain garden.

My favourite plants vary from season to season—what's out! I do like hellebores and I am doing a lot of hand-pollinating to get new strains. I have a bit of a passion for pulmonarias and epimediums, which do well in this garden because of the trees, and I need a lot of those sorts of plants. Euphorbias, naughty euphorbias, seed about wickedly, but on a dull late winter afternoon when a shaft of sun lights them up and the river and sky behind are dark grey, they are wonderful.

My little alpine plants, like the hoop petticoats and reticulata irises and the fritillarias, are a joy. The two little alpine rockeries have become my most treasured spots because I had nowhere to grow these plants for years.

The yew topiary on the edge of the lawn came as a seedling from my old home. I had it by the front gate until someone broke it in half and it was moved back here. I was clipping it as a bit of a column but when I went to England I saw the topiary at Great Dixter and it's really a steal from there. I got up there on a ladder and started to clip, and I am not quite sure what it is, but it's some sort of bird. I am reminded of that story about someone clipping a holly into Lord Montgomery, and it got out of control and had to be turned into a turkey! Topiary's like that—you never quite know what's going to happen with it and it has a life of its own.

I don't know whether I ever feel this garden is really mine. I gradually claimed it from the family over the years. I remember at one stage Roger said, 'You are taking over too much of *my* garden,' being a lovely old male chauvinist you couldn't change. And I said, 'I'm terribly sorry, let's go for a little walk and you can tell me what you'd like and I'll tell you where I thought I might go next.' So we wandered

round and divided it up—you can have that bed, I'll have this, and so on. Then the following year he came to me and said, 'You know my bed outside the billiard room?' (which he hadn't done a thing to the whole year and was in a terrible state). 'Well, I think you can have that one.' And over the next few years he handed me back all the beds he had decided to take away from me.

But even now that I am on my own, I still don't really feel ownership. I enjoy working in this garden but I rather like the feeling that I am only the steward. I am really privileged to be here and when I leave I hope it'll be handed on to someone else who'll look after it and put their stamp on it.

I have put a few little stamps on it here and there but I don't have a huge feeling that this is mine and no one else can have it. And it is inevitable that when I go it will change enormously. There aren't many idiots like me left who would want or have the time to work over an acre of garden almost entirely on their own seven days a week.

Barbara Jennings and 'Chevy'.

setting the stage

WALLCLIFFE HOUSE CATE HOHNEN

Wallcliffe House is at Margaret River, 300 km south of Perth in the southwestern corner of Western Australia between Cape Naturaliste and Cape Leeuwin. The 2 hectare (5 acre) garden faces north across the Margaret River. The soil, which is coastal sand, is neutral but the combination of limestone and bore water greatly exacerbates its alkalinity. Average annual rainfall is around 760 mm, falling only in winter. With its coastal position, the garden is frost free and summer temperatures rarely exceed the mid-30s, but salt-laden winds are a challenge. Although the house dates from the middle of the nineteenth century, the garden is very much the creation of the Hohnens and their gardener, Colin Thomson.

A guard of four clipped olives leads down to a line of topiaried lilly pillys along
the back of the house. Formal santolina domes tone with the old limestone walls.

WALLCLIFFE HAS A fantastic rich history. The house was built in 1865 by Alfred and Ellen Bussell. Alfred was a member of parliament, so Ellen was virtually left to run the property, a dairy and grazing farm, with her daughters. The dairy is still in the garden and has been renovated. That was where they made cheeses that were shipped to the Swan River settlement, or traded with the American whalers who used to come down this coast on the way to the Southern Ocean. Part of the reason, it's believed, that Wallcliffe always had corrugated iron on the verandahs was because it came down in the whaling ships as ballast.

Nothing much remains from the early garden. The only thing we can verify from letters is probably the old mulberry trees down by the dairy that came from cuttings from Government House. We had cuttings taken and sent to a specialist for propagating, and out of twenty they got two to strike, which we have planted down by the old mulberry. So we are keeping the strain going.

Mark and I came to Wallcliffe in 1987 and planned a complete restoration of the house. We started with vague ideas for the garden. First we needed to get some terraces made because the block slopes steeply down to the river. At that point we found Thommo—Colin Thomson. He was building some stone fireplaces for us and he became our gardener. For the next two years, all he did was build stone walls. He finished the first of his limestone retaining walls in 1988, creating the wonderful long main terrace in front of the house for the croquet lawn. Terracing to establish the levels meant we lost that sense of always falling down the hill. And it gave the house a stage, set it on a platform, rather than just having everything floating away from it.

There was no overall plan for the garden. It has just developed year by year and is still evolving. I haven't done any formal design training but I am a bit of a stickler for balance. Things that are not right or easy on the eye tend to annoy me. I have learnt by trial and error.

I think you start off with a principle. We have made it a formal layout, so you work from that, with the odd folly just to break up that very formal feeling. Then it lapses from being formal to informal, being surrounded by the native vegetation. We don't have a boundary, so you get that melding of the two. There is flexibility and a bit of looseness in the planting.

The Bussells had a real eye for a site. There is the profile of the windswept hill as a backdrop and a melaleuca on the waterline, which is a wonderful shape. In those days the most important thing to get surveyed was your water, so the first title was just a long narrow strip that ran both sides of the river. Then Alfred was given extensive grazing and pastoral leases.

Our water supply now is actually ground water. The river is estuarine in these parts. The Bussells must have pumped water from the wells, so a garden would have been an impossible luxury for them, apart from a few fruit trees and vegetables.

We thought hard about the colours of the plantings and tried to maintain different themes in various parts. The greys and blues tone with the limestone and the landscape and the garden at the side is principally blue and yellow. Lower down we have used mainly dark reds—camellias, alstroemerias and the darker azaleas. Then we have an area of white 'Iceberg' roses and on the far side of the croquet lawn there are mainly blues. I plant a lot of salvia for summer colour because it does well here and the rabbits don't eat it. And with the foliage, I try to alternate greys and greens.

Thommo has made several herb gardens. He designs the layout, which is very creative. He is now on herb garden number three, below the terrace at the back of the house. We had santolina bushes around the outside, balled and looking like limestone forms, but they lose their shape and die off after about four or five years. So we have put in golden oregano as an experiment. And there is lemon thyme, germander and rosemary. It is designed a bit like half a wagon wheel, with the plants dividing and intertwining.

Below the herb garden there is a hedge of myrtus (*Luma apiculata*) and the vegetable garden, where we have used materials that were on the site to reconstruct a surrounding post-and-rail fence. Thommo's a great vegie man. It's his favourite part of the garden and he keeps everything up to date.

There are four beautiful formal olives, which have got a bit too large, so I am moving two of them to the fence-line and pleaching them. An enormous amount of wind comes between the house and the hedge. We get a lot of burning from the wind and

I thought this would make almost a two-hedge effect with the myrtle in front of the pleached olives.

We have created a vista on the slope behind the house, with an avenue leading up to two concrete sculptures of a kangaroo and an emu at the top. They are actually in *Barry Humphries' Treasury of Australian Kitsch*. The line of yuccas on the back driveway and the agaves down the front are probably original and are very architectural.

Beyond the cypress hedge to the west of the house we have planted silver birches and bluebells, with wisteria and the echiums the same colour. I used to worry every year that the bluebells wouldn't come back but now we have thousands spread around to put on a show.

You follow the path down to the dell where Mark's folly is. He let the local tiler Edgar have his head. It is a mosaic that is supposed to be a water serpent or a dragon, and was meant to be in blues and greens, but Edgar was a bit keen on the reds and oranges, so it's quite vibrant. In the middle is an Indian salt-evaporating pan, which is a lovely architectural piece. The dell has acanthus and forget-me-nots naturalised on either side of the steps. There is even a little hellebore, which is a thrill because we've had such bad luck with them in the past.

We have a few roses that were in the garden when we came, including 'Lorraine Lee', which Thommo has moved a few times, and it flowers and flowers. The kentia palm was also here and it has done fantastically well. It doesn't get burnt by the wind and is particularly handsome.

The winters are very wet here and the reticulation is on all through summer, so we do lose plants that prefer to dry out—like rhaphiolepis, which can look really healthy and robust and then all of a sudden does a total collapse. Yet they are so hardy and are often the last things surviving in abandoned gardens.

There is a wonderful vista east of the house from the old dairy, of the distant grey stand of yuccas. By the dairy we have made a sweet little formal area. It was a natural glen and Thommo used the contours to put in circular steps and a pond which we planted Louisiana irises around. They have a fantastic colour and I love that strappy leaf in contrast.

We have used low hebe hedges to make a formal entrance to the east of the house. Originally we planted box but it was highly unsuccessful and we had to pull it all out. It is heart-wrenching when you think of the time and effort and expense. But the hebe has been a great success. It survived being cleared and everything else, so Thommo propagated more for the hedges. And we have two weeping mulberries pruned to a great shape.

We have started cleaning up the dam and put in a stone wall at the far end. I'll put some trees at either end of the wall and plant around the edge. There is a huge clump of castor-oil plants (*Ricinus communis*), which we think of as dreadful noxious weeds but they actually look good as a little stand of glossy red foliage in contrast to the background of peppermints (*Agonis flexuosa*).

Violets grow everywhere here. We get very few flowers from them but they make a constant green backdrop. And Thommo has established veltheimias—the South African lily of the veldt with pink pokers—and aristeas, which are a great blue and were growing on the site originally.

It is a crazy environment to garden in, with the wind. It's a northwesterly that really hits the plants. I had no idea I was taking on such a challenge. My triumphs here have been funny things, like getting the liquidambar to grow. Getting autumn foliage seems like a strange thing to aspire to. The birches and poplars lose their leaves very quickly with the winter winds. But the liquidambar for the last three years has had the most wonderful reds and it has been a great triumph because we thought we'd never do it.

Cate Hohnen and 'Harley'.

LEFT: Limestone steps descend to a small round pond defined by semicircles of box and Italian cypresses.
RIGHT: The low roof of the old dairy is framed by a generous arch in the cypress hedge. Rising above is a pair of golden gleditsias.

guilfoyle's champion

WIGANDIA   WILLIAM MARTIN

Wigandia perches halfway up Mount Noorat, an extinct volcano in Victoria's Western District, 200 km west of Melbourne.
The 0.8 hectare (2 acre) garden is landscaped with heat-retaining, free-draining scoria—the local volcanic gravel—and with its
elevated position is virtually frost-free, enabling a wide range of semi-tender plants to flourish. Rainfall is around 700 mm and
is winter dominant. William Martin is a gifted plantsman who concentrates on little-used southern hemisphere plants that revel in
the region's hot and largely dry summers. His strongest inspiration is the rich-textured tapestry of William Guilfoyle's masterly
plant groupings in the Royal Botanic Gardens Melbourne.

Scoria paths link Wigandia's richly textured garden to its backdrop of Mount Noorat. The architectural forms of a splendid *Cordyline kaspar*, furcraea and a young bunya (*Araucaria bidwillii*) set off bold groupings of succulents including *Aeonium arboreum* and sedums. The upturned iron vat repeats the rounded form of the hill behind.

I LIKE THE way this garden sits in the landscape. There is a tiny pocket of indigenous vegetation left here with half a dozen manna gums (*Eucalyptus viminalis*), casuarinas (*Allocasuarina verticillata*), which are the dominant tree and would once have covered this hill, and even some native poa grasses, which are very rare in this dairy-farming district.

The traditional way of gardening in southern Victoria is about enclosure, covering things up and creating a canopy, putting walls around if you like, and working within that space. There is a great fear of having things open to the elements and the sky.

I find people's reactions to the garden intriguing. They'll see a plant they are quite familiar with and they'll comment: 'Look what you've done with that.' In other words, they wouldn't really have considered using it because it's too ordinary, but in the different setting, growing alongside something that they wouldn't have thought of, they find it exciting. I grow a lot of 'usual' plants. 'Usual' plants are as good as rare plants, which are often not widely grown simply because they are boring.

I still feel a bit weak at the knees when I walk into the Botanic Gardens. There is just such magic there and I don't think there is any other garden I've been in that can move me as much. I often don't look at the detail, it's the overall scene. And I think that is pretty well how I have done this garden. I don't concentrate too much on the finer detail, even though that is important.

What Guilfoyle created in the gardens he designed impressed me because he used plants from such a broad base. In the nineteenth century, when that sort of English park thing was very prevalent, he was an exception because he had such a great appreciation for plants from different areas, not just the usual northern hemisphere woodland plants. And he slotted plants together like no one had before and I don't think anyone really has since.

I have taken Guilfoyle's lead in the way he blended his plants. Southern hemisphere plants are in the main far more suited to our climate and conditions. And a lot of those plants have that exotic touch that I think we badly need in our gardens. The English would kill to grow the range of exotica that we can.

We tend to take our leads from overseas and if we don't fully understand what we are working with, more often than not it is doomed to failure. The bulk of southern Australia's gardening comes from northern hemisphere woodland-style gardens. This underlying principle is still with us today as a hangover from the past.

If we use southern hemisphere plants, which can tolerate heat, they'll still get a belting and lose some of their good looks, but they hold well enough through to the next spring and we don't have to look at a garden that is below par.

In this part of the world we can have a garden that looks good for the whole year. The models we follow are models that are designed to look good for certain seasons and look far less than that for the rest of the time. That suits colder climates but here we don't have to live with gardens like that.

After Guilfoyle, I think the influence of the English Arts and Crafts movement with its emphasis on woodland-style gardens took over and has been with us ever since the 1920s. To a large degree you could say Edna Walling set back Australian gardening fifty years because she compounded that early woodland style and gave it an extra lease of life. There are still people who think that early Walling was the greatest thing that ever happened in this country. We have never really been able to grasp anything of that earlier substance that Guilfoyle created. People are fiddling around the edges but even gardens planted two years ago still have pretty well the same rather clichéd, tired groups of plants.

Recognising native plants as a way to go was Edna Walling's most positive contribution to the Australian garden scene. She made people realise we should be growing plants more suited to our climate and made it okay to plant Australian natives, and she loosened us up a bit in our gardening, which was important.

Apart from Guilfoyle, the thing that really kicked me along in gardening was that my wife Robyn's family had an old homestead perched on one of the lakes over Camperdown way, and it was filled with plants from South Africa that someone in the past had collected and put together. Robyn's mother added to the collection but rarely turned on the

On a knoll surrounded by remnant casuarinas and manna gums, Wigandia gazes over the great plains of the Western District. In the background is the entrance to Dalvui, one of William Guilfoyle's grandest commissions.

hose. The lawns would turn brown and she wouldn't worry. That garden had a large influence on me in the way I put together my own concept and plant collection.

The garden here began by plonking the house, an old groom's cottage, up on the hill. The original cottage had been moved off in the 1940s. There were still the old stone stumps the floor sat on and a bit of a wall. There was a little circular bed with a Spanish broom in the centre and African boxthorn.

Guilfoyle used a lot of what are now considered second-rank Victorian shrubbery plants. These are underused now but a lot of them are worthy of dragging out and giving pride of place. Osmanthus is beautifully perfumed and perfect for all sorts of places, and *Olearia paniculata* from New Zealand, which was once used a lot there for hedging, is very, very tough and has a great presence all the year round, and you can smell the perfume at forty paces. But the flowers are insignificant, so most people don't use it.

Iochroma from South America and the southern African sparmannia, which has single and double flower forms, are not used much any more. Sparmannia copes with terrible frosts and bounces back again. It is the same with wigandia, once it's established. They can be hit to the ground, black, and within the first few weeks of spring there'll be new shoots, and a new bush by the end of summer. I called the garden Wigandia because *Wigandia caracasana* is the most asked-about plant I grow.

Teucriums are favourite plants of mine and would certainly go into any garden I made, along with melianthus and *Buddleia salviifolia*. I could not live without *T. betonicum*, which is often mistaken for a plectranthus. It can be used everywhere and the leaf texture and colour in winter is as interesting as the violetty flowers. In this district it's a hanger-on in the old nineteenth-century pastoral gardens. It doesn't get a decent spot, it's there because it's a survivor, and most gardeners would pooh-pooh it.

I have a lot of buddleias in the garden. As well as my favourite *B. salviifolia*—both the common one that is found everywhere and a form with a much more silvery leaf and a deeper-coloured flower that comes out a month earlier—there is *Buddleia crispa*, with a great long flower, and some interesting seedlings, crosses with unusual colours.

Calodendrum, the Cape chestnut, is another great plant. It has an attractive leaf, and the flower is very like an orchid. *Hibiscus cannabinum*, as in leaf cannabis, is a wonderful species hibiscus. It is cream with dark-brown or nearly black markings. It is worth growing even as an annual—it drops so many seeds, and will make quite a little thicket from just one plant. It flowers for months and months.

Melianthus grows brilliantly here and I am putting in several new species that I got as seed from South Africa. *Echium pininana* loves growing on nothing but scoria, no soil at all. We have a four-acre former scoria pit here, where I am establishing different echiums. And I am also using a grass that has fallen from favour, *Arundo donax*. It's a beauty and the English love it but it won't flower there.

In some quarters my garden is known as the garden that doesn't have flowers, which is not true. It's just that I go for a gentler floral year, rather than the big bang, punch you in the eye display followed by flat foliage. The whizz-bang flowers are often on plants with boring leaves and structure.

I plant colonies and like to see things fill up a space. I can't abide shrubs that are wrongly chosen for a position and have to be butchered at least once a year. It is very institutional. You see a lot of that happening in public gardens. More often than not the garden is overplanted. We plant too many shrubs and definitely too many trees. We are overwooded. If a plant isn't doing its job, get rid of it.

I use a lot of spiky plants and big leaves, and again my influence is Guilfoyle. It was his use of contrasting forms and shapes I've followed because I rely on a good body of foliage rather than a show of flowers. I've always loved different-shaped leaves and I don't think we appreciate as we should that we can grow a great range of semi-tropical looking things.

There is great variation, even in strappy leaves. For instance, *Phormium cookianum* has fairly lax leaves, whereas *P. tenax* is up in the air. A lot of the earlier cultivars in the sixties and seventies had both *P. cookianum* and *P. tenax* in their blood, so they were a mixture of upright leaves and flopping leaves, and I have always really liked those older cultivars. They don't have the brashness of more recent ones. I often find when I am working on an area I have a spot for something with strong sword-like foliage but I may not want the leaves sticking up like a shock of hair. I want something that is a mixture.

I don't know why *Doryanthes palmeri* isn't grown more. It is Australian but the most unlikely looking native. They look like they belong in New Guinea. They grow to five metres plus and they don't take very long to flower. I liken the flower to a giant toothbrush—a great curving banana covered in coral red flowers. The other species (*Doryanthes excelsa*) that is normally grown has a stem that goes straight up and a flower shaped like a giant red football—an extraordinary thing. They are so tough and you'll find them wherever Guilfoyle trod.

And I've got a heap of agapanthuses, grown from about ten different batches of imported seed from private gardens. A lot of the old 'aggies' that have been around since the year dot are rather muddy and boring, but these are very exciting, like nothing I've seen before. One has the palest blue flower and stands very upright at three feet. It should be out there in everyone's garden.

I also use a lot of self-sowing plants. They are very useful for loosening up permanent plantings. One of my best-performing plants of the moment is bronze fennel. I think I could sit in an acre of it. It's such a fantastic plant and works with just about everything. I like it particularly with the casuarinas, which set the scene to a fair chunk of my garden. I am also quite taken with *Achillea* 'Terracotta'—one of the German hybrids with a strong colour, which, like a lot of the achilleas, fades nicely.

Understanding the plants I use is an important part of the equation. I know how wide they will grow and I know which ones are slightly invasive and I often use that quality to create a natural colony. It is understanding what the plants will do for you in your plot, understanding your material.

Being too greedy is a great trap. In many gardens there seems to be one of everything and two if the tag says rare. If you are trying to put together a harmonious picture, you've got to curb that collector's 'must-have' urge, or you will probably end up with a motley collection of things you don't really want. I used to save everything, grow everything I could get hold of and then hate everything, but the more I garden, the less I want.

I am a collector of numerous things but I would never let my collecting take over my aim to have a harmonious garden. It is impossible to grow everything and I don't think we should fight and push and pour all our energies into growing things that don't belong. There is enough challenge and work to grow things that do grow well and to put them together well.

I've discarded heaps and heaps of plants. And there is not one plant I've used in the past and don't have now that I miss at all. At the time I probably thought it was wonderful but there is so much out there. When I do find something good, I might discard a whole group of plants to make a place for it. Some plants in my garden don't pay their way and I know there are better-performing plants to do the same job, so one day I'll replace them. But there are very few plants now that I feel I really have to have, that will move me to alter parts of the garden to slot them in. And I am not interested in putting in a garden bed and tweaking it over a couple of seasons, then getting bored with the concept and getting rid of it. My whole garden is a single garden bed. It is forever being tweaked.

I think I've got one more garden in me. I wouldn't mind gardening a flat, boring patch with no view. I would like the challenge! I might just cover it with casuarina, add some teucrium and melianthus, and that might be enough.

William Martin and his son Rory.

in their element

AUSTRALIA PROVIDES SOME OF THE SWEETEST-TEMPERED PLACES FOR PLANTSMEN AND WOMEN TO INDULGE THEIR INTERESTS.

Minnie Thomas surrounds herself with the roses for which South Australia is famous. The climate and the site itself, open to sun and fresh winds that discourage pests and diseases, are ideal for an unbridled love affair with roses. Pergolas, formal areas and borders that follow the natural contours of the slope give the shape and structure often lacking in rose gardens.

The northwest coast of Tasmania is another gardening paradise. At PIGEON HILL, Fairie Nielsen soon outgrew the garden surrounding her house. Now over seventy, Fairie has spent the past few decades clearing and planting a series of spectacular natural gullies, which begin below the home paddock and follow a network of creeks down the valley. Here, exotic woodland trees and huge rhododendrons flourish among native blackwoods, leatherwoods, sassafras and tree ferns.

Bob Griffin moved from Sydney to country New South Wales originally to farm, but a horticulture course switched his interest to gardening. At COORAMILLA, he has built a hillside garden around bold drifts of perennial plants, basing his plant groupings on a knowledge of natural plant associations. The combination of fertile soil and a long growing season result in phenomenal growth of herbaceous plants, and in Bob Griffin's talented hands, they provide the structure and architecture of the garden by themselves.

A similar idea—exploiting the fast growth of perennial plants to provide both form and substance in a short time—led to Michael McCoy's triumphant experiment in 'instant gardening' in his small town garden. The experiment appealed to Michael's inner scientist; its success relied on his knowledge and skill with plants. He came to garden design through a love of botany, and his approach bridges what are often yawning gaps between botanists and gardeners, and between gardeners and garden designers.

Gardeners with a passion for plants do not have to enjoy the most favourable gardening conditions to be in their element. By exploiting to the full their deep understanding of plants and how they perform, they can make less-than-ideal sites seem like the chosen place of the plants they grow. Stephen Ryan grew up on Mount Macedon near Melbourne. The grand gardens of the area were his childhood playground, where he picked up a fascination with plants almost by osmosis. He calls his jungly, rich-textured garden of rare plants 'the other Mount Macedon garden'. Making the most of a site with a smudge of topsoil on pebble-dashed clay would test any gardener. Yet at TUGURIUM, Stephen's 'plant Picassos' look so at home that non-gardening visitors assume they are natives.

After a tough horticultural apprenticeship in the north of England of his youth, Dennis Richardson swore off gardening for life. Years later the innate plantsman won out in a bold, confident garden that celebrates the heat of summer. The discipline of Dennis's early training is revealed in his scrupulous ground preparation and highly discriminating plant selection which underpin the seemingly effortless tour de force of his huge summer borders.

OVERLEAF: Shapely Himalayan cypresses (*Cupressus torulosa*), rhododendrons and hundreds of choice woodland trees and shrubs clothe a steep-walled gully at Pigeon Hill.

down among the roses

MINNIE THOMAS'S GARDEN

Minnie Thomas's 0.8 hectare (2 acre) garden is 15 km east of Adelaide at Stirling in the Adelaide Hills. Average rainfall is 1100 mm occurring mainly between April and October, while the 500 metres elevation of the garden ensures cool nights and only an occasional 40°C day in summer. The garden is frost free with winter temperatures rarely falling below 2°C. The fertile acid loam over clay is an ideal medium for the roses that are Minnie's chief love and the garden's focus.

Beds of toning pink roses surround a standard 'Sally Holmes' encircled by catmint. In the foreground are 'Bonica' and 'Seduction', leading round to 'French Lace', 'Ambridge Rose', 'Pristine' and 'Bredon'. 'Pinkie' provides a strong backdrop to 'Temora' and 'The Countryman'.

I THINK I started to become a gardener when I worked for a florist. I used to help people do flowers and then began growing them for my own use. I started collecting gardening books and from that I got obsessed.

When the children were young, I used to escape into the garden, and I think they knew my bottom more than my face because I was always head down. Just walking round the garden looking at flowers is the most peaceful feeling I know.

Working in other people's gardens helped with my own ideas, and my sister and I have helped each other. We've always swapped plants and knowledge. She is obsessed with curves and lines, so she has straightened or curved my lines a little bit more to her liking. And my husband Andrew cleans up my messes. Wherever I garden I leave little piles behind me and I hate clearing up. He also builds all the constructions to grow my roses on.

The garden has gradually got bigger over the years. I had no idea when I first started that it ever would get to this stage. When we came, there was a post-and-rail fence that was too close in. It was really hugging the cottage but I stuck within the confines to start with. There were a few old camellias, an old *Magnolia grandiflora* and two oak trees near the driveway, but no real garden.

I felt there was no connection between the house and the dam, so the fence started moving out into the horse paddocks. We then joined the whole thing up and it just got bigger and bigger. Then a tennis court went in, which opened up another whole area.

I did a horticulture course and became more obsessed. Probably the most valuable thing I learned was to use a space rather than plants and I think that shows here.

I've grown roses from the very beginning. I found they were so adaptable, they could be treated very harshly, and there are so many varieties. Most of my plants have been moved a million times and roses move so easily. I also adore perennials and I found the two work extremely well together, so every time I plant a new rose I buy more perennials. Then I buy another book on roses and one thing leads to another.

The roses get very little disease except a bit of powdery mildew. Unless I am opening the garden I try not to spray them. I looked at one rose the other day, covered in aphids, but every single bud had a ladybird on it. So they are doing their job. It is quite windy and open here, so disease is not a great problem and I don't mind the blemishes.

It is a very kind gardening climate and I can grow most things. I have used plants that are rather thirsty but I mulch well and try to toughen my plants up by not watering too much. We use bore water, which has lots of iron and stains everything orange, but it's low salt. It was really great having the bore put in because it enabled me to plant lots more garden and made watering a joy.

The soil on the slopes is very good. In some areas it was thin and I had to use a crowbar to put the plants in through the rock. I put mushroom compost on it for two years and it is beautiful now. I fertilise in spring religiously with a dynamic lifter or blood and bone and I have good intentions of doing it in autumn but often don't make it. I put all the leaves back on the garden; we have a compost heap and I occasionally get horse manure and pea straw.

I didn't plan the garden on paper. I just sort of started in one area and worked my way around the house. I still get surprised by how beautiful some of the plants are. You see them in books or in other people's gardens and you go out and you buy them, but you are still amazed when they come out in your garden. Especially the roses—each one is better than the last.

I am very particular about colours and as I made my rose beds I grouped them together. There are pinks and creams in one area, apricots and yellows in another. I love grey-leafed plants such as artemisias, nepetas, lambs' ears and bearded irises with the roses, and there are heaps of forget-me-nots and love-in-a-mist that self-seed everywhere.

The heritage rose garden faces northwest, so it gets the afternoon sun. On one side is a very rampant 'Wedding Day', and I have the yellow species roses 'Canary Bird' (*R. xanthina* f. *spontanea*) and persiana (*R. foetida* 'Persiana'). 'Penelope' goes all along the front mixed with irises. And on the other side there is 'Lamarque' climbing up some tripods and David Austin's 'Dark Lady', a deep-red rose. My favourite rose is 'Gruss an Aachen', which is just loaded with buds. I've also mass-planted some roses, such as 'Cornelia', which runs the whole length of one bed.

I choose roses first of all for colour. I find a lot of the old-fashioned ones are very fragrant anyway, so I try to find one with a good form and colour and the fragrance is a bonus. I have one area where I've planted roses purely for their hips.

On the old barn there is 'Meg', which is a soft apricot climber. I also have it on the tennis court wire. Over the large arbour I've planted all pink and blush climbing roses, including 'Constance Spry', 'Mme Alfred Carrière', 'Blossomtime', two 'Zéphirine Drouhin' and 'Sombreuil'.

The garden above the tennis court used to be a horse paddock and now has a sweep of lawn surrounded by curving beds. I've got very interested in contrasting foliage colours and shapes and I've got into stronger colours. I like purple-coloured foliage. I also like growing succulents and big architectural plants.

There is a huge trellis covered with 'Kathleen Harrop', 'Ophelia', 'Pinkie' and 'Clair Matin'. They form a framework for the beds of pink and apricot roses and I've gone into quite a few hot colours.

A rose I really like is 'Bishop Darlington', a very soft tea rose about seven feet high, but strong and self-supporting. There are some David Austins, which are fairly recent additions, and salvias hanging down over a dry stone wall, with 'Nozomi', which is a little single rose.

In the new rose garden that I've mainly planted for the hips there is 'Complicata', a single pink. I've also got 'Geranium' (*R. moyesii* 'Geranium') and *R. forrestiana*, which has interesting pear-shaped hips. There are a couple of rugosas and *Rosa glauca* with dark foliage.

Susan Irvine [the Australian rosarian and writer] has been a great influence on me. I could relate to her books and how she made her gardens and I've been to see every one, even the new one in Tasmania. I think it's incredible that she leaves those beautiful gardens behind her and moves on to create another one.

I like to choose roses after seeing them in other people's gardens, like the little *spinosissima* 'Single Cherry' I saw in Tasmania. It's got an attractive black hip and I didn't realise its flower would go so well with the one next door to it that has dark red hips.

I travel quite a lot to look at gardens. I have a particular friend and we leave our husbands behind and off we go and totally indulge ourselves. We visit gardens here, interstate and we've been overseas too.

It is very important to see other gardens because even if it's one tiny spot in a garden or two plants together, you get different ideas. And you get to know plants and where they will or won't grow.

There are many garden seats because I walk around the garden a lot. Nearly every morning I go off with a cup of coffee. I might just sit down for a few minutes on a bench somewhere and think, what am I going to do today? In the early years I was caught quite a few times in my nightie, still out in the garden at ten o'clock in the morning.

I was looking through one of my many gardening books the other day and I came across an ancient Chinese proverb and this says it all: 'If you wish to be happy for a day, get drunk. If you wish to be happy for a week, kill a pig. If you wish to be happy for a month, get married. But if you wish to be happy for ever and ever, make a garden.'

OVERLEAF: 'Nozomi' spills from a stone bowl amid a sea of the hybrid rugosa rose 'Frau Dagmar Hastrup'.

Minnie Thomas prunes 'Autumn Delight', a vigorous free-flowering hybrid musk rose. In the background is David Austin's 'Leander'.

fairie's folly

PIGEON HILL   FAIRIE NIELSEN

Pigeon Hill, on the northwest coast of Tasmania at Burnie, enjoys one of the best situations for gardening with its elevation of 180 metres, superb chocolate soil and an average rainfall of 1000 mm. Summer temperatures are mild, and in winter there is only an occasional frost and snowfall. The thirty-five-year-old garden has been built in two stages: the relatively mature area around the house, and a series of woodland gullies which Fairie continues to develop.

The fresh young foliage of a beautifully formed *Cornus kousa* var. *chinensis* is delineated by the dark mass of evergreens behind.

DURING MY EARLY childhood in New South Wales during the Depression, we had no garden at all. It was hot and dry and people simply had no time or money to indulge in gardening, except vegetable gardens. Then we moved to Woodburn in Burnie, where there was not much of a garden, although my mother was knowledgeable and always comfortable with gardening. But the inspiration I think came from my grandparents on my father's side. Mother's grandparents in Victoria had a very formal garden with a huge hideous South African boxthorn hedge around it. But Dad grew up at Culzean [a historic Tasmanian garden at Westbury] and that was very different.

Our grandmother had nine grandchildren at any one time in that garden. It was not formal and organised as it is today. We had the run of it, we played croquet non-stop on the croquet lawn and we lived in the trees. The avenue to Culzean was a tunnel of green. For all those grandchildren that garden became quite a focal point. My two sisters and my girl cousins all became really keen gardeners and I am sure that was Granny. She didn't go on about it, she just said, 'Do you mind chasing the peacocks out of the vegetables?' Could you do this or do that. Granny was a good gardener. They were short of money and labour but they made a wonderful arboretum. They used to get their plants from a nursery in Sydney and it all came down by boat. It was a big garden, not exactly overgrown, but it was wild and ideal for children.

Now my nephews and nieces come here regularly. They are not gardeners but they walk around and play in the creeks and I put them to work as well. I believe in stopping every now and again and saying, 'Isn't this good, all this moss or this particular flower? Isn't this intriguing?' I think if you teach small children how much beauty there is in the native bush, which I've got tons of, and how beautiful things are in their own right, they might not do anything for twenty years, but you have sown the seed.

Years ago in *The Englishwoman's Garden* [by Alvilde Lees-Milne and Rosemary Verey] I saw a photo captioned 'The Folly'. There was a very steep gully with lots of rhododendrons. Now the children call this Fairie's Folly. Rhododendrons do so well in this climate and are the one thing wallabies and possums don't eat. It is very handy, as you can put big clusters together. I love them, though I must admit there are things I would like just as well if they weren't eaten. The wildlife has been the most difficult thing in making this garden.

I always remember John Buchan's *The Thirty Nine Steps*, where the character gets lost in a thicket of rhododendrons. At that time we had one lone rhododendron on the lawn—we all jumped over it. I wondered how you could possibly get lost in a thicket of rhododendrons, until I got to Scotland and saw for myself. It was actually that same *Rhododendron ponticum* I planted down in the gully. And it did make a true thicket, so much so that I had to take it out. I thought I was there for life! I thought, I hope someone will find me if I die down here.

When I first got my own home and garden, I thought of flowers for the house and lawn for the children to play on. Danny my husband was an engineer and he was away a lot overseas. Mother wasn't well, I had two young children and was running the farm and it was hard work for about seven years. But I did a little bit of garden around the house. Danny put up a fence and, typical engineer, set every post in concrete and made sure not even a spider could have got through the netting. Everything was straight and square—even in the vegetable patch every onion and lettuce was in a straight line and if it leaned sideways out it came!

My mother encouraged me a lot. I had a 'birthday present' of a plant every month from her for the first few years. She'd give me a cornus she had just seen, knowing I liked them. She gave me a lot of plants that she knew well from books, even though she had not grown them herself.

Danny was Danish. He knew all the European trees, many deciduous trees and conifers that I hadn't heard of and he was very keen to plant them. We got quite a lot of seed from his parents and relatives in Denmark and Norway, including some of the conifers you couldn't get in Australia. We learned by experience that the trees that grow in Europe stop growing in the cold icy winters, but here in Tasmania on the northwest coast, with good rainfall and soil, they just go on growing. So while it takes a hundred years for an oak to reach a hundred feet in Europe, here it will do it in forty. You think you have plenty of room but I find I am now having to take things out.

People kept giving me plants and cuttings, knowing I was a keen gardener. Once the children were at school and I was a bit freer, I soon ran out of space to plant things and Danny said, 'Well, there are all those gullies down there. I can't use them for anything, have those if you like.' I said, 'Thank you very much!' But I did go down there and investigate and we cut the first gully and burned a bit away and he and I planted the first trees—which I like so much now—the conifers and the oaks.

When Danny died, I considered selling but I thought I could manage it as I had grown up on a farm. I decided to make more space and asked my son Peter and a friend of his if they'd like to pull the fence down to earn a bit of pocket money. I thought it was a weekend job. Well, we started in September and it took six weeks. Each post had to be taken out with the tractor and hoist. It ruined the road, ruined the watering system, which I didn't know was there, and made an appalling mess. Everyone came and asked what the hell I was doing and I said, 'I'm just extending the garden. Go away!' And it took another year to cart the stone for the wall to replace the fence.

Then I said to Peter, I don't think this looks quite balanced, so we took out the fence along the road and extended over there. He said, 'Now do you think this is enough, Mother?' But of course it wasn't and in the end I was going clip, clip, clip down into the gully. Every time I thought, I'm not going into it, well, I'll just go a bit further. Then I got to where two creeks joined and of course there was another creek going off that. And Peter—this was his fault—said, 'You know, I think there is a waterfall there. It would be nice if you could uncover that.' That took two years, but when I saw the potential there I thought there is nothing for it, this is gully two.

So now I've got two gullies and I could go on for ever, but of course common sense has caught up with me at last. And I did learn that it's no good clearing without planting straight away because all the rubbish comes up and you've got the job all over again. So I've always cut by hand and the following year the blackberries come and I can walk through and spray them. Then things grow up and you learn and read and visit and you say 'Ah! Couldn't live without that tree!' And so it goes on. The first gully is now mature and almost everything we have

planted has gone well, so I know the next one will work, if only I can live long enough.

People have said I should get some paths down there. But it is not a path sort of garden. It was never intended to be a garden open to the public; just my indulgence. I am not a path-maker and don't actually want a lot of people down there. I put a main path to walk along and the idea is to stay on the high ground and look into the gully, which, with careful planning, you ought to be able to see. I am very conscious of not planting out my sightlines. People keep asking when I am going to finish planting. I tell them I have finished and they can't see it.

I like my visitors to stay on the high ground but then, of course, the keen ones go down and ask 'What's this?' and I say 'Well I am rather pleased, it's a so-and-so cross, quite rare.' And then down we all trek, taking our lives in our hands!

I know I am a very greedy gardener. The first davidia (*D. involucrata*) I got, I was besotted with. Now I've two more. Then I saw that beautiful *Magnolia campbellii* in the Mount Wilson garden of Peter Valder [the Australian gardener and writer]. I had read it doesn't flower for seventeen years but mine has flowered in six and this year it was absolutely beautiful. Now I have two more of those.

I love trees the most because they'll go on. This garden isn't really about flowers. You have flowers for the house and there are actually quite a lot of flowers here with the bulbs and shrubs. But those gullies are only suitable for trees. The first time I opened the garden I was criticised for not having flowers and that meant beds of flowers.

Probably I've been most influenced by the gardens at Mount Wilson in the Blue Mountains [New South Wales] because of the trees. Going to those gardens with a similar rainfall and climate to mine really opened my eyes to mass planting.

But my great teacher was a friend of Danny's, a Danish landscape gardener called Harry Frederiksen, who settled in Australia. He never practised landscaping here but he eventually came to live in Burnie and used to stay with us. He knew his trees, and what something would look like in twenty or thirty years and he would say, 'No Fairie, that's a big tree and it's a pyramid shape so it's a mistake to plant it there.' Or that I needed more blue or gold somewhere.

The greatest lesson I learned from him was that when you plant trees you must look at the long view and be sure you don't muck up your sightlines. We'd be planting and he'd tell me to run back to the house and look from the upstairs window. And he also told me never to buy just one tree. You've got the space, he'd say, so buy ten magnolias or ten camellias and have done with it, or you'll get a spotty garden. Sometimes I would think it looked a bit sombre but he could always picture how it was going to be.

Another very important thing I learned from Harry was to use conifers. You need them to tie everything together. It took me a while to come to grips with that because I kept thinking of radiata pines, not those beautiful European conifers. You can see how conifers really set other trees off, like that michelia against its dark background.

I wish I had started earlier, so I could have been where I am now when I was thirty-five. I am now finding it hard going getting round the second gully. Getting the blackberries out is the hardest but also the most rewarding work. Because it is on a slope, you are looking up at it all the time. You can't spray, or walk through it or use a whippersnipper or burn it. It has to be cut by hand. It is the hardest, slowest and most frustrating job but it's also often where the best soil is. So I have to get down there.

But having had some success at seeing what lies underneath all this blackberry—like the manferns— and knowing that the soil's good and that plants will all do well down there, encourages me.

I wish I had done all the hard work first and left the garden around the house for my old age! But it has all given me tremendous pleasure. I think gardening is a lovely occupation.

Even if I drop dead tomorrow, the trees are now big enough to live by themselves. The small stuff will probably go because people won't want to be bothered with it but the trees now are of an age to look after themselves. What happens next doesn't fuss me. I've had all the fun and made all the friends. It's amazing how many friends you make through gardening.

Anything you do yourself is so satisfying. You think, how clever, I did this all by myself! You have disasters but I think if more people had even a small patch of garden there'd be less stresses and strains. And for children a garden this size is absolute bliss.

I still visualise it in another thirty years. People say, haven't you finished? And I say well, I haven't done the last parts yet. I want three or four pools with hostas. I haven't got the stream quite to my liking with the small plants along it. And of course there are still trees to plant.

The magnificent white trunk of a *Eucalyptus viminalis* sets off the brilliant foliage of a group of maples. In the foreground, massed daboecia makes a showy and long-flowering groundcover.

Fairie Nielsen against one of the garden's giant gums.

making associations

COORAMILLA BOB GRIFFIN

Cooramilla is a 1.2 hectare (3 acre) garden near Blayney in central western New South Wales, 250 km from Sydney. Bob Griffin's main interest is in growing perennials, for which Cooramilla's conditions are excellently suited. A high altitude (1000 metres) ensures that summer temperatures rarely exceed the low 30s. The soil is a fertile basalt clay and grey loam, and the rainfall of 800 mm is distributed through the year. Cold winters, with weeks of −4°C frosts, also suit the natural conditions of the cool climate plants grown here.

'Reclining Figure'—a metal sculpture by Peter Gibson—is sited behind a huge drift of *Scabiosa* 'Butterfly Blue'.
The low-growing *Berberis thunbergii* 'Atropurpurea Nana' (syn. 'Little Favourite') adds depth to the composition.

Shrubs and trees planted to create the effect of a natural woodland clearing shelter a host of cool-climate perennials. In the foreground are healthy clumps of gooseneck loosestrife (*Lysimachia clethroides*) and golden *Telekia speciosa*, with a tall eupatorium waiting in the wings.

WHEN I MOVED from Sydney to Blayney to farm, I didn't touch the garden for the first three years. It remained a bare paddock, with 300 sheep to keep the lawn down. I was busy out in the paddocks. The rest of the farm was very much like the garden—it needed a lot of attention.

But like most farmers here, I had to diversify. I studied propagation so I could afford to have the size and scale of garden I wanted, and I started a nursery. The nursery gradually took over from the farm. Now the nursery is my main commercial activity and the garden is my consuming pleasure.

I garden in grabs. Whenever I've got a bit of time I pop out and do something. At times I am so busy with the nursery and farm I don't garden for six weeks. Then I get intensely involved and do a lot in a short time.

The defining characteristic of gardening if you compare it with other artforms is that it is a process rather than an object. Sculpture is a three-dimensional form, it's about space. But what defines gardening is time and change. We are dealing with something that is in a constant state of change. It is not an object that we can slightly rearrange and this has got all sorts of ramifications. The easy part is planting the plants. The hard part is keeping it looking good, keeping it full of interest.

I am not inhibited by all sorts of philosophies about what a garden should be like. I started off pretty fresh, and so haven't been self-conscious about gardening. I've been able to do things and then stand back and say that looks good, or that needs something else.

When I studied horticulture, I became interested in the huge range of plants there are. I came to appreciate their diversity, their similarities and differences, and what they need in order to grow. One writer who had a big influence on me was Beth Chatto. She works on an ecological basis. A wonderful designer with the skills to win gold medals at the Chelsea Flower Show, you'd expect her to talk about the way plants are put together, whereas her main concern is that they should be planted where they'll do best. English gardening is so sophisticated and they take gardening very seriously. It is a serious cultural pursuit. But her voice speaks to me in a language I can understand.

The beauty of planting on an ecological basis is that you get plant associations that really work because the plants tend to look right together. Plants in a particular group have to love the same conditions. That way, you get natural association and a lot of your job is done for you. Then it is worrying about form and working on detail. You have to be very careful to select plants that balance so you don't put thugs with plants that are delicate.

One thing I've found, which I still haven't read anywhere, is that plants chosen for a similar situation tend to flower at the same time of the year. I've got a series of garden beds that shine in winter, early spring, mid-spring, mid-summer. They are seasonal gardens.

Gardeners who truly recognise the individuality of their particular location and try to create a garden that suits it and thrives in it, are likely to have successful gardens. It is arguable whether that then becomes an Australian garden, or whether it becomes just part of a world gardening culture where there is a lot of individuality both in design and plant choice.

One of the main reasons I live where I live is not so I can garden here, but so I can live in the countryside, in the landscape. Both the house and the garden are sheltering in this little fold, and that is the way we survive. There are all sorts of aspects to how you relate to a landscape, and part of it is how you stop the elements blowing you off the soil. At the same time you don't block yourself in, because you then block out the very reason why you are here. So I try to have it open as much as I can, to leave vistas. Deciduous trees work well. In winter you can see more of the landscape through the trees.

The garden was designed in stages. The front area really came about through the natural need for a driveway to make the whole place accessible. That created an island, so I had a road and natural beds that gave me the basic structure.

Up the hill behind the house I wanted to reverse the normal relationship between lawn and garden and have virtually all plants, with lawn pathways to bridge the plants. The picture I had was of a very full area. Once I decided that, a lot of the pathways were made by walking around and gaining access to different parts. This gave the garden a very easy, natural feel. I was trying to do something I thought wasn't following anyone else's lessons. I was trying to work out a few things for myself.

When I ploughed the paddock up, the water ran down into the gully and it became a series of ponds. If you can go with the landform, then your garden will fit the landscape. You couldn't have a formal garden on a slope like this. You need billiard-table flatness or retaining walls. But you can have strong structural elements with plants, which I've tried for throughout the garden.

Although the garden has almost independent segments, they are linked together visually. The sorts of colours I used, I kept on repeating. I am less interested in colour than in form and texture so I repeated the same colours in different combinations with different contrasts.

There are always floods of new ideas and it will always be changing. I would hate to think I ever had a finished garden but I would like to reach an equilibrium within my physical limits. I don't want it to become a monster, something I haven't got time to maintain.

I have two very basic requirements for plants: one, that I can grow them easily, and the other that they are gardenworthy. I am not interested in a plant because it's another salvia or something I haven't got. I am interested in the best plant.

Plant combination is often serendipity. A lot of the time your eye is looking at the picture just the way an artist does when looking at the composition of elements in a painting. It's out of balance or it's in balance.

My main interest is in perennials, partly because I get such quick rewards from them. Perennials reach maturity in two years, whereas shrubs and trees can take a lifetime. Perennials create their own framework. Some will grow a couple of metres in a year and will do that every year because they are herbaceous and die right down. When I first came here, I planted all natives but I couldn't take them

very far. I found with perennials, and shrubs to give me a backbone, I could create something far more interesting. Now I grow natives if they are gardenworthy plants here—so I have things like the gorgeous little *Acacia cognata* 'Green Mist', which is one of the most exquisite plants in my garden.

Apart from Beth Chatto, my biggest inspiration has been Barbara Cottee's garden in Orange. It wasn't just her planting—she also inspired me to garden on that scale. When I talked to Barbara, I discovered that although she had an incredibly well-structured design, she was completely unconscious of it.

Gardening is a bit like grammar in a language, a structure in the way we speak all the time even though we are not conscious of it. A child can use the most complex grammar and not be aware of it. There are all sorts of strong structural elements. The whole thing inspired me—it got me out of the suburban constriction and allowed me to garden on the scale that this huge landscape of ours demands.

Sandra Russell and Bob Griffin.

a bold experiment

MICHAEL McCOY'S GARDEN

Michael McCoy worked professionally in Melbourne and Mount Macedon gardens for several years before embarking on his own 0.1 hectare ($1/4$ acre) garden at Woodend, 70 km northwest of Melbourne in the Macedon Ranges. His summer gravel garden of drought-hardy plants was designed to peak in just eighteen months.

LEFT: Grouped with a masterly sense of colour, form and texture are flaming *Gaillardia* 'Mandarin', a fine-leaved stipa and *Eupatorium maculatum* 'Gateway'. In front of the rustic trellis, *Miscanthus sinensis* 'Gracillimus' arches over bronze fennel and bronze-leaved *Dahlia* 'Clarion'.

MIDDLE: Intensified by the rich blues of *Nepeta* 'Six Hills Giant' and *Salvia azurea*, a magnificent clump of *Sedum* 'Autumn Joy' picks up the warm

tones of an oil jar nestled among nasturtiums. Creamy yellow *Achillea* 'Hoffnung', purple *Verbena bonariensis* and a silver mound of *Artemisia ludoviciana* play supporting roles. RIGHT: Dark purple plantain gives weight to a grouping of *Kniphofia* 'Maid of Orleans', lime green nicotiana, *Achillea* 'Terracotta' and verbascum.

I HATED GARDENING with a passion as a kid. I remember being forced to come out and help weed and just hating it. Then there was a period between school and university when I was stuck at home and I got interested in propagating. It just fascinated me that tips of plants put in water or soil would grow their own roots. So I came to gardening via propagating and then got interested in the context of the garden and became a fanatic overnight. Gardening just got me.

I was doing a science degree and intended shifting to veterinary science and never did, because I discovered botany and it was sufficiently related to my passion for gardening to keep me interested. After I finished my degree, Professor Carrick Chambers [Professor of Botany, University of Melbourne and later Director of the Royal Botanic Gardens Sydney] assisted in getting me an apprenticeship at Rippon Lea, the National Trust property in Melbourne. He could see that there was a great rift between people in garden administration and those actually doing the gardening, and he was hoping that I and a girl doing similar training might begin to bridge this gap. That never really came about but Rippon Lea was probably the best place I could have started.

The head gardener had been taught at Burnley Horticultural College in the days when Burnley taught people how to garden hands-on and he had a wonderful grasp of basic principles. As a scientist, I always want to go back to the universal rule. I am never happy just learning specifics. And he was able to help. But I became very disillusioned with gardening as a profession. I had come to it because of a personal passion but the education level after doing a science degree was a joke and I didn't find anyone there with anything like the passion I assumed they'd all have.

Then I made contact with the Australian gardener and writer Jean Galbraith when I was researching something. We started corresponding and she put me in touch with friends of hers, passionate gardeners who helped me to see there was some real enthusiasm and interest out there. Then someone gave me one of Christopher Lloyd's books. I had no intention of reading it, I was that cynical about the gardening world. I thought I would keep it for a polite length of time and hand it back, but just before I did I thought I had better have a quick

glance at it so I would know something of what was in it. I started reading and just couldn't put it down. I thought, this is the way I want to garden and to think about gardening. From that point I devoured everything Christopher Lloyd wrote.

The big problem for professional gardeners here is a general lack of recognition of gardening as a craft of extraordinary skill. The things that I've been taught, I've only learned because I've been so passionate about wanting to learn. A lot of the stuff that I have had to extract through years of experimentation would have been taught to me in my first year in one of those big English gardens.

The technical skills of gardening are essential before you can begin the art of it. I am constantly finding something I want to express but technically don't have the ability to do and if I am finding that, with the huge opportunities I've had to learn, how many other people are?

In discovering Christopher Lloyd I realised that any amount of inquisitiveness and questioning is valid. I think that is what attracted me about his writing and kept me going at Rippon Lea. Then the head gardener set up a job for me with Lindsay and Paula Fox at their garden in Toorak, which I thought was the most fantastic thing that had ever happened to me. And the very first day I arrived to work there, Paula told me they'd bought Hascombe, one of the great old Mount Macedon gardens, and wanted me to take that over as well. We worked together very effectively for nearly ten years and while I was carrying out their vision, I was able to play with a lot of things on the side, trying out plants I didn't know and so on.

Meanwhile I had made contact with Christopher Lloyd and we started to correspond. He asked me to come and work in England. I went to Lindsay Fox in a moment of passion and said I wanted to go overseas. They didn't want me to resign so they paid me while I was over there, which meant I could volunteer to work for Christopher Lloyd. My time at Great Dixter was the pivotal point for me, not in anything specific that he taught me, but just in validating my approach and the way I thought about gardening. At Dixter, the conversation always centred on gardening in one way or another.

I came back and worked for the Foxes for about another five years at Hascombe. I was more confident. Christopher had taught me to lighten up, that there weren't really any rights and wrongs. It was a matter of getting in there, having a go and, above all, having fun. I used to read the English gardening books, and the photos and captions gave me the impression that gardening, combining plants, was a very difficult thing to do and that it would be years and years before I even came close. But having worked with Christopher Lloyd I realised it was a nonsense. If something works, great, if it doesn't, try something else.

It has taken me fifteen years of gardening to realise that in general, if you are going to create a good garden you have to be thinking always about the bigger picture and the broader effect. But interestingly in my own garden, I deliberately chose to overthrow a lot of the stuff I learned to revert to the plantsman in a sense. I think it's because it's the first garden I have had and although I wouldn't do this in gardens I make for other people I still had to go through that stage in my own garden. But I am already seeing the need to simplify. It's quite scary, I am going so much the other way now in my design for other people that I start to panic. Perhaps my planting is too simplified, to the point where I think if I can do the job with three different plants, why would I choose any more than three?

What excites me as much as anything is technical virtuosity. Powis Castle in Wales did that for me. It was an extreme example of the sort of thing I was trying to achieve. There was the highest level of technical ability and it was so fabulously energetic, with all these half-hardy things put out at the beginning of summer, so it just powered away with incredible vigour.

I was greatly affected by a garden design conference which made me realise there was a whole world out there using totally different materials to create outdoor spaces. I saw that plants are just a spatial tool, and the strength of the garden is about its volumes and three-dimensional quality. That is the main contribution of the plants, rather than their flowers or anything else. There is a spatial potential of gardens that could be much more explored. At Sissinghurst, for instance, there is not a single spot where you'd want to lie on the lawn and look. It's just this fantastic display of technical achievement. So I came to realise that if I have technical skill, it's only so that I can better serve the creation of this spatial element.

The starting point of my own garden was that we didn't intend to be there for very long, and I didn't want to wait two seasons, I wanted a garden in the first year. For ten years I had been living in somebody else's garden and I had this desperate need for my own. So I launched into it with the aim of a good but quick garden purely for myself. And the more I was convinced it could actually work, the more I thought the Open Garden Scheme might be interested in opening it to the public. I was prepared to accept it as an experiment, knowing it could be a dismal failure or a huge success.

It was crazy but tremendously exciting to try and create a garden that would peak in under two years—I wanted to put it to the test.

I knew what perennial plants are capable of here and I knew I had access to a good range of plants without having to buy much, which I couldn't afford. So the aim was to create a sense of structure and within that have all sorts of plants that would look good in February. I had a few reasonable-sized fruit trees and worked the design through them to give more of an established feeling.

I was forced to do some things that I wouldn't have done if there had been a longer time-frame. I had to skip the woody plants that normally mature over a few years to form the permanent evergreen structure of a garden and I just jam-packed it full of really tall perennials for fast impact. It was a good experiment, it was lots of fun and it proved that plants can create huge volumes and define spaces in a very short space of time.

I wanted to show what plants are capable of and I managed to do it for about $2000 including gravel and compost. I wanted to do it on a very low budget. I actually only watered the gravel garden once over a period of eighteen months. It stretched my experience to the absolute limit. I had to rely heavily on my knowledge of how plants perform, how high each would grow and how they would all relate to each other.

There was no room for trial and error, so some plants I would quite like to have used, I chose not to. I only put in things I knew would work. And interestingly, it caused a complete about-face for me: I am just not interested in growing the difficult stuff, the stuff that isn't going to succeed now. I have discovered that I am a garden lover rather than a plant lover.

What I aim for now is to stretch the boundaries of when the whole garden feels right. It can't be twelve months but let's see if it could be eight. That is why I have moved towards things that are absolutely reliable.

Christopher Lloyd has been a great influence on me but I don't see his gardening philosophy as typically English. As far as Australian gardening style goes, perhaps we are not best placed to identify it. A French photographer told me he loved our incredible, generous sense of space, the way we think about space and use it in our landscape.

I think perhaps we are too self-conscious to recognise what's truly Australian. But I think that national or local cultures are dissolving. What happens is that individual landscapers, like Thomas Church or more recently van Sweden in America, come to the fore and do something new, and then it is regarded as belonging to that country.

What excites me, whatever style of garden it is, is technical achievement and craftsmanship. In my case, it took constant exploration to make my 'instant' garden. It may have looked easy but it was mighty hard to do. Gardening is a journey and it's great fun along the way. I still have as much fun now as I did in my first year of gardening but it's a whole lot harder than it appears. I don't think any gardener ever attains the skills to fully reach their vision. The trouble is that people start off feeling they won't be happy until they achieve a certain level, and that is not the case.

I love gardens that are incredibly simple and show one idea carried out to the extreme but I don't think I would ever create one for myself. Those beautifully simple courtyards, for instance, look nice but they are not a lot of fun for a gardener. The gardens I admire most aren't what I want to live in. My place will always be a bit of a hotchpotch because I want to experiment with different things and have fun, and for me that is playing with plants.

stephen's weeds

TUGURIUM STEPHEN RYAN

At the foot of Mount Macedon, 60 km northwest of Melbourne, is the garden of plantsman, nurseryman and writer Stephen Ryan. In contrast to the great gardens of Mount Macedon, Tugurium is small (0.3 hectares/$3/4$ acre) and is built on the poor, gravelly clay soil of a site burned out in the 1983 Ash Wednesday bushfires. This has necessitated extensive building up of beds and mulching to accommodate a vast and ever-increasing collection of plants, whose exciting textures and shapes enclose the garden.

Close planting enables a huge range of rare and interesting species to be accommodated at Tugurium, and creates a sense of depth and mystery that belies the garden's size. Here, lush-leaved bog plants including *Cyperus alternifolius* and *Salix x erythroflexuosa* contrast with orthrosanthus, *Onopordum acanthium* and *Helleborus foetidus* 'Wester Flisk'. The autumn tints of *Acer japonicum* 'Aconitifolium' echo the tones of variegated box in the foreground.

I THINK I was meant to be a gardener. The family moved up here when I was about five, right up the top of the mountain opposite Duneira, and I used to play in all those big gardens. The owners and gardeners never knew I was there. When I was ten, my father decided to open a nursery. From the early days I can remember being enthused by plants I had never seen before. That has always been my interest, to have something I haven't got in plant life. Ours was a large retail and wholesale nursery; we used to grow 30,000 rhododendrons a year.

Dad used to give me a cheque once a year—filled out to fifty dollars or something so I couldn't overspend. And I could go for a little tootle up to the Dandenongs and buy some things I wanted. Dad saw them as completely useless, Stephen's weeds basically, because I would bring these obscure plants home that nobody would ever ask for. I was always keen and on the mountain everybody assumed that I would end up in horticulture—that was the way it was going to be.

There were some good gardeners at Mount Macedon. The one that really sticks in my mind is Hamish McVinney because he was one of the few who had grown up in the old world and had been trained by the head gardener on a Scottish or English estate somewhere and had worked his way up, so he knew gardens inside out. When we first came to Mount Macedon, he was head gardener at Duneira. There were lots of others who had grown up and been trained in the area and I got to know all of them.

This is my first garden and I am very happy where I am. When the family moved away from the old nursery, I opened my own nursery business but I didn't have anywhere to live. So I started madly scrambling around to find somewhere and this was a vacant block that had been burnt out in the Ash Wednesday bushfires and I could afford it. If I'd had the money, I probably wouldn't have bought here—but the bad points about the block are outweighed by a lot of its advantages.

The worst point is that the soil is absolute rubbish. There is no topsoil except a smudge under the gum leaves. It is just a sort of whitish clay with pebbles through it. When I came, there were a few old messmates (*Eucalyptus obliqua*), some of which are still here, and almost nothing was growing on the ground. There were a few tufts of grasses, some seedling blackwoods and gums coming up, but not a blackberry or a thistle or a dockweed, or anything that suggested fertility.

Some of the advantages are that it is a nice quiet little street and our neighbours are all fabulous and do what they are told. If I want to plant something in their garden, they accept it! So I can sort of impose plants on them willy nilly. It's amazing what you can get away with if you say it with conviction.

I was working seven days a week—in the nursery and in everyone else's gardens—and I didn't start seriously gardening here until my partner Craig came on the scene in 1988. He couldn't understand why this person who grew all these fantastic plants didn't want them around him at home. But I just couldn't cope with them at home. I hadn't got things to that level.

The people who used to own the house next door when I built this funny little weatherboard cottage said to a mutual acquaintance, 'Isn't it a shame the young bloke next door's built that little hovel.' I was highly offended and I was going to get a piece of corrugated iron and some red paint and write 'The Hovel' on it and nail it to one of the gum trees out the front. But my sister said, 'No, you've got to be more subtle than that. You work with Latin, so find out what a hovel is in Latin.' And that is what Tugurium means.

My interest in plants includes everything I can find out about them. That is part of being a professional in your field. Just as doctors have to learn all the names of bones and diseases, a horticulturist needs to know the names of plants. The plant name isn't just a reference point, it also gives the plant personality.

I can pin onto the name all that really fascinating historical data and all the things I love to know about something. You know, there is nothing more exciting to me than to read about a plant and find somebody fell to their death while collecting it!

I did a three-year apprenticeship in horticulture when I was starting out because I wanted to get the papers. The course was actually called Gardening and Turf Management and we visited lots of golf courses and crematoria looking at grass. I breezed through the first two years without even having to study because I had been in the family nursery for so long I knew most of what they were trying to teach us—except about turf grasses. I still don't know what dollar spot disease looks like. Then I got a couple of overseas scholarships that were great fun. I spent twelve months in New Zealand and three months in England, working in parks and gardens.

But the nursery was what I always wanted to do. I wanted a small specialist nursery, a sort of boutique nursery growing a few of this and a few of that. Lots of people in the nursery trade told me I would go broke because there was no economy of scale in my nursery. But it doesn't have to support anybody else, and it gives me a great lifestyle.

I didn't design the garden. It was really a matter of trying to plant with the site in mind. We had to select plants carefully because of the shade. And the only way I could see of making the site feel a lot bigger than it was, was to make a really rambly, undesigned sort of garden, so you felt like you were wandering miles within a smallish area. Many designers will tell you that small spaces need to be carefully handled, but I think small spaces need to be really exuberant if they are going to feel bigger than they are. You've got to really fill a garden up if you are going to make do with a small area.

We wanted to blend the garden into the surrounding bush but we didn't want a native garden. Australia is the only country in the world where people ask where something comes from before they ask whether they can grow it or not.

You have two camps. You have the Australian native environmentally conscious group, who think we should do nothing but plant Australian native plants, and then you have the other camp who say, 'They don't mix well together, so we are just going to have our weeping cherries and our standard roses.' People don't see that you *can* mix them.

I started with a basis of gums and blackwoods, and then it was a matter of planting underneath. Some of the things I planted are in the broader sense native because 'native' puts a very man-made geographical boundary around things. You know, New Zealand could have been part of Australia, and New Guinea was a Protectorate for a long time, so New Guinean plants could have been considered Australian natives. I select plants because I like their texture and their look, and where they come from doesn't matter.

You've got to work within the character of the site. I want to collect rare plants and have interesting things in the garden. I am passionate about foliages and textures and forms, more so probably than flowers and colour. The plants don't need to be rare. The garden is full of forget-me-nots and foxgloves and honesty, all common garden plants I wouldn't be without. But then I've got *Sophora toromiro*, which has been extinct in the wild for seventy or eighty years. So I've probably got one of the world's rarest plants growing surrounded by forget-me-nots.

I want to have rare plants because they give the garden another aspect. Few of us can afford a Henry Moore sculpture or an original Picasso but we can have a plant nobody else in the street's got. You can buy a very rare and interesting plant for little more than you probably paid for your golden diosma or your 'James Stirling' pittosporum. We can make our gardens individual and unique with interesting plants. I've probably had more plants come through my hands that have since gone to the compost heap than most people and it doesn't worry me at all. I've enjoyed them while they've been with me, it's all part of the fun of it. And if something does die on me it gives me a gap in the garden. A garden's got to be fun.

When we get a dry summer, I spend an enormous amount of time out there with a hand-held hose. I couldn't do that in a five-acre garden with all the precious things I am trying to keep here. And there is no way I could have anything but dry barren areas in the summer if I wasn't prepared to water.

But I don't see plants as something precious. Sometimes I let a plant get swamped because I am bored with it and the space could be better taken up by the plant next door. I am not precious about how far apart I have to plant my trees either, because I figure trees will take up the space you allot them. If in twenty or thirty years they are too big, I've got a chainsaw.

I don't want a garden that takes thirty years before I enjoy it. The garden's for now. I like to get fairly quick results, so I overplant like mad.

I am not planting a botanic garden that is going to be here in a hundred years. I would be very surprised if any of my gardens survived me.

Viburnum macrocephalum f. macrocephalum 'Sterile' is a choice form of this popular flowering shrub. Its huge greenish-white flowers are a voluptuous accent in a garden where foliage plays the dominant role.

This will disappear when I go from it. Some of the plants will survive and people might make the effort to try and keep it as I left it, but it will never be like I had it because of what I do in it.

I get an idea of what colours I want in a particular area, what textures I am looking for, and then I try to find plants that will fill it, but I don't plan ahead. Often the colour combinations in the garden are accidental and then they are extended because that is what happened to be there.

Sometimes it's fun to do things that other people don't like. I have the same attitude as Christopher Lloyd there. This border out the front is a whole area of magenta, purple and puce, which most people hate. I feel terribly sorry for all those tasteful people who limit themselves in colour and say I am only going to have a pastel garden or I can't have any yellow. If there is something that I am not sure how to use, I'll go out of my way to try and do it, not limit myself by what other people say I should do. I try to make sure every colour that I can think of is in the garden somewhere.

Colour is one of those things that you can get so locked up in. I think texture's far more important. I try to steer away from throwing really screaming colours at each other unless that is the effect I am trying to get, but I make sure I've got my strappy foliages and my fluffy foliages and my platey leaves and all those things that go through the border, and then the colour becomes incidental.

I see this as my own version of an Australian garden, if you want to put a label on it, but I don't see any point in an Australian garden. I can't see any point in a Tasmanian garden or a Western Australian garden, let alone an Australian one.

When non-gardeners see this garden, their overall impression is that it fits within the environment and therefore it must be a native garden. The people who appreciate the garden most are firstly those who perhaps are at the same stage as I am—where they've got sick of the obvious, of the pink and white collectors and the garden mafia types. And secondly, children. Small children love it, just as I loved the old gardens of Mount Macedon as a child.

And this is one of those gardens you don't have to be precious about. I don't panic when I see children running down the path here. They might step on the leaves of something or on the odd bulb, but it is not one of those gardens that relies on being neat and tidy and it doesn't matter if things get a little bit knocked about.

I can't say I wasn't inspired or excited by most of the gardeners that people are excited by, the Christopher Lloyds, the Beth Chattos. I have been excited by their techniques, I have been excited to see their gardens, I have been excited by their skill as growers and the depth of knowledge they've got. And the annoyance of going there and finding they not only have a particular plant that I've always liked but they've got the superior form! But I still wouldn't say any of them directly influenced me. They're inspiring because they give you the enthusiasm that you need to be a constant gardener. They are kindred spirits.

I was very lucky to grow up in a horticulturally interesting area, so that I got to love plants almost by osmosis. I would really never want to garden anywhere else. I am too deeply rooted in Macedon.

Stephen Ryan.

the reluctant gardener

DENNIS RICHARDSON'S GARDEN

At McLaren Vale on the Fleurieu Peninsula, 40 km south of Adelaide is Dennis Richardson's 0.8 hectare (2 acre) garden. The rainfall of 500 mm is winter dominant and the close proximity of the Mount Lofty Ranges effectively places the garden in a rainshadow. The site is flat and the alkaline soil varies between sand and red clay over a limestone reef, which is often encountered at less than a spade's depth. With its close proximity to the coast, the garden is frost free with winter temperatures seldom falling below 6°C. Dennis is a highly disciplined plantsman who concentrates on growing the best forms of a few top-performing species. During summer, when temperatures regularly reach 42°C fanned by northerly winds, his garden is at its most spectacular.

Matching decorative value with surprising resilience, the highly scented snail creeper
Vigna caracalla from tropical South America is a staple plant in Dennis Richardson's garden.

WE DIDN'T PLAN to start a garden here. I just put a few plants in and it sort of went on from there. And I never intended to be a gardener. Back in England when I left school, there wasn't a lot of choice. It was get out on a farm or go down the pit. My mother got me a job in the garden of the place where she worked. The flower gardens alone were several acres, there was a large vegetable garden, greenhouses, woodland—everything you could think of in an absolutely beautiful place.

Two gardeners were employed, the head gardener and me, and there were sixty boys aged up to sixteen, so we sort of had unlimited labour. There were always three or four of them working in the garden and on Saturday mornings every boy had to turn out and work, raking the leaves and digging.

I was born around there and had always known the garden—I used to pinch apples out of it. But I really hated the job. The pay was poor and the conditions were poor. I was there for nine years. I did learn a huge amount about gardening there, although I didn't realise it at the time.

When we first came to this property seventeen years ago, there were lots of native trees, and it was very dense. It had a spectacular view looking over the vineyards to the Willunga Hills but there wasn't really a garden.

The first thing we did was to plant lawn to keep the dust down in the summer. This new grass, Santa Anna couch, came on the scene and we liked it. So we planted a lot of grass to tie the whole area down. We started off with nine square feet and then did one big area each season. It is so green, visitors often ask if the lawn is real.

We planted masses of canna lilies because they were cheap and you could split them. We had lots of agapanthus, yarrows, huge Jerusalem sages, red-hot pokers, snail creeper (*Vigna caracalla*) and hibiscus. We were stuck with a limited range of plants, all hardy tough summer flowering perennials, because we didn't have any manure or quantities of mulch in the early years.

Now we bring in grass clippings and chicken manure and each year we can grow more different plants. So you could say the garden's got softer in a sense.

We specialise now in plants that flower from November through to May. We try to stretch the seasons as much as we can and look for new plants

because the garden and nursery are our livelihood. But generally it's a hot-weather garden. We aim for our peak in the middle of January.

The north wind is our big enemy. In England it was frost, here it is a forty-two-degree northerly in January. And if you get a huge hailstorm through, like we did late in the season one year, it just shreds everything. One thing we've learned is that to live on this piece of dirt we need to cut back the garden in winter. The storms and the winds turn through it and generally things don't get hurt.

The soil seemed terrible after England, but it could be a lot worse. It's light, sandy soil on the south side and on the north there is a bit of topsoil, then you are into red clay, which grows plants beautifully.

What makes a successful garden is choosing the plants—using the plant that works, rather than something you like. With any site, there are certain plants that are going to work well and plants that aren't. You have to make your choices out of what will perform for you. It is no good buying a camellia and sticking it on limestone. And when you find a plant that works, learn to love it.

I have developed a particular style of gardening through the plants I use, which you see in the gardens I've made for other people too. You could drive past a place and you'd know that I had put the garden in. That comes through finding out what plants do and using the best. For instance, *Hibiscus syriacus*. I cannot replace that plant. I would love to say to people, 'Look, for the hedge at the back we can use a choice of four plants.' But unfortunately I can't—I'll give them the hibiscus because that is the best plant for the situation.

In some areas of the garden we can change quite a lot, in other areas we can't, so this definitely does set your style. Even when I was buying plants from a nearby nursery, my garden looked different from theirs, which I was thrilled about. I had used plants in a different way and it was mine.

Most of the plants here have a very long season and I cut back a lot to keep them flowering. There are days when you don't want to do it but you've just got to get in there and you know within a month you are going to be rewarded with a whole new batch of flowers.

In the garden at the front of the house we've got cannas as a background, then red alstroemerias,

hippeastrums and a bluish-purple agapanthus that we got from seed. The alstroemerias look after that bed for most of the season. It is cut back just before Christmas, it regenerates in a very short time and we chuck a few lilies in just to cover that down spell. So I hardly have to touch it, I just deadhead it and it works fine.

Agapanthus is green all the year round; nothing touches it. And if you are English and you've never seen one before, the flower is absolutely spectacular. It flowers at just the right time in summer and holds all the rubbish back off the roads. We do a lot of edges and hedges now because the blackbirds were bringing everything onto the lawns. We've used a lot of different plants since then to do the same job but there is just nothing to dislike about agapanthus. Other favourite edging plants are catmint, curry bush, dwarf cushion bush, some of the lower growing salvias and pink rosemary.

We often get people saying they couldn't possibly use the colours we do because the colours 'don't go'. My answer to that is, God's cheated you if you only like pastel blues and pinks. I don't have a favourite colour at all, I look at hardiness. Everything revolves around the north wind and whether a plant can stand forty-two degrees.

We accept that there are many plants we can't grow, but it's not a problem. We were right on the Scottish border and there is stuff here you just couldn't grow there. It really doesn't matter. You've just got to garden where you are. The only thing you can do to help things out is improve the soil, which gives you a bit more range. But at the end of the day, you are still stuck with the temperature.

The whole key to the place is mulch, laid on about a foot deep. It's all lawn clippings. You learn how to use it. At different times of the year it performs differently and you'll use it in different ways. At the end of October, it's between breaking down and dehydrating and as the weather gets hotter it totally dehydrates: it's just a big fluffy mess and you throw it on and the blackbirds work it through the beds. But from late autumn, the clippings are stored to rot down and by mid-spring they have broken right down and drained out, and you are dealing with a really beautiful black material. From then on you might use them every

three or four weeks. Then once a year in winter I spread chicken manure around.

This is basically a low-water-use garden. We have got a bit softer and probably use a bit more water than we used to but generally it does have to be water-efficient. We get that through the plants we choose and the heavy mulching. We try out new plants and if they don't stand up to our water regime we just scrap them.

We try to keep watering down to once a week and the lawns every two to three weeks. If we get a few days of forty degrees we'll move the schedule in two days and if we get a cooler spell we can move it out two days.

The garden at the eastern end is one of my favourite new areas that we are developing in a different style. It is much more formally laid out, with curving lines of plants. At the back we've got tree dahlias and there is a fence covered with Allard's lavender, which has got perfumed snail creeper going through it and will take it over in time. In front of that is a pink hibiscus, then ballota mixed with blue statice and *Salvia* 'Cyclamen', which is a medium size and suckers, so we'll get a huge life out of it. Then comes pink rosemary in a long curving hedge, then curry plant and right in front, dwarf catmint.

So within a very small space we've got all these different edges and hedges, yet there are actually very few plant species to mess with. When people say formal, you think it's a lot of work but in a bed like that it's easy. You only need to trim. The hibiscus won't be touched until winter and the catmint gets trimmed with a whippersnipper. We trim back the salvia in December, deadhead the statice and the rest takes care of itself.

The job I hate most is mulching, and moving eighty cubic metres of chicken manure. I also hate digging agapanthus out. Honestly, I hate most jobs in the garden. It hasn't changed since I was fifteen!

What I enjoy is Friday night walking around with a bottle of wine. Friday night I never see a weed. And I am always happy to try a new plant like these salvias, just waiting to see the first flower. Watching seeds come through that I've never seen before, that is always exciting. I just feel lucky to be able to do this. It just doesn't get any better.

Boldly massed agapanthus and bright red canna lilies are framed by columns of snail creeper.

going troppo

THE FREEDOM TO CREATE DISTINCTIVE STYLES WITH PLANTS STILL AT THE FRONTIER OF GARDEN USE GIVES AN EXCITEMENT AND ENERGY TO TROPICAL AND SUBTROPICAL GARDENS.

As garden designer Phillip O'Malley says, this is largely uncharted territory. His suburban Queensland garden successfully mixes elements and plants from Mexico, South America and Asia. Bottle palms are used as classical columns, and ochre-washed walls give a jewel brilliance to zinnias and cosmos.

Gillian Elliott's courtyard garden, with its strong Asian influences, was well before its time when she designed it in the 1950s. Balinese and Indian doors, lanterns and antique statues set off a garden used as an outdoor room both day and night.

Queensland is home to a growing number of passionate plant collectors. Dennis Hundscheidt's love of tropical plants stems from a childhood spent in Brisbane's Oasis Gardens, which were managed by his father. An early interest in palms provided the framework and canopy for his garden of beautiful foliage plants with its special collection of cordylines.

Peter Heibloem's safaris into central Africa in search of rare cycads have a flavour of high adventure reminiscent of nineteenth-century plant-hunting. His obsession with these ancient plants from remote places has resulted in a unique specialist garden of landscaped rockeries, where about eighty per cent of the world's known cycad species are represented.

For many, tropical gardens invoke images of paradise. At WATERFALL COTTAGE, a piece of true subtropical rainforest is set against Sydney's characteristic sandstone cliffs. Boardwalks allow access right into the heart of the garden, where understated planting plays a supporting role to tall rainforest trees, luxuriant vegetation and water cascading over mossy rocks.

The garden of ILLALANGI VILLA, set on one of the coral-fringed islands of the Whitsundays, is also designed to enhance rather than compete with some of the world's most beautiful natural scenery. Spindle palms and strelitzias around a rock-edged pool frame views of the ocean. Informal borders mixing exotic and native tropical plants and trees create a lush backdrop of dark green leading down to a palm gully. Flower interest is confined mainly to the house terraces and verandahs, which are lined with huge pots of clipped bougainvillea.

OVERLEAF: A great fallen coachwood and mossy rocks back a secret pool at Waterfall Cottage. Surrounding the water are irises, impatiens, monstera, orchids and ferns.

fearless with colour

ALBA   PHILLIP O'MALLEY

When garden designer Phillip O'Malley moved to Burleigh Waters on the Gold Coast, 100 km south of Brisbane, five years ago he chose a twenty-year-old garden with established shrubs. Working with these, he has created a 20 × 35 metre courtyard garden of vibrant colour using a surprising palette of tropical and subtropical plants. Many of the plants he chooses have fallen from favour due to inappropriate use in the past. Phillip is excited by the possibilities open to gardeners in the tropics.

Textures and colours are skilfully balanced in this grouping of cosmos and agaves against an adobe wall.

I KNEW I was going to do the front courtyard instantly. The flat site was easy to work with and didn't eat up heaps of money, so it allowed me to spend more on the wall. I had a guy do the bricking and I rendered it myself. I have always loved rendered walls. They are uneven and have someone's personal signature and energy in them. I like the primitive or naïve look rather than perfect traditional European forms. A wall is a brilliant canvas or backdrop for plants. Against a soft-textured and coloured wall, plant colours come out beautifully. I love colour; it never ever scares me, it excites me. And having such a strong light in Queensland you get better value when you use it boldly.

The gates are Mexican, and some hand-painted tiles are inserted in the wall, and there is a plastered archway on top. Style-wise the garden has been labelled 'Mayan' and I suppose it could be described as Mexican in its structure and wall colouring. Really it's too moist and tropical for Mexican, although somewhere like Puerto Vallarta, where frangipanis grow wild, is more like Cairns.

This was a twenty-year-old garden with shrubs, big port wine magnolias, gardenias and sasanquas all against a brown fence. They looked so dead against it. What I have tried to do is respect the history. You don't walk into a place and annihilate it. That is really ignorant and power-mongering. People make the mistake of coming in and just trashing everything.

I enjoyed working with this place because I was recycling. It is great to reuse things. Any place that someone has really cared for and put together well has a specialness, it has a history and a story which give it an added dimension. I have tried to work with things here, even the three Cocos palms (*Arecastrum romanzoffianum*) and the crucifix-shaped lavender bed in the front.

This is old swamp grassland, so it's quite sandy. It had been built up when they did the development so it varies from a beautiful sandy loam to a pure sand. My very first thought was to put a straight path through but the two sasanqua camellias were so perfectly sited they determined the curve in the path.

The borders down the front path are *Dracaena marginata* 'Tricolor', tillandsias and about thirty other different bromeliads and *Zephyranthes candida*, with clumps of eucharist lilies (*Eucharis x. grandiflora*) either side. A border of cordyline hybrids mirrors those colours.

The crucifix bed is filled with 'Sidonie' lavender in the cooler months. In November I switch over to chillies and basil. There is a large murraya in the southwest corner—murraya is great for hedging off bland fences in the city —and a hedge of plum pines (*Podocarpus elatus*). On both sides of the courtyard against the house are two very big old port wine magnolias. The lawn area is surrounded by a pineapple hedge (*Ananas* sp.). Against the street boundary wall between the sasanquas are small-leafed strelitzias and here I plant zinnias or cosmos for seasonal colour.

Millions of pink *Zephyranthes grandiflora* surround the octagonal blue pond, and these are echoed by zephyranthes edging the side bed of bromeliads, gingers and heliconias. Along the carport there is a very narrow bed up against the courtyard wall of a moderately dwarf form of mother-in-law's tongue or sansevieria.

Beneath the large eucalypt is a border of *Tulbaghia violacea* with *Agave attenuata*, which does really well there. The tulbaghias continue round the corner. The violet flowers against the wall have *Aloe barbadensis* dotted in among them. Outside on either side of the gates are pale pinky-white dipladenias (*Mandevilla sanderi*) in pots. Being west facing, it is very severe, but it suits a lot of plants. I've got gazanias and in the warmer months there are scattered cosmos and other annuals. At the very front on the footpath are two nice fat bottle palms (*Hyophorbe lagenicaulis*) with *Rhoeo* 'Hawaiian Dwarf' underneath.

What we have in this subtropical climate is totally uncharted territory. There are parts of Africa, South America and Mexico that are very similar to us, plus certain parts of Asia. It is so exciting what you can do here, so many combinations of plants, sculptures, styles that just haven't been put together, whereas in temperate climates, it's more limiting. In Australia we are insane not to have enough guts to go out and do what we intuitively feel might work rather than following overseas styles. This was very big in the eighties. Anything from overseas—especially Europe—was glamorous and 'We'll have all those, thank you very much'.

In a really practical way there is an Australian garden style. Just look to the suburbs. Actually it's

LEFT: In the back garden, spindle palms in decorated tubs form an outdoor temple for a Mexican god.
RIGHT: Between dracaenas wreathed in Spanish moss, a statue watches over an octagonal pond.

really strange living in seventies suburbia in Burleigh Waters on the Gold Coast! When I am driving around, some things just stand out— whether it's a combination or a single plant. I think the essence of Australians generally is nicely raw, true and honest. We have an honesty and simplicity, we are not too complex and neither are our gardens. They are not like the French gardens, which are layer upon layer hiding reality, so clipped and unnatural and controlled.

Once you get verandahs and outdoor living spaces, that is when gardens can be really sensational. We should live indoor/outdoor in Queensland. We have got heaps to learn from traditional Asia. If I had to name a designer who's a world leader, it would be Made Wijaya [Michael White, Bali-based Australian garden designer and author of *Tropical Garden Design*]. He has done sensational stuff, but of course he has every ball in his court because he is in Bali!

The water and the tropical luxuriant element in this garden are somewhat similar to a Balinese garden.

The mood of a garden is determined by both hard landscaping and plants. I don't think you could say one is more important than the other until you look at the site and see what's required.

I like to use plants with distinctive sculptural form, for instance an avenue of bottle palms, a hedge of bunyas growing into each other, and my favourite hoop pines (*Araucaria cunninghamii*) scattered on a hillside. I also plant avenues of spindle palms (*Hyophorbe verschaffeltii*) which are like Grecian columns so they have a traditional form with a tropical twist. They have a white trunk, they are fat and short and their fragrance is like osmanthus. I love olive trees and have used them for years. Used correctly the colour and form are sensational.

I tend to use plants that don't necessarily have a peak flowering season but hold themselves for most of the year. That's how you get a small garden to look good. If we forgot about wanting the tradition of spring flowering, I think there would be more interesting gardens in Queensland in summer, autumn and winter as well as the spring. We have a climate that allows virtually year-round gardens.

One favourite is frangipani. I've got a collection of about seventy different colours. They flower in this climate for six months and they are a very manageable tree. Each one has a very distinctive fragrance and with them I am like a rose connoisseur in love. Frangipanis have a sense of pure indulgence, they are so exotic.

I think a successful design looks right. Even when it is outrageous it holds its own, it melts into the site well and marries with it.

Phillip O'Malley at the gateway to Alba, flanked by welcoming tubs of *Mandevilla sanderi* and coleus.

shades of asia

TAN JUNG SARI GILLIAN ELLIOTT

Tan Jung Sari is at Clayfield in Brisbane's northern suburbs. The 0.2 hectare ($^1/_2$ acre) garden, now 50 years old, reflects the Elliotts' shared interest in Asian cultures. Each garden area is designed to flow from the rooms of the house. The sunken walled courtyard at the front is the heart and centre of the home. At night it is lit by lanterns and the many white-flowered and night-scented plants come to the fore.

A tibouchina arches over chequerboard paving interspersed with *Zephyranthes candida*.

MY HUSBAND MURRAY had lived in Japan and was very Asian-oriented. My ideas of gardening were very anglicised at the start but Roy Smith, the Brisbane-based landscape gardener, really helped me. A long time ago when I was trying to grow grass under a jacaranda, he looked at me and said, 'Dig it up. You know you can't grow grass under a jacaranda.' I said, 'I can't dig it up.' I thought about it for about three days and I rang him up and said, 'If you do it tomorrow, you can do it.' He came and ploughed up the whole front garden while I sat there crying. It took about five years before it worked. And people would come and say, 'What have you done? It was so nice before!'

We had seen a lot of courtyards in Bali and in Greece and Yugoslavia and had always thought how beautiful they were, so I decided to make a courtyard. It is actually a room, and that is what I always wanted, for the garden to be an extension of the house. A garden has to have water and should be part of your house. There is no point for me in having a garden that I can't step into any minute of the day. There is a garden off our kitchen and even one off our bedroom where I have huge plants of the absolutely magic night-blooming cactus (*Hylocereus undatus*). I've counted as many as thirty-eight flowers on any one night. In the middle of the night I wake up to their exquisite scent and look out the window to see the flowers trembling, which is their way of attracting every possible insect.

I knew exactly what I wanted and Roy knew the proportions. He just stepped it out and said, 'This is where the wall should go.' I would have built it right out to the footpath but he said that was too much. I trusted him and he was right.

One day I was working in the shrubbery and thinking how pretty the house looked from where I was and how you didn't see it from there, so I put a path through. And I said to Murray, 'We need a pair of doors.' And because he haunts antique places, he found these old Indian doors, but of course they were too small so we got slats put on the bottom.

The house doors also have an interesting history. In Bali I saw these doors and I thought they were fantastic. I said, I'm buying some Balinese goods and Murray said, you're not and I said, I am and he said, you're not and so I bought them. But when I got them home I realised they'd only fit a very small person! We got an architect in and he modified them.

Later in Surabaya we went to the house cum shop of a Dutchman. He must have had thirty or forty lights around his courtyard and I bought two. Murray said, don't and I said, I would and he said, 'you'll carry them'. I carried them on my lap all the way back. They are really meant for candlelight but we electrified them and they throw a very soft light. We sit in the courtyard every night, with rugs around us if it's cool.

These days I say to Murray I've had a fantastic idea but we won't do it of course because it will be too expensive, and he says oh yes. And I'll say wouldn't it be fantastic to do this, this and this and of course we won't do it because it will be too expensive or because it's not sensible, and a week later he'll say to me, you know you were talking about doing such and such, and the next minute we have done it! It is an elaborate ritual! But we have never been sorry about anything we have done.

The statues on either side of the front gate were a present. They are Chinese and we don't know their provenance. The tiles are Persian, although I've been to Persia and I have never seen tiles like them. Murray saw them first at a Spring Hill Fair about twelve years before we bought them. We kept following them around until one day I went in to see if the dealer still had them and he did. But I really couldn't think what we'd do with them. As I was driving away someone on the radio said if you want to do something don't put it off, do it today so I went back and bought them.

I love white flowers. The zephyranthes flower from the end of January and they are still there about April. I started off with six and now I have a blaze of white all around the courtyard offsetting the deep blue tibouchina, if the possums spare them! Other white flowers I really value are my eucharist lilies, lovely November lilies, and the crinums which coincide with the jacarandas that carpet the garden in mauve. I also love white scented flowers like murrayas, frangipanis, gardenias and white ginger (*Hedychium coronarium*).

An Indian woman once told me that we use white because you can see it at night. I notice that you can't see blue or red at night, they disappear. If you have blue flowers in a vase you don't see them at night unless they are well lit.

The flowers in one part of the garden were almost all white but I put in a few dark red azaleas and

I suddenly realised they gave depth to the garden. They gave warmth and character. I don't like red but I put in a little bit because it warms your heart, especially in winter. It leads your eye and gives the garden a bit of guts. You realise that green and red are complementary colours and you suddenly see why it is so beautiful.

There is always a creeper flowering—white thunbergia (*T. grandiflora* 'Alba'), white and blue wisterias, the deep scarlet ipomoea (*I. horsfalliae*), *Allamanda carthartica*, herald's trumpet (*Beaumontia grandiflora*) and the star jasmine (*Trachelospermum jasminoides*).

The soil here is not good, in fact it is a terrible clay field. My father used to swim in a clay pit at the end of the street. It used to be full of water and it held the water because of the clay. I fertilise it with blood and bone, and it also needs plenty of water. After all, that is what a garden is—it eats just like us. Vita Sackville-West said you need to listen to your garden—when a plant wants to live somewhere let it be. I planted the Japanese windflowers somewhere else and they just walked and sowed themselves all over the place.

We were in Amsterdam a few years ago and went to all the art galleries, and the thing I remember best was a little staircase and window we passed on our walk to the galleries every morning. Through the window we could see a marble hallway and a garden. One day a woman tapped me on the shoulder and said, 'Please excuse me. I want to go through my doorway.' I said, 'I beg your pardon but we look at this every day because it is so beautiful.' She asked if we'd like to come in and see it. We walked into the hallway and there was an ancient courtyard with these huge walls around it and with an old sundial in the middle. It was filled with white and blue hydrangeas.

I hardly remember the art galleries, I just remember that garden. And that was just a courtyard. That is all you need. I don't need a whole garden.

A reclining Buddha finds paradise among white lilies and impatiens.

throw away your fork

DENNIS HUNDSCHEIDT'S GARDEN

Dennis Hundscheidt's garden is at Sunnybank, a southern suburb of Brisbane. Over the past fifteen years, the garden has burst its boundaries and now spreads over 0.4 hectares (four $1/4$ acre) blocks and spills out onto the nature strip. The natural sandy loam has been extensively built up with mulch. The maturing canopy of palms minimises evaporation and limits the effects of temperature variation on an understorey of tropical and subtropical foliage plants gathered from all over the world.

Light filtering through palm fronds plays on an understorey of bromeliads, cordylines and many other foliage plants that provide both shape and colour in the garden. A Balinese pot is an attractive accent.

MY DAD WAS the manager of the Oasis Gardens of Sunnybank, seven acres of beautiful gardens and one of Brisbane's major tourist attractions. We lived there for about fifteen years and growing up in such a beautiful garden surrounded by palms and tropical plants was where I cut my teeth and more or less determined what I was going to do.

Whatever I have done has been related to gardening in some shape or form. I was going to go into business and by golly am I glad I didn't. I did a Business Administration course at Queensland University of Technology and my desk overlooked the Botanic Gardens, but I was more interested in looking at the gardens than in listening to the lecturers. In the end this passion for gardens got hold of me and took over.

I had a very keen interest in palms in my early twenties and was co-founder and first president of the Palm and Cycad Association of Australia. I did a few trips to Kuala Lumpur and it was there that my fetish for collecting began. Local people thought I was absolutely crazy going into the jungle and collecting fruits. I brought back all these wonderful palm seeds and grew them in pots because I was living on someone else's property. Later they became the basis of this garden.

Each year I introduce new cordyline cultivars into cultivation and I am president of the International Cordyline Society. I have collected in Tahiti and I was in Thailand last year, but Hawaii is my main source. We have a quarantine house on the property and plants stay in there for three months.

As you become more restricted for room you have to be much more selective, so I am whittling out some of the ones I collected six or seven years ago and introducing others because they are better.

Although cordylines are my main thing—I have 250 to 300 cultivars—I am also interested in other colourful foliage. Last year in Bangkok I collected some crotons. Anything with an interesting texture, an interesting colour or foliage I will collect. There is a whole world out there of wonderful plants.

I am a very disciplined collector and the greatest restraint on a collector is design. There are lots of gardens that I have seen that to me are just botanical zoos. They are just collections of plants, and if I want to see a collection of plants I would rather go to a nursery. I also won't grow anything in the garden that is not going to perform. There are some wonderful palms that grow in the tropics and look good here for perhaps four weeks in the year, but for the rest they are just struggling. That is not for me, not at all, and I would soon turf those ones out. So while I am a collector and I look for something different, it has to work well within the garden, and the cordylines that I bring in are trialled here before we release them. But generally I have a pretty good idea that whatever I collect is likely to succeed here. It takes a lot of discipline because sometimes you see plants overseas and you want to have that but you just know they won't grow. This doesn't just apply to tropical plants—lots of people who migrate from Melbourne to Queensland try to grow rhododendrons or lavenders and they find the same thing—they just won't do.

I don't think there is an Australian style of garden in the same way you might be able to say there is an Italian style. This is because we have so many climate zones in Australia. It is very important to choose a style of garden that suits the climate. I don't think we should be aspiring to cottage gardens in Brisbane or tropical gardens in Hobart. When you are travelling, gardens give a city or a town a sense of place. There is nothing nicer than to fly into Brisbane and see palm trees, and for me it's equally important to see liquidambars or camellias or azaleas in Hobart or Melbourne. I don't want to go there to see palm trees. We are so lucky in the tropics to have a wonderful palette of plants to chose from, and not to use it is such a sin!

The garden was built in stages. I did the front first about fifteen years ago. The back garden was all under shadecloth because at that time I was very much into propagating. I gradually took the shadecloth down because I got sick of seeing the plants in pots and got much more satisfaction out of seeing them planted in the ground. Over a period of five years we gradually planted the garden as you see it today. I always knew I wanted a lush tropical garden with foliage and pathways, but it was never planned as such, it just evolved.

Six years ago we bought next door so we could extend the garden and I have utilised the back for my collection of cordylines and other plants. We are

A tiny lawn and pool beckon at the heart of the garden.

on a very sandy soil here and there aren't many nutrients in it. I bring in garden loam and mushroom compost and mound the beds slightly to create a bit of interest. By doing that and having a fairly regular fertiliser program in the first couple of years, we get tremendous vertical growth. Each year I put on six or seven inches of mulch, which decomposes rapidly into humus. I come in with a bucket and whenever I find a space I spread it around—that and a little bit of blood and bone are basically the only fertilising I do.

One of the biggest bugbears in gardening is maintenance. Not only mowing but spraying, fertilising, maintaining a lawn and replanting with annuals. In more temperate style gardens they get colour through annuals but we don't need them in a tropical garden. This garden relies on foliage for colour. It's probably one of the lowest maintenance gardens you can get because you are not digging. In a tropical garden you throw your garden fork away—you just keep mulching.

The top storey is all palms. I don't use anything else. When the palms are swaying in the breeze and the sun is blazing, you get wonderful moving light patterns, with shadows dancing on the leaves. Palms allow filtered light to come through and that is very important when there are so many levels of foliage. A canopy should not be too dense, otherwise it gets too shady to grow anything underneath.

In the mid-storey I have used different palm species—there are many undergrowth palms. Then underneath there is colour from cordylines, bromeliads and pleomeles. The closer you get to the equator, the more you rely on foliage rather than flowers for colour. And once you get into a shady environment you have to forget about flowers because they just won't grow.

You have to know your palms. A lot of them are just too big for suburban gardens, like the Cocos palm (*Arecastrum romanzoffianum*), which grows to sixty feet. I'm lucky to have a horticultural background that has enabled me to transfer ideas and principles into this garden. I am constantly learning and always changing and adding different things. If you had a garden that always stayed the same, it would be boring. Tropical gardens are so vibrant, so dramatic and constantly evolving.

A garden is like a painting but it is more difficult because it's forever changing and there are so many variables. I am a keen photographer and I tend to see the garden in terms of its being worth a picture.

I try to keep the garden as natural as possible so that you could believe you are in a tropical rainforest. It is escapism, this idea of being somewhere else. And that is the illusion. It is almost like having a resort in your own backyard. In summer you come in off the street and it's four or five degrees cooler. It takes your mind off the ordinary everyday work strains. It's a fantasy really. A garden should be relaxing. Once a garden becomes a burden it loses its purpose.

I am particularly interested in some of the tropical plant designers, for example the Brazilian Roberto Burle Marx. I very much like his style of landscaping. His designs mainly involve vast open spaces and mass plantings of a few different plants. I borrowed his design principles and applied them to my quarter-acre block. Throughout my garden I use a basic palette of tropical plants which I repeat in groups of five, seven or nine, changing the combinations. But I am really a 'put and look' man. I'll stand back and look at it for a little while and if it works I'll plant it, but nothing ever goes on paper.

I would like to be known as a good gardener. I would like people to say, oh yes, I remember him, he was a good gardener. I get the greatest satisfaction from imparting my enthusiasm and my passion for gardening to others. If someone comes to me and says they saw the garden and did something like it at their place and it worked for them, that is fantastic. That is the greatest reward of all.

Dennis Hundscheidt with some of his cordyline cultivars.

hunting the big game

EUDLO CYCADS PETER HEIBLOEM

Peter Heibloem's extraordinary collector's garden spreads over 2.4 hectares (6 acres) on the north facing slope of a sandstone ridge at Eudlo, 90 km north of Brisbane. In this subtropical climate, minimum temperatures rarely fall below 8°C but the most significant challenge for Peter has been the humidity and rainfall (annual average 2300 mm), as a large number of the plants in his collection originate in arid or desert conditions. Hundreds of tonnes of soil and crushed rock have been used to build up the cycad beds, while succulents and cactuses are protected from direct moisture by clear plastic roofs.

LEFT: Hundreds of cactuses grown in a carefully controlled environment create their own fantastic landscape.

RIGHT: The ancient forms of cycads garnered from remote corners of the world cover acres of hillside.

IT ALL STARTED when I saw an ad in a newspaper for a plant for $500 and I thought, I'll go and have a look at it because either he's a positive thinker or it's a really nice plant. It was a big rainforest cycad *Lepidozamia hopei* that a retired nurseryman had been growing for twenty years. It was taking up too much space—the leaves were ten feet long and stretching out in all directions.

It looked magnificent, a bit like a palm but it was sufficiently different for me to know it wasn't. I bargained hard and bought it for $350. We built a special house for it because it had been growing in the shade, and when you move them into the sun you have to give them some protection. When it got bigger, we put a big pitched roof on it. It's thirty years old now and the leaves have hit the roof.

In those early days when I knew nothing about cycads, I couldn't even say the names of the plants. I went along to the meetings of the Palm and Cycad Society and the people there were friendly. I saw all these books and magazines with pictures of different cycads that grow in Australia and overseas, and I thought, wow, these are really nice, and so I started asking questions. I didn't get very far. I was told, 'Oh, they're difficult to find and they're hard to grow ,' so I thought it might be a challenge to start a bit of a collection.

I heard about the journal of the South African Cycad Society, which is the best cycad journal, and persuaded a friend to loan me his entire collection. I would sit up in bed every night and read through them. There was no real supply of plants in Australia and I wondered how I could manage to get some. So every time the journal mentioned a visit to Mr Schmidt's garden in Pretoria, I would get on the phone and ring up international directory and say I want to talk to Fred Schmidt in Pretoria. And they'd say there are twenty of them and I would say, well give me the numbers, and I would ring them all up. I'd say, I would love to send you some Australian seeds, have you got any African seeds? That's how I got started. It cost a fortune in phone calls, but I got contacts and people were stunned that someone in Australia would ring them up and want to send them some seed. I started growing seedlings and also swapping with people in America. There was once a collection that came up for sale. I ended up buying dozens of plants and we built a quarantine house for them.

There is a world conference on cycads every four years and the next one to come up was in South Africa and I thought, wow, I might go to that. In the meantime I had been talking to a botanist at one of the botanic gardens in South Africa who was going on a safari to Kenya looking for cycads. I offered to go with him and pay the costs. I have done more trips into central Africa looking for cycads than anyone.

I began exchanging with the botanic gardens in Australia. Then an article in the cycad journal mentioned a botanical gardens in Zimbabwe that had more African cycads than any other garden in the world. I rang up the curator and said, 'I'm from Australia, and how would you like to get some Australian plants, and I would like to get some from you.' We had to deal with the government of Zimbabwe and after more than a year they eventually agreed to the proposal as long as I paid all expenses, so I sent them 800 plants in exchange for a thousand kilos of rare African cycad seed.

There are different families of cycads. It's a little bit like Holdens, Fords and Volvos. Different ones grow at different speeds. There are little tropical ones that grow in the rainforest, that will start producing cones after three, four or five years.

The two African families, which are perhaps the most ornamental, are found nowhere else. They are slower to cone and the quickest you can get cones is at about eleven or twelve years old. But these plants will live to five, six, seven, eight hundred years. One in South Africa is a national monument and has been aged at 2000 years. They are like living fossils and go back to the age of the dinosaur. A cycad collection can be passed from generation to generation.

There are cycads in China, in Central America— in Panama, Ecuador and Cuba—and one species in North America. In Australia there are four families, and fifty or sixty species. They grow in remote places, in the Kimberleys and around Darwin, Katherine, Cape York and Western Queensland. Some grow at Alice Springs and in Perth.

With the exception of lepidozamias, the Australian species don't transplant easily and are hard to get. They are adapted to dry situations and not very vigorous. Some of them are subterranean— a big bulb is hidden underground and the leaves just come out.

When you move a cycad, it goes into a coma and it can stay in shock for seven years. And while it is in shock, it doesn't want any water. You have to make sure all the bugs stay away from it because it gives out a signal that insects are attracted to, saying, 'I'm in stress, I'm suffering.' And the insects say, 'Great, let's eat you.'

I feel a heavy responsibility for the plants because some of them are so rare. Even the major botanic gardens in South Africa don't have some of the specimens I've got reproducing in colonies now.

In a viable colony there need to be enough males and females, and a special insect gets attracted to the perfume given off. When the male cone comes up, it gives off an intoxicating perfume. The bug gorges itself on pollen and then the female opens up a little bit at the top of the cone, which is like a big pineapple. The female cone opens up and gives off a different perfume and the bug finds that intoxicating and goes into the female cone covered in pollen. There is a spiral staircase winding down the centre of the cone and as the bug walks down there is a sticky spot on the end of each seed that is fully developed but infertile. It is a bit like a baby that is ready to pop out. All of a sudden the pollen gets drawn in and the seed is fertilised.

When you take cycads from one country to another, you lose the bugs so you need to do it by hand. If the bugs die out, the cycads die out. And in some of the colonies we found in Africa there is no pollinator, so there are big plants hundreds of years old but no young ones.

There are restrictions on exporting plants from Africa. All endangered species around the world are governed by an international treaty that transcends national boundaries, the Convention in Trade of Endangered Species (CITES). There are three categories: the ones that are rare, those vulnerable to extinction, and those that are critically endangered. All African cycads are on the critical list.

The CITES rules are designed to stop people from ripping cycads out of the bush and destroying colonies. In Mozambique on top of a huge outcrop like Ayers Rock there were a couple of hundred originally but there are now only about ten left. So when they discovered a new species in the north of South Africa they put a twelve-foot fence around it and an armed guard.

I am not really collecting cycads any more. I have most of what I want and a lot of the rarer ones are just too difficult to get and most of them, like the ones from Columbia, require very tropical conditions.

I decided to create a specialist garden that people could come and look at and get inspired. It was a big project. It took a D9 dozer hundreds of hours to excavate the site and all the soil and rocks were brought in. The garden now extends over six acres of landscaped rockeries with raised beds.

Probably eighty per cent of all known cycad species are in the garden. There are also all sorts of other foliage plants. I have started getting interested in cactus and euphorbias and caudiciforms—desert plants from the Namibian desert with great big trunks that store water.

There are pachytodiums from Madagascar and Africa. Madagascar is extraordinary. Most of its plants and animals are not found anywhere else in the world. It's a little botanical ark.

There are about 300 different species of aloe, beautiful things, of which I have about eighty. Some grow into trees and some have huge leaves and flower stems that go from floor to ceiling.

Most of these plants look good, and they are rare or endangered—you put that together and it makes an interesting project where people can come and see all these things they couldn't see anywhere else in Australia.

My garden doesn't have a plan. It evolved as my interest evolved. If I built it again, I would make it more botanically elegant. But when you are collecting, every time you get something beautiful you make a feature of it and then one day you have got something that is ten times better.

the heroes of the garden

WATERFALL COTTAGE   JEANNE VILLANI

For seventeen years Jeanne Villani has lived at Waterfall Cottage at Bayview on Sydney's Northern Beaches. The 3.2 hectare (8 acre) paradise garden is set in a subtropical rainforest gully whose natural features include a magnificent rock amphitheatre, huge old coachwoods (*Ceratopetalum apetalum*) and a creek with waterfalls. Summer temperatures seldom exceed 30°C and rainfall is spread throughout the year, although there are frequent spring droughts.

Among lush subtropical rainforest greenery, a beautifully sited summerhouse looks down the gully.

Sinuous trunked palms and a spreading crepe myrtle shade the stone path to the house.
Scarlet salvias and shrimp plants (*Justicia brandegeana*) add splashes of warm colour.

SEVENTEEN YEARS AGO I saw an ad for a house in the paper that sounded as though it had been written by a very clever copywriter. Being cynical I decided to go and have a look at it. It was a Sunday morning and it was drizzling and usually a place doesn't look as good when it's raining but this was far better than the actual ad and I immediately said, 'Oh I've got to have it.' There was a small house—the only solid thing was the chimney. And that sank after a heavy fall of rain undermined the foundations! I then built this new stone house and made it look old.

There was lantana all down the gully, and jasmine up the hill between the house and the road. I had no particular ideas, I just wanted to get into it. I suppose the fact that I bought this place and a huge amount of land was the real reason I became a gardener. I had always been interested in plants and in gardening but I hadn't ever had a proper garden before.

The garden's design has been influenced by the natural features. Sandstone cliffs and rocks are something you could not build however much you wanted them. An incredibly rich man came here once and said, 'I'm going to have all that.' But that was impossible—it's either there or it's not. We have cleared around the rocks so they sort of stand up as heroes of the garden. So the things that make it the way it is were here. I couldn't have made it, but I have added to it.

Originally there was nothing except the path and the front lawn, the level area with palm trees, which is the only really formal part of the garden. There was a tiny bunya pine (*Araucaria bidwillii*) that is now sixty feet high. Palms had been planted to pretty the place up for sale, so there were little two-foot high Cocos palms (*Areacastrum romanzoffianum*), which are now an enormous stand. I wish I had removed them because they throw millions of seeds, and every single one seems to grow.

In front of the house was a large crepe myrtle and surrounding it big old coachwoods which gave a sense of intimacy. In the years when they flower they are an absolute picture.

The only part of the garden you could get around was the part from the house up to the boundary. There was just one bridge and one path and a rubbish dump with an old car and acres of lantana and jasmine.

In the past somebody had made attempts to get around the garden because when we cleared we discovered flights of steps and walls and the odd hydrangea or camellia or abelia. I had a really wonderful site but no access, so we put boardwalks in with the idea of getting right down into the core of the garden. This was mainly to be able to get around to clear, to actually be able to see the site, and to look for the cats when they were missing. It's so wonderful, particularly the bottom two bridges. But you can't see it unless you are actually down there standing on a bridge.

The bamboo stands are sixty to eighty feet high. They are several levels lower than the house but they tower above it. It is *Bambusa balcooa*, one of the clumping varieties. The clumps are getting bigger but it's not invasive. It grows within itself.

Part of gardening on a very big canvas is that you can't afford to have little fussy beds of treasures. It is really broad-sweep gardening. Something small can easily get overwhelmed before it grows to its right size. There are masses of impatiens, and we rip it out but it just grows and grows and grows, and often I get a surprise when something that I have forgotten suddenly pops up above it. In one way the impatiens are good because they conceal delicious plants from the wallabies.

Over the years things have been planted in the wrong place, so sometimes it is more a case of cutting things out to make the picture. I hate cutting plants out—you have to wait so long for them to grow—so Tony Seager my gardener always asks when I am going out and does it while I'm not there.

The light factor is important because the garden is quite shady. At different times of the year the sunny parts vary, so we choose things that are happy in semi-shade.

I am almost ashamed to say that the worst thing that has happened in my life was when one of the coachwoods in the amphitheatre outside the house fell down. I thought, isn't that terrible—you've had a mother die, you've had a husband die, and the worst thing in your life is a tree falling over. Most things you can fix with money but when a 200-year-old tree falls over there is absolutely nothing you can do.

I had Phil Hadlington [Australian consultant and writer on pest control and tree care] out to advise me on all the others that were broken off. He said, 'Look, Jeanne, I don't know what you're worrying about, it will fill in. Not in your lifetime, but it will fill in.' I thought, that's not what I wanted to hear!

It was Phil who first identified the area as rainforest. I had asked him to come and see it and he said, 'When you rang me and said you had rainforest, I thought yes, girlie, you might think you have—but you really do.'

It's fairly unusual to have a real rainforest garden in Sydney. A lot of the land is dry bush but there is a rainforest band running down through the gully.

In the big bushfires in 1994, the garden was burnt out right up to the rainforest. There were even spot fires right up the waterfall. The thing that stopped the fire getting to the house were the rainforest trees, so we extended the band further.

Tony is always clearing more areas. He is knowledgeable about rainforest plants and most trees we have added have been rainforest trees.

We have also put in tabebuias and other tropical flowering trees, so the garden is more like a Queensland garden than a traditional Sydney garden. Tony brings plants down from Queensland. I have got about eight different varieties of ginger, which do very well here. We have tried heliconias but they won't flower, probably because it's not quite hot enough.

The thing that made me realise the garden was special was years ago when Sydney gardener Brian Donges rang and asked if he could bring the Friends of the Botanic Gardens. I told him there was nothing here they would want to see but he said he'd heard differently. After they came and exclaimed over it, I thought I've got to make this better and better and better. And when Brian came to work here I told him I wanted it to be the best garden in Australia.

There is no other garden quite like it. But the reason it is special is that even if you did nothing to the site it would be fabulous.

island paradise

ILLALANGI VILLA   GRAHAM WILSON

Illalangi Villa is on Hamilton Island in the Whitsunday Passage off the coast of north Queensland, 1000 km from Brisbane. The 0.3 hectare (^{3}/$_4$ acre) hillside garden enjoys spectacular views of the ocean and the Whitsundays, and has volcanic gravelly shale soil which is non-moisture retentive. Winter daytime temperatures average 23–24°C, and nightime temperatures seldom fall below 15°C. Summer temperatures are constant at around 30°C. Rain falls mostly between January and May, when it averages around 750 mm. Graham Wilson moved to Illalangi Villa fifteen years ago and finds gardening in the tropics a continuous voyage of discovery.

Palms underplanted with strelitzias overhang the pool and frame vistas across the Whitsundays.

COMING FROM A cold climate, gardening with tropical plants was all quite new to me. I really didn't know what grew here, so a lot of it in the beginning was by sight. I would walk into a nursery and if I liked the look of the leaf or it looked tropical, I would buy it and put it in. I lost a few plants by doing it that way. Then I got some books and read up on things. I can only read during the winter weeks. During the summer I am far too busy.

The site wasn't landscaped until 1988, and at first it was all planted with natives—grevilleas, bottlebrush and baeckias. As the trees grew, it became very shaded, and although I persevered with the natives for about three years, they didn't come back the way they should have done. So I have been tackling a section of the garden at a time, gradually changing it over to a tropical theme, except for a few drifts of natives for the birds. It is about half exotic tropical plants, from places like Madagascar, and half Australian rainforest plants.

The block is very steep on all sides of the house, and to plan the garden took quite a bit of thought. With any project like this you have got to stand back and visualise. We used rocks and sleeper walls to retain the slope. At the bottom is what I call the ring garden: a big central garden with a surrounding walk.

There is very little topsoil here, and we brought about ten semi-trailer loads from the mainland. Everything has to come over on the barge.

The garden is towards the northern end of the island, facing east. On the northwest and in the gully, it is very protected. You can look right down onto the garden from the verandahs and decks. There is a dark-green backdrop, then the lime green of the golden durantas (*D. repens* 'Sheena's Gold') underneath.

All along the terraces and verandahs on both levels there are big terracotta pots of different coloured bougainvilleas, which I have trained into standards. They look quite dramatic when they are all out in flower, which is most of the year.

The idea was to get colour and variety into the garden, so I have chosen quite a few variegated plants with different coloured foliages like the variegated miniature umbrella tree (*Schefflera arboricola* 'Jacqueline'), cordylines, crotons and dianellas. These have contrasting shapes—weeping forms next to upright ones and so on. I have always

had an eye for detail, and I think it's important to have contrast and variety to keep your interest.

Hamilton Island is known as a dry island. The wind sheers up between the rainclouds and they go off to either side. So we can be bone dry here while it's pouring rain on Whitsunday Island.

The watering system is an absolute must. There is a large dam and two reserves for the island but we have to conserve water from about mid-November.

We also have regular tropical storms. I have been through five, but fortunately just the tail end, so there has been no damage. Down the back, the gully garden is protected from the wind, but if we were closer to the eye of the cyclone I would still get damage down there. But I have been very lucky.

Before the property was fenced, I had problems with the wildlife, especially wallabies and deer which we have on the island. They have a habit of just wandering in and ripping out plants completely, and they'd eat big circles of lawn. Now all we have got to combat is the possums. But I don't mind them. I actually feed them. They are my pets.

The native trees here are mainly spotted gums (*Eucalyptus maculata*). I have taken out some to open up the garden and to let the rest spread out to their beautiful shape. They give a lovely canopy and keep the garden flowing right down to the gully.

I have never seen gingers this high. I actually thought I had planted them in the wrong place, and I never dreamed they'd get to that size.

There are a few plants here from my grandmother's garden at Glen Innes in New South Wales. I brought a lot of things here on trial and they have all grown—canna lilies, gladioli, and surprisingly lambs' ears. And my mother, who's an extremely good gardener, swaps plants with me. I find it quite amazing because of the different climates that they grow here, and mostly grow a lot bigger.

I worked to a plan for the area near the house, with the tree ferns and impatiens, but the new section has never been planned, and that will be a completely different garden. There'll be some tree ferns there too to tie it together but that is the only planting I'll repeat.

I have been gradually shifting the fence further down the gully but I think the garden down there is big enough now. I'll grow vines over the fence, and then outside I will put stag horn and elk horn ferns up in the trees to give the impression that the garden goes on and on down the gully.

I have used lots of bromeliads and tree ferns, which are very adaptable. Bromeliads of course are virtually air plants. You don't even have to plant them as long as you keep them watered.

The pool area is framed by spindle palms and strelitzias, and there are big bush rocks overlapping the pool. I have used island rock all through the garden. Below the terrace the ground just seems to drop away, so you get that wonderful clear vista of the ocean. I have extended the area to bring the garden towards it and make it entice you. The huge rock steps are planted with little yellow Dahlberg daisies (*Thymophylla* sp.) to make it look quite natural.

My worst enemy here is the wind on the eastern side, which is quite severe at times. On the exposed east facing bank, after having to replant it four or five times, I eventually went in for extremely hardy, common plants that I knew would grow. There are tamarisk trees, the lantana hybrids, dwarf and standard oleanders, lomandra (which is very wind tolerant because it is reedy), and grass trees (*Xanthorrhoea* sp.). They are in there among the rock mounds and it is very steep and very dry. They only get water when it rains and they seem to thrive. And some Mexican cycads, which seem to be the most wind-tolerant ones.

Down the steep slope away from the house on the northwest I have planted lawns of very hardy Queensland blue couch. I was very keen on the idea of being a greenkeeper when I left school!

To one side of the lawn, I have planted about twenty different crotons, with varied leaf forms and colours to add texture and interest. In front of them is the yellow daisy that is on the stone steps.

Looking down through the canopy, you can see the silver trunks of the gums, and the standard lilly pillys (*Syzygium australe*) along the sides of the lawn. I don't normally like to shape things like this but I really do love them now. They bring some formality to a rather disorganised area of the garden, contrast with the wildness of the rest of it. And I have used *Cuphea* 'Mad Hatter' as edging.

Near the big informal rock bank there are tree ferns and variegated hibiscus, which does extremely well, and is underplanted with different ferns and impatiens. They are in full hot afternoon sun,

and they don't seem to mind at all. There are a lot of doubles and different single colours.

I am becoming a bit of a collector of certain things. With the bromeliads in particular, every time I see one I haven't got I write the name down and try to get it. I now have over a hundred. And they throw pups like you wouldn't believe! I have lots of different canna lilies too, which are just outstanding plants here, they are such hardy old things. I don't think they are something many people would associate with a tropical or subtropical climate but they really suit. The flowers remind me of irises, which I love but can't grow here.

I have just started planting bird's nest ferns which are really taking off under the canopy of trees. There are around thirty palms too—carpentarias and several kinds of livistonas including a huge Chinese fan palm (*Livistona chinensis*). The spreading poinciana is less than ten years old and twenty-five feet tall, and there is a leopard tree (*Caesalpinia ferrea*) and a flame tree (*Brachychiton acerifolius*) which is spectacular with its huge fat leaves contrasting with the weeping palm.

The steep slope leads down to the lower level, and the ring garden. From there you look back northeast up into the main garden. I have planted a lot of rainforest trees, like Davidson's plum (*Davidsonia pruriens* var. *pruriens*) which are still very small, with tree ferns, special palms and purple cordylines. The tall plants with huge elephant ears are *Alocasia x. amazonica*. The flowers look like wrapped cigars, and the leaves are a wonderful blue-grey green.

I've got white and purple jacarandas, and this stunning yellow-foliaged tree which I bought as a poinciana but I am sure it isn't. When you stand up at the house on a moonlit night, it just glows.

The totem in the back is carved out of tree fern trunks; the ferns were taken out for the pool area.

I just love gardening, I don't find it a job at all. The guests really enjoy the gardens; I invite them to come down and they'll spend up to an hour with me in the garden. They seem to love it even if they are not gardeners.

If I was taken away from my garden, I would go mad. I have to have that space to get out and do my own thing. I think gardening at its best is really an artform; you are like a painter working with colour. You think, well, I'll have pink in there, then over here I'll have a blue bush or a mauve. You plan it as if you are creating a picture.

a frame for living

AUSTRALIA'S WARM TEMPERATE AREAS LEND THEMSELVES NATURALLY TO OUTDOOR LIVING.

Pat Gaffney's Fremantle garden, complete with cricket pitch, is designed for a family to live and play in. It was inspired by travel memories of French and Spanish gardens and villages, and realised through his skill as a craftsman with a sure eye for scale and proportion. The materials used—rough limestone, old bricks and weathered timber—give structures and ornaments a settled, comfortable feel, while freely seeding annuals soften the formal design.

A formal parterre in the bush sounds an uneasy juxtaposition. At BRINKHURST, it succeeds because of the care taken to line up the central axis of the design. The long main path runs due east with absolute symmetry from the central hall of the house, through the bush clearing, to a distant prospect of Mount Dale. Halfway down, round steps introduce a change in level and mark a cross-axis whose paths lead to seats under the gums. The parterre, originally designed as a fire barrier between the house and bush, is planted with drought-resistant Mediterranean plants whose soft greens and greys harmonise with the bush surroundings.

Because of our fiercer sun and more brilliant light, Mediterranean-style courtyard gardens with large areas of paving and few plants are often more pleasant to look at than live in here. Courtyard designer Penny Rudduck admits to being plant-driven from the planning stage. Plants provide both architecture and soft furnishing in her garden; predominantly dark green foliage is a background for splashes of vivid colour.

The gardens of the Alhambra in Spain inspired REVERIE's walled gardens, on an elevated site with vistas of the Blue Mountains. These gardens for the senses are deliberately separated from their bush surroundings, but include framed views and glimpses of the landscape in each part. The Rembels have carried out landcape designer Andrew Pfeiffer's concept in stages, building a walled potager, a citrus garden, a tropical pool garden and, at the centre, a large cactus garden. The rich yellow walls were their own touch, providing a marvellous background for the citruses, a wisteria tunnel and wattle blooming in the surrounding bush.

Walled gardens offer the chance to create a self-contained fantasy. In THE MOSAIC GARDEN, Margot Knox combines an artist's imagination with accomplished landscaping skills. Mosaic flows along walls, paths and steps, covers vases and a sculptured settee, and encrusts mock boulders. Tropical plants and desert succulents rub shoulders in the high-walled microclimate, echoing the primitive and naïve style of Margot's paintings. She sees her mosaic as a scaled-down version of the paving and walling learned from master landscaper Ellis Stones.

DOMAINE DU CASTELLET was deliberately conceived as a fantasy: a stage set on which idealised elements of Tuscany, the Cote d'Azur and the tropics are improbably brought together and, through sheer strength of imagination, come to life. The formal mood of gardens strongly defined by clipped hedges, gravel walks and terraces shifts into wild romance with paths winding into semi-tamed jungle. This piece of theatre has the advantage of incomparable natural scenery, looking across a mountain range to the Whitsunday Passage.

In the main flower garden, hollyhocks, delphiniums and poppies throng a limestone fountain inspired by travels in France.

perfect pitch

PAT GAFFNEY'S GARDEN

Pat Gaffney's simple, stylish family garden is in the historic seaport of Fremantle, 12 km south of Perth. The 720 square metre garden with European influences has been developed around a Federation-era cottage over the past eleven years. Pat is a furniture craftsman, and the garden and its structures reflect his natural flair for design and building.

WHEN WE MOVED here eleven years ago, there was a basic structure of Mediterranean trees and plants typical of Fremantle gardens. There were old fig, olive and lemon trees and some very old grapevines, so we expanded on that.

Before that I travelled around Europe and the UK for about a year and a half, and I gained more of an appreciation for architecture than gardens, though I am sure the garden thing was there in the background. I liked the really simple architecture in Greece and the white towns in Spain were fantastic. I noticed the plants that survived with minimum care, like oleanders, which I love.

The garden took shape slowly. I wouldn't know what was going to happen until one morning I would wake up, and I might have thought about it for weeks, and all of a sudden things would start. I was trained as a carpenter and love designing and making furniture. I suppose I have a natural eye for getting proportions and dimensions right.

This was always intended to be a family garden. It's divided into four separate areas. There's a shade area out the back with a buffalo grass lawn that gives the kids somewhere to play, then an outdoor eating area with grapevines over a pergola, which is nice and shady in summer. From the lawn you go down two steps into the main garden area with the central fountain. Leading off that there is another shady area with a circle of paving around a plane tree, where you can sit on hot days.

The paving is just second-hand footpath slabs, broken and laid on sand and grouted with white cement. I have put periwinkle there because it doesn't compete with the roots. I tried a few things but nothing would grow, then at the front of the house alongside the shed I noticed a bit of periwinkle that nothing would kill.

I think you can try too hard to grow the wrong plants. You have failures and you keep trying but you are probably better off finding out what does survive and reverting to that.

Most important of all is the cricket pitch! I surfaced it with blue metal fines, which is pleasing on the eye. It feels good to walk on because it is soft, yet it makes a firm surface to play on and it is low maintenance. The kids love it and all the kids in the street come and play there.

The line of *simonii* poplars along the west facing side boundary was the first thing we planted.

It gives shade in the summer and performs pretty well as a windbreak from the south-westerly sea breeze going through.

The back terrace is lined with pots of box. There was a little path along the side of the building that I raised up to be almost level with the back door. And to separate the terrace from the lawn I made a wall out of pots. The lawn was on a slope with angles all over the place, so I levelled it all out.

I also built a pizza oven, which is very important—every house should have one! That was another whim. I had seen one in a derelict house in Portugal and I woke up one morning and had have one.

The long pergola was put in to support the old grapevines. I lowered an area to make a courtyard, retained it and then raised up the area where the lawn is and paved under the pergola with rough limestone.

The main garden began with paths, laid out using second-hand bricks. When I decided to put the fountain in, I made the paths meet at the central point, which gives that little bit of formality. The garden itself isn't really formal. There is a real mixture of plants in each square—daisies, irises, agapanthus, rosemary and lavender, and lemon and bay trees. A lot of it is self-sown, like the poppies and hollyhocks, which do really well. And we are always adding to it.

The idea for the fountain came from our last trip to Europe. We took lots of photos of fountains in squares in the south of France. The rondels came from a fountain in Provence. A friend of ours with a few red wines in her took a casting off it in the middle of the night and we had those done here from the casting. They really make the fountain.

The design of the little wrought iron pergola at the back of the house also came from our last holiday. It is a fairly typical French pergola.

There is also a Spanish influence in the garden. We saw some fantastic Spanish gardens, like the Alcazar in Seville, again with water and fountains. I like the mixture of formality and informality those gardens have.

The two sets of rustic timber gates, at the street entrance and leading into the fountain garden, are unusual. I got them from a friend who imports furniture and architectural pieces from Sweden, and made the gateposts myself.

The plumbago (*P. auriculata*) hedge along the front replaced an ugly salmon brick wall. When the hedge got high enough, we knocked the wall down.

The soil here is really poor, limey sand and it retains no water. I have just built it up over the years with my own compost, which is made from horse manure, sawdust and fine wood chips, leaves and lawn clippings. At the start I brought in some soil conditioners, which I now regret because this introduced weeds like onion weed that I can't get rid of. There is also the compost from the vegetable garden, which has been really successful for summer vegetables and herbs—tomatoes, zucchini, eggplants, basil and so on.

The important thing for me about the garden is that it's a place of relaxation and it's always there in the background whether you take notice of it or not.

You do notice increasingly the lack of space around you—even big houses are being built on small blocks so the whole block is taken up by building. And there are not that many parks. So having the garden is like having our own private park in a sense.

Sonya and Pat Gaffney with their children Ben, Finbar and Ella.

a bush parterre

BRINKHURST JILL KEPERT

Brinkhurst is at Roleystone in the Darling Ranges, 40 km southeast of Perth. Surrounding bushland shelters the 0.4 hectare (1 acre) garden from wind. With an elevation of 250 metres, there are occasional light winter frosts. Summer brings at least thirty days when temperatures are higher than 35°C. Average rainfall is 1000 mm but occurs only between June and September, so the garden's size was determined by the quantity of available tankwater. Twelve years ago the Keperts moved here from Perth and set about translating foreign designs and inspirations into the setting of marri (*Corymbia calophylla*) and jarrah (*Eucalyptus marginata*) forest.

A timber bench and swing provide a place to relax in the shade of the gums. Dutch irises have naturalised throughout the garden.

A brick path bisects the parterre filled with Mediterranean plants and remnant grass trees. The formal path with its traditional half-circle steps, used to manage a change in levels, translates remarkably well to the bush setting.

WE DESIGNED THE solar house and the garden very much as one. We looked on a map and saw that Mount Dale was absolutely due east, so we lined the house up with the mountain to be sure it was correctly aligned for the solar effect.

When Dave and I came here, the land was thick with waterbush (*Bossiaea aquifolium*) and you couldn't see ten feet in front of you. We pulled it all out but it still seeds everywhere. We had to have a clearing round the house because of the bushfire risk in this area—we had two fires in the early days—and we started by putting in a few fruit trees and a firebreak walk. For water we put in a 30,000-gallon tank and at the end of the first year we found we still had some left, so we thought we could plant some more. We have now got a second tank and we water once a week.

We made lots of mistakes in choosing plants that needed more water and we now restrict ourselves to things that are drought-resistant. There is no lawn, it would be terrible here. Azaleas flourish—they don't need a lot of water and they flower beautifully —and we have lots of roses. I have realised there are lots of plants, the traditional English ones, that I can't grow. I have tried delphiniums, foxgloves and verbascums, and lost them all. It is better to use what you know will grow, and a garden looks better if you repeat things around it rather than try to have everything.

We only mulch with the natural stuff like gum leaves and bark, which we collect and put round the plants. We have never bought any.

Most of the plants we have used are Mediterranean but the garden's design influence is definitely English. We go to England each year and have visited a large number of gardens. Sissinghurst, Hidcote, Bodnant and Hestercombe have all inspired us.

The formal design was directly inspired by Hestercombe, an English garden designed by Lutyens. There is a huge soak well or leach drain under here, which left us with a problem flat white sand area that is a little incongruous in the bush. I thought, we can do something here, and we came up with the brick parterre, which Dave has extended with straight laterite paths from all the rock on the property. We excavated huge slabs of laterite for the big round steps and made slightly raised beds so they are above the soak. We have used jarrah sleepers for edges and garden seating, which have gone beautifully grey.

Each side of the top of the steps is clipped box. It is fantastically hardy and I have grown lots from cuttings that I put in a couple of inches high. They thrive through the summer, in sun or shade. We have two or three hundred plants in now, including the hedges.

The symmetry is carried through with pairs of daphnes and persimmons. The persimmons (*Diospyros kaki*) have a large oval-shaped leaf and an attractive form, with the branches coming out almost horizontally, and they turn a brilliant orange in the autumn and have orange fruits. They were hard to get going until the tap root got down and we had to hand-water them fairly carefully in the summer.

The beds are planted with irises, dietes and grey-leaved plants—santolina, rosemary, lambs' ears and Italian lavender. We have some ageratum right on the edge of the soak well—that is why it's doing so brilliantly.

The little hedge going round the edge is 'Hidcote' lavender and beyond that are echiums and a self-seeding euphorbia, a white-flowering cistus, Jerusalem sage and convolvulus. Poppies and a sea of pink and white everlasting daisies just seed themselves all over the place.

We have planted apples that will be formally pruned into lollipops and a 'Granny Smith' that lines up with the path. 'William Lobb', 'Fantin-Latour' and two other old roses are trained over bush poles. We have planted lots of Dutch irises around the garden. They are fantastic and flower without the need to water them.

Then there is artemisia, dianthus and *Plectranthus argentatus*, and we have planted quite a few proteas in a new raised garden, where Dave has cleared the bush back from the path. We are going to put a narrow brick path down the middle going to the gate to make more of an entrance.

A nectarine gives us about fifty kilos of wonderful white fruit, even after the kangaroos and parrots have had their share.

I am going to have box domes going all the way down the path—the light reflects beautifully on the domes. The idea either side of the steps is to have a centre of grey and a surround of the yellowy green euphorbias as a contrast, and thornless 'Bridal Pink' roses, which last for ages and gradually change colour.

Below the steps Dave made a bog garden that is planted with Louisiana irises. It is not really a bog but it is less arid than the rest of the garden in summer. And there are lots more bearded and Dutch irises, mostly blues, and hebe and ceanothus. The euphorbias make little mounds everywhere. Their reddish stems and lime-green flowers make a terrific contrast, and go with the diosma.

The south side of the garden is in shade, so instead of grey it's all done in yellows and greens. Sisyrinchiums (*S. striatum*), with creamy flowers all up the stem and spiky leaves look good here, with *Cistus salviifolius*, euphorbias, hypericum and big clumps of yellow Dutch iris. And asparagus fern makes a very good filling groundcover.

We have made a formal garden with edgings of box, santolina and 'Sidonie' lavender around lemon and quince trees surrounded by herbs, including golden marjoram, green santolina, winter savory, germander and lemon grass.

On the southwest side are plums with 'Iceberg' roses in front, and further down the walk are silver mounds of santolina and native grass trees (*Xanthorrhoea preissii*). I like the combination of informal planting within formal borders, which is very English, and also the straight paths and long vistas.

Against the garage walls are 'Yellow Charles Austin' roses and old yellow wallflowers. The citrus trees have orange fruit, so this area is going to be all yellow and orange with a bit of blue from the echiums and lavender, and three pencil cypresses at the back.

The Manchurian pear (*Pyrus ussuriensis*) has made a gorgeous tree, with wonderful red autumn foliage, and the silver maple is aligned with the central hallway.

On the northern side, there is a fig that grows monstrous, the 'Kathleen Harrop' rose going up the wigwam in the middle, and the delicate *Prunus* 'Elvins'. This part of the garden is a perfect circle. It's the shadiest part, right under the marris. This side of the block is mostly marri and further down the hill it is mostly jarrah.

There are several bird's nest ferns and I am trying to introduce some red foliage just into this area of the garden. I have planted *Euphorbia characias* ssp. *wulfenii* and there are red camellias, dark-leaved berberis and prunus, and a cotinus with big red leaves. I was very nervous about red until a couple of years ago but providing you put it with strong green and you don't have any greys among it, it's okay. The best camellia for here is 'E. G. Waterhouse'—they are quite hard to grow here as they need cold.

There is a chair we made out of the big tree we had to fell to build the house. You sit inside it and get quite a loud echo. It's like listening to a seashell.

There are grass trees around the garden. They really tie everything together and they go out into the bush. And I am pleased with my trim hedge of peppermint (*Agonis flexuosa* 'Nana') which is a foot high.

On the north side we have a formal rose garden inside a box hedge, with nine santolina domes parallel to the roses, which breaks up what is rather a mixture of colours.

There is quite a lot of pruning to be done in this garden. Dave is the official pruner. He does the sawing and hedge clipping, and I do the snipping. He says when he retires he'll do nothing but come out in the morning and snip his box bushes into little peacocks!

building with plants

PENNY RUDDUCK'S GARDEN

Garden designer Penny Rudduck has gardened around her small nineteenth-century Italianate house in Norwood, an inner suburb of Adelaide, for twenty-two years. Her 8 × 30 metre garden relies on a rich variety of foliage plants to soften areas of hard landscaping. A spreading Manchurian pear and vines provide summer shade.

I HAVE ALWAYS lived in Adelaide. I got hooked on growing things in pots after I married, and when we got our own house in 1978, it became a passion.

Gardening in my own garden is all fun. I treat it very lightheartedly. Things can be created from very little. You don't have to use imported objects or architectural pieces—you can make things happen simply. I always admire green-thumbed people who can create something from nothing, who get a cutting and turn it into a huge thriving expanse.

The writer who has most influenced me is probably Roy Strong [English art historian and garden writer]. This garden is an attempt to create a classic Roy Strong small garden, so I defined quite strong geometric shapes in the front courtyard that relate to the bay window and give good clear access to the front door. It is a patterned parterre, using hedging and brick paving.

I like a lot of repeat planting, hedges and now foliage plants, and I have been particularly thrilled with the Manchurian pear (*Pyrus ussuriensis*) that engulfs my back courtyard. I have put one into nearly every new garden I have designed. It's a perfect tree for the Adelaide climate. I have always been excited by jacarandas in flower but they lose their leaves at the wrong time of the year for our climate. Manchurian pears suit our seasons so well, with beautiful blossom in spring, a glossy green leaf that gives shade and good autumn colour in the right position. And you don't have problems with the roots, so you can underplant them.

Fruit trees like apricots and loquats are taken for granted, but they can work really well as ornamentals in small gardens. I encourage people to consider those rather than the purely ornamental crab apples, prunus and magnolias, and move back to that productive gardening a lot of us knew in our childhood. I think apricot blossom is as pretty as some of the ornamental blossom trees. And in winter a citrus with all its fruit can look fabulous.

Adelaide gardeners have always been a bit self-sufficient. I think people have hung on to that tradition and I think it should be encouraged.

In designing a garden, I generally prefer plants over structure and built elements. If shade can be provided by a small tree, I would always advocate that over a pergola. I think our houses are becoming very built up and hot and reflective, so where we can introduce trees that is what I tend to prefer. With me it's always the plant that gives ideas. Some people have a gift for hard landscaping but I always get plant-inspired. I think there is a bit of a divide between people who are plant-driven and people who see in terms of stone or other hard elements.

A lot of gardening is experimental. You have a brainwave and you want to give it a go. Often it fails but it can lead to stunning results. A good gardening idea will sometimes come like a bolt of lightning in the middle of the night and you can't rest until you have tried to bring it to fruition.

I think there are a lot of lost opportunities where people just follow fashions. Where they try something different and make a bit of a statement, they bring identity to their whole house and the streetscape. But people shouldn't be inhibited about copying ideas and taking them further. I have made a wall of 'Iceberg' roses by having standards underplanted with bush 'Icebergs'. You get a two-metre wall and it looks incredible.

You can't ignore plants that work. I think you are being a bit foolhardy if you do. 'Iceberg' roses in Adelaide are fantastic, there is no doubt about that. It is a good rose that performs better than others in partial shade. French lavender is another standby plant. I use it again and again, it's a good hedging lavender and at the moment I can't improve on it.

I don't think there is an Australian garden style. If you look at a range of American, English and Australian gardening magazines, you'll see the same sort of plants being recommended and a lot of the same spatial concepts being espoused. We are looking at global gardening, with a huge range of garden styles as a palette that you can select from. But Australia has a wonderful indigenous plant repertoire and I think it is underused.

I have tried a lawn in this garden and given it up. It is not just the problem of watering but also the insects that invade lawns in small areas like this. So I decided to pave. We need to discard the old cultural cliché of the big lawn. There are some wonderful parks in Adelaide if you want to enjoy lawns.

Earlier on, I suppose twenty years ago, I was mad about flowers as most new gardeners are. But now leaf shape and colour and texture are the things that

In a garden devoted mainly to foliage, small areas of jewel colour have maximum impact. Here, an urn of variegated *Phormium tenax* surrounded by alyssum rises out of a mound of daisies and rich red geraniums. In the background, ivy is the foil for wisteria, red impatiens and begonias.

excite me and there are very few flowers here. I rely almost entirely on foliage. It's a heady feeling when you get a wonderful combination of some strappy leaf with a palmate one, or a dark colour with a variegated leaf. Some of the plants are so beautiful in themselves, you can look at them as if they were pictures on the wall. All the plants are either repeated in other sections or grouped in threes or more, to unify the garden.

There is so much potential in foliage for compiling elements. Often you don't see or appreciate things properly. Like mother-in-law's tongue (*Sansevieria trifasciata*), which most would find hard to appreciate—I just see it as very architectural and statuesque. It's not the plant, it's all to do with presentation. Sometimes plants are treated a bit shabbily, as a poor relation, and they respond in kind. Good gardening is recognising the appeal and limitations of each plant.

Although I concentrate on foliage I still play with colour. For instance, I've contrasted strong pink impatiens with yellow variegated box and I think it works. I am becoming a bit of a colour anarchist. You can put just about anything together, and if it's looking healthy and in the right position it will work. There are underlying principles. I group 'jewel' colours: orange, purple and red can look wonderful together with gold and yellow.

I use lots of climbing plants. Slow-growing climbers like Chinese star jasmine (*Trachelospermum jasminoides*) are invaluable: I include it in most of the gardens I work on, either to create pattern or just a wall of green. It has a lot of potential. The flowers are very understated, it's the perfume that makes its presence felt, and it has a marvellous rich green leaf.

I try to think spatially when I am approaching a garden but invariably three sentences later in my mind I am thinking about the plants I can picture there in the long term.

What I have tried to achieve in my own garden is a predominant dark green. I started various areas using box hedging and then moved into the whole garden. I realised the parterre needed to be uniform, so I created coned box shapes up the front path, with standards in a formal setting at the end of each bed. There are paired topiary ligustrum as centrepieces for two of the triangular beds. In the centre of the garden is an urn of dwarf variegated New Zealand flax (*Phormium tenax*), with cerise

geraniums tiered below it. The flax has a wonderful maroon margin on the variegation, so it's quite an unusual leaf and complements other variegated plants in the garden. It is a good contrast to the formal clipped shapes and is like a fountain overflowing out of the urn. It looks a bit explosive and it's rather irregular and erratic. It is one of those plants that creates the unexpected in the garden.

In the back courtyard most of the plants are succulents, planted in different shaped pots with a rich green glaze. I've chosen a plant to complement each pot. And I filled a large square pot with water and put in waterlilies and fish, and nestled it into a clump of mondo grass.

I do think there is a tendency towards too much hard landscaping, large expanses of paving and monolithic sort of fences. I am a plant person and I am often brought into gardens where the hard landscaping has already taken place and the planting is an afterthought. It really is a bit of a battle in those gardens to create good planting.

For me there must be something softening, pouring out of pots or growing over a wall, that gives a bit of joy and seasonal interest. Our climate is not always understood by people in the eastern states, where the humidity is so much higher. Here, it's so glary and stark and reflective, and if you are looking at large areas of hard surface constantly, it's unpleasant as a living environment.

Rhythmic planting and the use of overhead space for vines make the most of the narrow side passage. Pots of pink impatiens and agaves are nestled in a border of mondo grass.

Penny Rudduck.

dreaming walls

REVERIE GITTA REMBEL

Reverie stands on a 2 hectare (5 acre) bush block near Dural on the outskirts of Sydney. The natural soil is sand over sandstone, and copious amounts of soil have been brought in to build up garden beds. The garden is 400 metres above sea level, but still close enough to the coast to enjoy sea breezes and to be almost frost free. Begun twenty years ago, Reverie is the result of a continuing collaboration between the garden's renowned designer and its dedicated owners, Gitta and Gunther Rembel.

In the first of the walled gardens, bright pink standard roses are surrounded by box-edged beds of vegetables and herbs. A circular bed of colourful daylilies forms a centrepiece.

GUNTHER AND I had absolutely no idea about design when we decided to buy this block of land here at Dural more than twenty years ago. We fell in love with the bush, with the beautiful white-trunked scribbly gums (*Eucalyptus haemastoma*), and we liked this site because of its elevation and privacy.

This is quite a steep site. We didn't have to clear big trees, just scrub, and where the house is was a plateau of rock, which was very fortunate. It is quite a challenging environment, with the hot climate and droughts. Although we are on the coast we don't have a very high rainfall compared with the rest of Dural. We have sprinkler systems to water the garden in summer. There are no frosts to speak of and the garden is protected by the walls.

Shortly after we acquired the property my husband heard Andrew Pfeiffer talking about garden design on the radio and was very interested in his ideas. So we asked him up to the site and showed him our house plans so he could incorporate that into his design. I feel a garden should always complement the house. It should be a complete story. We actually began with a retaining wall for the garden along the driveway, even before the house was built.

We talked through various ideas with Andrew. We had the idea of blending slowly into the bush but Andrew said that with the kind of garden we envisaged, of exotic plants and lawn, it would never work. He said we should divorce the garden from the bush, not try to blend it. And he suggested we did it like the gardens of the Alhambra in Spain, with walls overlooking the countryside, and water elements, which are very important to me. We have fountains everywhere.

In summer when it's dry, the sound of a fountain gives you a sort of freshness. I think a garden without water is empty.

So the garden here is an extension of the house but it stands apart from the landscape. And the walls, which are roughly rendered and designed to match the house, are the main element. Everywhere you look you see walls! They serve to separate the bush from our cultivated area, to draw a line between the two. I found it very exciting to have the garden divided up into rooms like that. To go from one garden to the next is more mysterious; and you always want to know what's behind the walls.

There is a large open lawn in front of the house, with a line of orange trees and a copse of scribbly gums leading back towards the walled gardens at the rear. To contrast with the foliage of the orange trees, we underplanted arctotis, which is a good silvery green. When all the oranges come into blossom, the perfume is overpowering.

We painted the house and garden walls yellow—they had been boring white. Our son is an architect and he said we should have a strong colour, and the yellow seems to belong. It blends with the bush because of the wattle trees. We find it very refreshing and all the plants come to life against the yellow walls. We have also used red ochre for the walls in some areas and blue pots are used for contrast. So the colour use is very bold and some people think we are rather brave to do it.

Building the walls, which are quite high in some areas, was a mammoth task. We wondered if we could realise it. We planted a formal citrus garden first, then the herb and vegetable garden, which is completely walled in. I love cooking, so this is an important area for me, and it's also an ornamental garden with standard roses.

From the gardenia terrace along the back of the house you go down steps into the tropical pool garden. Coming from northern Europe, I love tropical plants. We used dark pebbles for the swimming pool because we wanted it to look green, a more natural effect. We planted Cocos palms (*Arecastrum romanzoffianum*) and Alexandra palms (*Archontophoenix alexandrae*) around the pool, which were small when they went in but are now about twelve metres tall. The 'Lady Finger' bananas, mandevillas and strelitzia have also done well. There is a large hibiscus, gardenias and large clumps of cliveas. A gate in the wall leads into the wisteria walk. In summer there is a lush green shade tunnel, bordered by clipped mandarin trees that give extra colour in winter. The idea came from a visit to France.

To the side of the wisteria walk is the citrus garden, where we grow mandarins, tangelos and two different kinds of orange, grapefruit, limes and of course lemons, so it's quite a variety. It extends into the new vegetable garden. In the original herb and vegetable garden, I planted the lower growing vegetables to make it more ornamental. But this will be a serious vegetable garden because we really want more produce. There are espaliered quinces and apples on the walls, and we'll add other fruit varieties. The new walls will enclose a formal native garden and we'll have screening fences of espaliered sasanqua camellias.

You come up the steps from the new garden and look across the cactus garden, which has really become the heart of the design, a colourful area in the centre. The area was originally allocated for a tennis court but Andrew Pfeiffer said we should do a cactus and succulent garden there. I think it's the most exciting design, though it was an enormous job to build, as we had to bring all the fill in by wheelbarrow. The cactus garden has water as its central point. There are ponds and a little waterfall and the rill which runs right down the garden. This is a real hot spot and the water just cools it a little bit.

There are hundreds of different succulent plants, and cactuses of all shapes and forms. They are wonderful. They give all-year colour and change colour all the time through reds and greens, blues and greys. There is a great sculptural quality, and the round cactuses contrast with the pencil pines.

You can look across and see the bush, with the beautiful white trunks of the gums everywhere. At night we light it, with lights even in the bush, trained against the trees.

The vistas through the garden evolved as we made new areas. We built curved arches to frame views. Wherever you are in the garden, you are actually looking into the bush, so even though you are separated from it, you still feel part of it. There is a creek down in the valley and after heavy rain you can hear it from the house.

The garden has evolved but still holds to Andrew Pfeiffer's original design. Over the years we have just added more. I spend a great deal of time in the garden and I enjoy working in it. That is the simple ideal for a garden, to enjoy it. We are always thinking about the garden and planning, and we love reading garden books. The garden has become a very important part of our lives. And the next step is always exciting.

Gitta and Gunther Rembel.

Moorish in inspiration, the
central cactus garden is laid
out in geometric patterns,
with a stepped rill flowing
down to a basin and fountain.
Beyond, a grove of clipped
citrus, the wisteria walk
and the palms of the pool
garden contrast with scribbly
gum bush.

LEFT: The lush leaves of Abyssinian banana (*Ensete ventricosum* sp.) and *Strelitzia nicolai* overhang a mosaic urn of aloe and a Persian-inspired bird feeder on a pedestal.   RIGHT: A window set into the mosaic wall at ground level blurs the normal division between house and garden. Jungly plants enclose the courtyard, their exuberant forms contrasting with the intricacy of the mosaic.

grandmother's paving

THE MOSAIC GARDEN MARGOT KNOX

Artist Margot Knox's little Melbourne courtyard garden is unique. Her ideas and skills reflect her gardening apprenticeship with some giants of Australian landscaping—Ellis Stones, her husband the architect Alistair Knox, and Gordon Ford—as much as her artist's vision. Hidden behind high walls on a busy road in Hawthorn, an inner eastern suburb of Melbourne, the 20 × 35 metre garden and the house both bear the hallmarks of Margot Knox's art.

Margot Knox arranges pots of agaves on ledges ascending to the roof.

I DIDN'T THINK of mosaic when I started this garden; I thought of tiling. There are millions of people doing mosaics and they are nearly all absolutely hideous, really kitsch and arty-crafty and awful. My mosaic comes from something older. What happened to me happens to a lot of naïve painters, when they have worked hard all their life and they stop. They have something to say and then they start doing something creative. But I think my mosaicing is a frustration because I really wanted to build or do something in the garden, and it's almost like grandmother's paving. I am not dealing with big pieces of slate, I am dealing with little pieces of tile but I still lay it in a very workmanlike fashion, and if I want a shape I'll make a shape.

So I am sculpting in a way. I curved the walls around. I thought, I've got to hold that soil back and create something. It's funny, it has just been *felt* all along. I don't wish to sound precious about what I do because it is really just ground out of me. I use what I can lay my hands on in the way of bricks and stuff, and I just sort of push it into the shape I want. I think about shapes a lot. If I was building another garden, it would have a lot to do with shapes and constructions and things.

I can imagine this work going on and on. The one nice thing about mosaic is that it can be totally over the top. If you jammed as much as that into a normal garden, it would look frightful. But I wouldn't mind this being so full that you had to pick your way through it.

I did make a beautiful big chair which I was very excited about, but in actual fact it didn't look good. It was too big and your eye went to it all the time. The rest of the garden just settles. Even though it is bright, it is pretty resolved, but when I put this great enormous beautiful chair in, using all the good stuff I had, it just looked wrong. There was nowhere I could push it into. If I'd had an old apple tree and it could have gone underneath, it would have looked wonderful. So we just got a crane and lifted it out, and it went up to my son's at Eltham, where it sits under a tree in the orchard.

That taught me a lesson. I keep saying you can be over the top, you can put anything in, but this fought with the other settee, which is very resolved. It is still a real learning curve. If something's not working, I am quite ruthless, I just get rid of it. Everyone said, 'You are mad. That chair's the best thing you have ever done.' But it just took over and I didn't like it, so it had to go even though a hell of a lot of work went into it.

You haven't got much room for mistakes in a small space and I've done a lot of building out there. The end wall just went 'oomph' and was very straight, very cut off. I've got a very good son who works in special effects in films, so if I say, 'How can I curve this round?' he just comes out for the morning and works with me on it.

It was a very strange site because in the seventies the whole building, which was once a warehouse, had been revamped. It had been well done but it was wild. It looked like a Kentucky Fried Chicken house. The floor was all black and the house was divided into cubicles in very strong primary colours. This was before people started buying warehouses. Alistair walked in and said, 'It's beautiful, it's like a French apartment.' Everybody else thought, now they have really gone off their heads. For me it was great because I saw it as a studio. The garden had a wall going across half of it, as was done a lot in the sixties and seventies, and the gum trees and everything were outside on the nature strip.

People would sit out there drinking at night and it was full of bottles. I thought, that's a very ugly shaped garden at the back, and I got the plan and found out I really owned the land. I thought, blow that, and I also knew from previous experience that if I had asked it would have taken a couple of years for them to have worked out that that was my land. So I just got two bricklayers and pulled down the wall and in two nights I had put up the curved wall to enclose it. Then I thought I would build a little seat to sit on or something. That is how the mosaics started—I thought I would cover the seat with tiles.

There was a very dark room, almost like a carport, so I bought a window at the wreckers. When I put it in, that was very illuminating because I could see what a great garden I could make. We built the settee and then I thought, I'll tile the settee. I didn't think of mosaic—the word mosaic would have made me feel a bit sick. I had all these old tiles and started tiling and thought this was a wonderful medium for the garden. So I did a bit of a wall and was really quite addicted to it. Then I did the windows inside the room.

I don't like doing pots but I did a line of white pots on top of the wall and I think they work. I did them just to hold the plants but I am very pleased with them.

I am thinking of having an enormous succulent garden on the flat roof, though structurally it is quite difficult to do. I used to hate succulents but now I've gone very keen on them. They are effortless. Last year I nearly fell over when they all flowered, all these mini-flowers sticking out of them. So I would like to have that look up there. It should be splendid. I just thought it would be marvellous to enclose the garden as skyline. I love roof gardens. I'll probably put a roof over the top so that I can put all those beautiful cactuses up there and just let them grow wild.

Someone once said that unless ninety-three per cent of the people who see a work of art like it, it should be destroyed. And that is what I feel about the mosaic. I have never had anything that is such a popular medium. I think it is because it's made out of salvaged pieces, it's to do with not costing a lot, and people think it's like a patchwork quilt.

It reminds lots of people of things they've had in their lives. So it is very nostalgic because nearly all the china is old and of course it's good stuff. That is why it has remained intact. I get given some enormously old stuff with those old lead glazes still as new as they were in the nineteenth century. People give me pieces all the time. I have got them everywhere, under beds and in boxes and I never say no because you never know what you are going to get.

People also like this garden because they think, 'Oh, perhaps I might do it.' And I always tell them how to do it. I am quite mingy really, but I just say yes, you do this, you do that, because no two people do it the same. It is actually quite easy to do.

Children are the best at it because they have no preconceived idea of what it should look like, just as I was with the first mosaic with white flowers. When I look at it now, I can see it is really very primitive, like my early paintings, and it's got great life.

My interest in plants has developed with the garden. There are lots of different shapes and textures, and the pot shapes are made to suit the plants. The agaves were my first love—in fact I nearly called it the Agave Garden. Which would

have been mad, but that is what I loved, and I thought I had just discovered them. So I thought of a pot that I could put some agaves in, and then I made another one for those mad aloes with the orange flowers. It has pieces jutting out and I want to actually make flowers on the end.

I think the garden looks better with the more spiky, architectural plants; it doesn't look good with soft sort of things, unless they are actually almost clipped into a shape. I also love the exotic quality that you only get with plants like bananas, strelitzias and succulents. I just love all those really sculptural shapes.

I became a gardener when I was about eighteen. I worked with Ellis Stones and that had a profound effect on me. Ellis had a little shop nursery in Ivanhoe where I was renting a loft from an elderly lady. I always had trouble with the rent and she said, 'You should do some gardening to earn some money.' At that stage I was at Royal Melbourne Institute of Technology doing painting.

So she asked Ellis Stones—Rocky as everyone called him—if I could work with him. He used to pick me up very early in the morning in his little Austin. He had this theory that women were great stonemasons, that they were really good at construction in the garden. He actually set me off paving. I did thousands and thousands and thousands of square feet of paving for Rocky and he also taught me stone walling.

He was wonderful to work for but he was funny. I'd never have any money and I'd always be hungry and I'd start work without any breakfast, so he would say, 'I'll go away and I'll get us both a sticky bun.' And he'd appear back about six o'clock at night. Just sort of go off and leave me!

It was very hard work but I loved it and I was very good at it. I used to do so many metres a day and in the end I was paid by the metre. I never thought of gardens really, I was more interested in construction—still am, in a way. I enjoy building and I love buildings in the landscape; follies and structures.

It was a wonderful apprenticeship. And Rocky and I were very, very close. He used to be slightly worried about me. I was pretty outrageous and he used to say I should try to tidy myself up a little bit for people. But we did get on wonderfully. Then after a while I met Alistair, my husband, who was building earth buildings in the landscape. And it all tied together. I started paving the inside of Alistair's buildings, he met Rocky through me and he started using Rocky for his landscaping.

It was a very interesting period. A lot's been written about Rocky that I think is wrong. They have eulogised him and made out that all this deep philosophical stuff was behind his work. But he was just a natural. He did things instinctively and he had a great feeling for the landscape and the rocks. No one had ever really taken him as seriously as Alistair did. You know, Alistair told him he was a genius. Alistair was making great cuts in the landscape to put a slab and build, and Rocky used to just sort of creep in and put a bit of a boulder in. They were a marvellous team.

Then I introduced Rocky to Gordon Ford. Gordon and I used to work on jobs a lot together—me doing the paving, Gordon doing Rocky's boulders and landscaping, so that probably was my first introduction to gardening, but I still really didn't think of gardens as such. I was still much more interested in the building side—steps, low sitting walls. I didn't even think of the planting side until we built our big earth house in Eltham and the garden somehow had to be resolved. I wanted to plant European stuff and I remember Alistair saying, 'No, you just can't. You are not putting any of that rubbish in.' So I had a big vegetable garden and within that I was allowed to plant my roses and things. And gradually it dawned on me that I should be replacing the bush again and we planted hundreds of trees.

So I felt very much part of this school, with Gordon, Rocky and Alistair, who really saw the Australian landscape. Alistair always said no one ever had the courage to put back a landscape. He felt everyone 'salt and peppered', and they should plant a thousand casuarinas, but no one would ever be game to do something on that scale. So there was a lot of compromise. Rocky was very much under the Edna Walling influence. He was really more European, in a way, and didn't start looking at Australian gardens for quite a while.

But it has certainly rubbed off on me. Those landscaping ideas are very deep in me. I unconsciously put those 'boulders' out there but I made them out of bricks and chicken wire. I thought, I've got to put some boulders there. I didn't bring in real boulders. That would have seemed stupid to me, to bring in boulders and mosaic them. But I wanted to make something to bind the garden to the earth. That is something that has just rubbed off on me through working with Rocky.

I have been here ten years now. I've come from a bush sort of garden to a very small, disciplined sort of garden, and I liked that because I was able to create something from nothing. But I do think the Australian bush is extraordinarily powerful. There is nothing like it in the world, to me. Nothing like it. I sort of hunger for it a bit here because I haven't been into the bush for a long time.

The two eucalypts and the camphor laurels (*Cinnamomum camphora*), which would have been planted in the 1970s, were in the garden when we came, and they are huge. I am lucky that the garden's got those bones. Camphor laurels are unbelievably mucky with the leaves but they have very good basic shapes. You don't take them out because they are irritating, you sort of learn how to handle it. Even though I know this one will get me at the sink one day.

a tropical opera

DOMAINE DU CASTELLET   GUY CUNNINGHAM

In 1991, Guy Cunningham began his villa in the tropics, Domaine du Castellet, at Airlie Beach 1000 km north of Brisbane. With an elevation of 140 metres, the villa's 1.2 hectare (3 acre) east facing garden has wonderful views of the surrounding countryside and the Whitsundays, while benefiting from the shelter of the forest range behind. Using native and introduced tropical species, Guy has contrived a striking and original formal garden in a rainforest setting.

Coconut palms give an unmistakably tropical feel to the villa's entrance. Formal hedges of murraya and native fig wrap the garden, serving the same purpose as laurel or box in European gardens.

I AM JUST a theatre technician who's run away from Sydney to the tropics. I wanted to take all this opera scenery from 'Norma' and 'Tosca' and 'Traviata', and find a farm or somewhere and live among it. It wasn't enough to see it painted on canvas and balustrades, I wanted to create a theatre in real life.

This villa is so simple really, it's supposed to be like some sort of old rustic house, built from raw materials but with an old established look and feel. In a way it was like a child's sandcastle. I actually drew the plans for this place before I got the land, which of course you should never do. You should always know your aspect.

I had to build it myself, which is great because it adds to the charm, and I made it up as I went. I knew there were key ingredients and how I was going to place it in the tropics. It had to have a terracotta roof with hand-made tiles and lime-washed walls, and it had to have sheds because I love them. I had an idea that I was going to build it just like someone paints a watercolour.

I went very slowly on the garden because I didn't want to make it twee, I didn't want to suburbanise it, so I had to be careful what I put in. I am not really a gardener, to me it's architectural. The hedges are architectural, very simple. So I just started plodding away, moving rocks and pushing wheelbarrows. I must have moved a million rocks. I slowly built around the key architectural things, the hedges and the pencil pines. If you shape things, you end up claiming them.

I am extravagant in the garden. I want rich colours but I am sensible enough to know that I am not an experienced enough gardener to try and create a Tuscan-themed garden in the tropics based on exotic plants. I would get into trouble and no doubt gardeners and botanists and neighbours would all tell me about it.

The framework is native. I have used murraya (*M. paniculata*) for some of my hedges and figs (*Ficus microcarpa* var. *hillii)* instead of box hedging around the villa. You can topiary it just as you can with box—it's a tropical version.

I don't mind if something native wants to crop up in the garden, as long as it doesn't spoil the character and I can shape it into something without killing it. It's a sort of taming the wild. I don't have the time, energy or money to buy and establish

many new plants. They are mostly ones that grow here, or they are exotic cuttings, which if they work is great, they become part of the feature. If they don't, I plant something else. Down the steps at the front of the villa, we have got poincianas going very well. They have had their heads chopped off and are constantly pruned so we don't lose the view. There is the dracaena, which was put in to hide the tanks and has made a wild natural scene, and pandanus (*P. tectorius*), which grows naturally along the creeks, but also seems to thrive up here too. I got little cuttings of parrot's beak heliconias (*H. psittacorum*) from my neighbours to fill out the area and they are just going wild too.

There are also some plants, like the umbrella tree (*Schefflera actinophylla*) at the edge of the grotto, that have survived in pots with me in Sydney for years and years and years, and have now gone back to nature in the garden, which is nice.

I have deliberately used fairly few plants. I have stuck with things I know and tried to keep it simple. It is something I learned from observation, that masses of one plant look much better. If I plant a hedge I make the line go completely around the house so it's wrapped in hedges. I like things a bit broken up but there has to be a basic continuity. So you have the coconuts in avenues and try and lean them out to grow towards the vista.

I agonised over the coconuts and didn't put them in for years because I didn't want to suburbanise the garden. But they so obviously create a tropical feel—just the rustle of the fronds means the tropics—and they grow so fast. These are already huge and they have fitted in well because the colour of the new green fronds tones in with the yellow of the villa. They have become part of the building and part of the environment.

My water source is two tanks, not much. During January, February and March there is an average of 300 millimetres each month, then very little rain until August, and from October to January no rain at all. I do hope to put a bigger water tank in because if you have reservoirs to catch the rain in the wet season you can collect enough in half an hour to last you six months. But I survive very well as I am.

During the long dry season I don't really water my plants. With three acres, it's hundreds of metres from one end of the garden to the other. Whenever

I plant something, I water by bucket from my gravity-fed tank. It takes a while, so there is time to empty one bucket while the other fills. But I only water to establish plants or when I think something needs some help, and because I have mainly planted natives it works. The figs, for instance, don't get watered, and they wouldn't want to because I have to prune them every blessed week! It is a lot of work trimming these hedges. I thought that by planting different varieties, I would find the pros and cons of what was going to work but the murraya and the ficus have both worked very well. The murraya generally is a lot slower to get established but it means less pruning, so I have a bit of a reprieve at least from one of my hedges. I have about 250 metres of hedges here to maintain, so I never really finish pruning or sweeping patios and raking driveways, but I find it soothing. Even watering by bucket, though it's a bore, is my meditation. It is the same with mowing. I like the simple monotony of mowing lawns, that is when I relax.

I read something about going to a spiritual place, a tree, a spot on the mountain, and getting the energy back from that place. I thought, that's me. I love all the labour of gardening. It is more rewarding than anything else.

I don't think this garden will truly come into its own for another ten years. The more I can make it mysterious, the more tunnels of trees and nooks and crannies, staircases and so on, the better. This is my childhood playground all over again, going down to the bottom of the block and discovering that bit of bush and that tree, and collecting frogs down the creek.

I don't read gardening books—I am too impatient. I am the sort of person who builds a model aeroplane and puts the wings on upside down, and then reads the instructions. But gardening mistakes don't matter because I can change them. It's a bit like a scene change in the theatre. I am constantly creating a look, and it's the shapes and colours that are important to me, not the individual plants. For instance, I love the colour contrast of the coconut husk mulch on the border against the green hedge.

I am still making it up as I go. People say, how do you know where you are going? And I say, I don't, the landscape tells me.

The size of the formal garden was really forced on me by the developers because they'd bulldozed a three-acre vacuum and I had to use it and make it work. So I made terraces and driveways and a garden, then I hedged the terraces to define the spaces. The coloured hedges at the bottom are technically to stop the hard rainfall hitting the bank. I planted a red shrub and golden duranta, which turned out to be a magnificent thing, and I am going to plant more.

The gravel driveways and terraces are very much part of that Mediterranean thing. I mixed together terracotta gravel with the local white stuff, which on its own is much too glary for the tropics. It is definition, because this garden is more architectural than botanical to me, although we do have the most fantastic trees —huge six-foot diameter bottle trees (*Brachychiton* sp.), Burdekin plum trees (*Pleiogynium solandri*) that the bats squawk in every night, and the yellow wattle-like trees with their long pods. You have to create a theme, so there is a long looped driveway through the jungle, and when people visit they can actually feel part of it.

The fountain was an afterthought. I looked at the terraces and realised I needed a centrepiece, so I decided to build a fountain. I played with rocks and sat there and thought about it for ages. Then the manager of a resort in town was getting rid of a couple of Grecian urn-type pots, and I got the fountain from him too. I designed the base and the pond around it and I put in plants according to the season. The Cato Suite, the little studio that is also a grotto, is just an outbuilding but it gave me such pleasure to build that it was like a form of art. It is very solid and simple, with an arch and then the pencil pines framing it. The mould was growing naturally at the bottom and when my scenic artist friends came up and looked at the garden, they all flocked around that mouldy bit at the bottom and said it was the best part. Of course, since that was the part I couldn't control! But they are paid to make things look old, so they just reproduced the mouldy look on the grotto and it has worked really well.

The best colour in this garden is white, which I particularly like against the walls, but there are touches of warmth, like the little patchy yellow mustard that is vibrant, yet tiny and delicate. Once I had got the raw ingredients, the vista and the shape with the pencil pines, I thought it was time to soften off the building. I went to the nursery and spent a fortune on different vines. I was trying to create a high walled garden to separate my living quarters from the villa. I made a structure and put in every possible vine I could, and what works, works and what doesn't, doesn't. I've got jasmine, I've got the orange trumpet vine (*Pyrostegia venusta*), and some I don't even remember, but it really softens the bricks and mortar romantically and ties the buildings in to the natural bush.

This is one of the greatest natural parts of the world and the block in itself is very special because it has both the jungle and the vistas. To the south of the hill you get the jungle vegetation and the other side is a drier landscape with gums and grassland where the soil is black and dry. But where the garden is, it's very rich red soil.

The front of the site faces due east, across a mountain range to the marina. But the view of the water I like best is not the marina but the estuary, Pioneer Bay. It is tidal, so it changes all the time. And I am interested in all the wildlife: crocodiles and taipans, echidnas, lorikeets and kookaburras.

This place is heaven. Architecturally it's perfectly sited. In the peak of summer the sun is straight overhead with not one bit hitting the walls so it stays cool. There's always a breeze because we are so high up, yet we are protected from cyclones by the mountain range behind. A cyclone can come from any direction and once they decide to hit the coast they'll start heading north again, but though I hear the northerlies roaring in the hills, and I can see the whitecaps in the bay, I don't get them here.

The springs are eternal—they just go on and on until mid-January and the beginning of the wet season. Even then it doesn't rain every day and it's almost like winter because there is moisture, there is cloud; and the temperature is beautiful— twenty-five to thirty-five degrees every day.

I guess a lot of the theatre has rubbed off on this place. I am very aware of effects, as if this was a set. Like the lights at the back of the villa at night, which by pure accident cast a perfect shadow of the fountain in the arch. The attention to detail is really important to me—the straight edges, the sharp, sharp lines of the hedges. People say I am fussy but to me it's a set and the lines need to be absolutely sharp.

With me it's all or nothing: it's either a Belmont ute or a Mercedes sports. It's Tuscanville in the tropics, or I don't want to live.

Guy Cunningham and 'Olive'.

the battlers

THE GARDENERS OF INLAND AUSTRALIA CONTEND WITH INHOSPITABLE SOILS AND CLIMATES AS UNPREDICTABLE AS THEY ARE EXTREME.

Two friends have found opposite solutions for gardening an unusually dry pocket in southern Victoria. JENOLEN embraces the vast landscape with radiating walks lined by tough Australian-bred roses and hardy fruit trees. June Stafford's garden is sheltered by enclosing high hedges and windbreaks. Inside, precisely clipped evergreens, intricate parterres and hand-mown lawns create rhythmic patterns of green on green.

Superficially, the fertile strip of the Riverland is a fine area to garden. The McClellands have learned that with the heat of the desert at your door and a gardening year consisting of two seasons, the plant palette is severely restricted.

Annie Moorhouse began by having to shovel sand off the verandah, but has now built up her garden soil to the extent that she can enjoy getting her hands dirty. The dramatic spires of native grass trees colonise this sandhill garden.

MYRABLUAN is an oasis garden whose sense of ease in a harsh climate results from its simplicity. From the 'gigantic garden ornament' of the house, the lawn's beckoning curve draws the visitor down to a shady hidden pond.

Moree gardeners share the hardships of drastic temperature swings, floods and drought. At COMBADELLO, century-old Canary Island palms and a tranquil lagoon provide enduring reference points in a garden that has to be largely replanted each year. ROCKDALE's favourable river is offset by flood risk, so the lower garden holds plants that survive being waterlogged. Flat, relatively featureless surroundings present another challenge at BOOLOOROO. Here, strong formal lines extend into a naturalistic parkland that gives vertical interest against the flat plains.

In Western Australia's Wheat Belt lies KARABINE, a garden made against all odds in an area where more than half the year is dry and summer temperatures wipe out all but the toughest plants. Kerrie Robinson concentrated on the few plants that would thrive, setting them off with Edna Walling-inspired paths, steps and walls of local stone to lead the garden gently into its landscape.

Extreme cold is rarely a problem for Australian gardeners, but in the foothills of the Snowy Mountains, freezing winds, unseasonal frosts and snowfalls can be the gardener's worst enemies. At MYALLA, large trees, solid stone walls and a thick wooden door on the courtyard shelter the garden during the long winter.

All the negative factors listed above—extremes of cold and heat, drought and flooding, as well as poor alkaline soil and saline water—conspire against gardeners in the central desert climate of Alice Springs. The advantages are a unique flora and abundant beautifully coloured local sandstone.

The dry creek bed in Geoff Miers' town garden is both a design feature and a way to harvest flood water. The sandy 'banks' of the creek provide an ideal environment for Centralian wildflowers to germinate after the rain. The Simmons' hillside bush garden covers a large area, making the distribution of water a challenge. They designed the garden around zonal planting, with exotics giving coolness and shade around the house, native plants in the main garden and only plants endemic to the site towards the perimeter.

OVERLEAF: Watsonias, arum lilies, love-in-a-mist and daisies edge the lagoon at Combadello. For inland gardeners facing harsh conditions, the presence of a stretch of water satisfies an almost spiritual need.

a dry tongue: southern victoria

Stretching between Bacchus Marsh and Geelong, in the vicinity of the Brisbane Ranges west of Melbourne, is a dry corridor of land about 10 km wide where the annual rainfall is frequently less than 475 mm, 250 mm lower than areas just 10 or 20 km away on either side. Rain falls predominantly in winter, summer temperatures regularly exceed 40°C and strong winds are also a problem.

JENOLEN   JENNY HINE

Jenny Hine's 1 hectare (2$^1/_2$ acre) garden, Jenolen at Bacchus Marsh, is built on an exposed southeast facing slope. The elevation is 275 metres and the alkaline soil is a mixture of clay and basalt.

THE HEDGES   JUNE STAFFORD

June Stafford began her 0.8 hectare (2 acre) garden at Bannockburn twenty-five years ago by planting thick conifer windbreaks and terracing the steep southwest facing site. The alkaline soil is heavy black clay over limestone, making mulching a necessity.

LEFT: At Jenolen, the glossy green foliage of a nashi pear tunnel shades a path between densely planted borders.
RIGHT: June Stafford with 'Spot' under her arbour of copper roses at the top of the garden.

Statice, cardoons, white valerian and artemisia in the sunken garden at Jenolen make a harmonious transition to the dry paddocks outside. Unusual statues are a distinctive element throughout the garden.

JENNY HINE: I GAVE UP teaching about ten years ago, played tennis for a year and then I started gardening. I did the front area and the back area and that filled up and I was exploring beyond the fence and my husband Noel said, 'I think you should have the paddock beside the house.' I thought long and hard because I knew if I took over the paddock my life would be gardening and not other things. And that is what happened.

I planned the garden on paper based on a view of the dam. It is usually empty now, so it's just paddock, but I always loved the view of the dam from the kitchen window. I planned the garden as a circle with that as the focal point and made a sunken garden at the bottom so it wouldn't encroach on the view. Then I extended the circle into walks.

The plants I can grow here are very limited, and I am much more interested in design and layout than plants so I have planted in sweeps rather than groups.

The first plants we put in were fruit trees and a few roses, and they all survived. So when I came back to the garden seriously, I knew I could base a garden on those. The soil here is heavy red clay and alkaline. When trees put their roots down they all seem to survive because there is moisture underneath.

I discovered old-fashioned roses and became passionate about them. But the paddock was so windswept. I decided to try the roses bred by Australians, especially those bred by Alister Clark because Bulla, where he lived, has a very similar climate and he bred his roses to suit these conditions. I am now growing quite a few and they have done well. They survive where nothing else would.

I have 'Courier', a wonderful rose. Some of my other favourites are 'Lady Huntingfield', 'Ringlet', 'Glenara' and 'Traverser'— which is so well named, it really does traverse—and 'Mrs Richard Turnbull' with its big white open flower.

That has a story behind it. June Stafford at The Hedges made a beautiful metal sculpture of a climbing rose over an arbour and used my 'Mrs Richard Turnbull' as the model. She welded little Richard Turnbulls all over it. And I've got the 'baby' of the sculpture in my garden.

Then there is another Clark climber, 'Golden Vision', with the pathway behind it. Here I've got three roses raised by the Sydney breeder Frank Riethmuller—'Carabella', 'Gay Vista' and 'Claret Cup'. Alister Clark's 'Milkmaid' is growing right over one wall of the house and along the fence-line. It is an amazing rose that thrives with no water, and you can even run over it with the mower and you won't hurt it.

They are all great roses and so little known. I have made a point of getting as many as I can just to build a collection and to make sure I don't miss out on any that are really good.

I have made billowing hedges of 'Tarrawarra', pink in the bud and opening to white. It is not commonly known but it's the best hedging rose you can have. It is evergreen and always in flower.

There are tunnels of nashi pears (*Pyrus pyrifolia*) that blossom and fruit almost too well—to the point where you never want to eat another nashi pear.

The area in the bottom corner was a real problem. Nothing would grow because all the topsoil had been washed off. So I made a sunken garden planted in blues and greys. Around the outside is *Artemisia* 'Powis Castle', *Perovskia* 'Blue Spire', cardoons and sea lavender (*Limonium perezii*). In the centre are potentillas and 'Little White Pet' roses surrounding my favourite blue sculpture and the high-backed chairs, which seem to just go there. I have quite a few sculptures around the garden. I think people should use them much more for focal points and links.

There's a row of espaliered Nottingham medlars (*Mespilus germanica*) with rugosa roses growing along the front, which have white flowers similar to the medlars. Then the orange hips tone with the medlar fruits and autumn leaves. Crab apples also grow well. I planted a few *Malus toringoides* and liked the shape and the fruits so much I put in a line of them.

And I am replacing the birches, which were a huge mistake because they are very shallow-rooted, with snow pears (*Pyrus nivalis*), which seem ideally suited to the conditions here.

There is a formal line of Russian olives (*Elaeagnus angustifolia*). It's a shame they are growing some thorns but it's a lovely tree, even in winter with the shiny black stems.

And at the bottom, I have planted *P. simonii* poplars—again, they are ideal for these conditions and the glossy green makes a lovely contrast with the greys in the sunken garden.

Under an arch of clipped privet, a herringbone path runs between sculpted hedges and a hand-mown lawn. In June Stafford's restrained garden, the precise patterns of green on green have a hypnotic effect.

JUNE STAFFORD: THE FIRST THINGS we planted were the cypresses at the front, to define the boundary and stop the wind. We had to create the shelter and the growing environment. Now the cypresses have grown up and give the garden a wonderful microclimate, with hardly any wind. You can see the tops of the trees moving but you can't feel it. The people across the river say it looks like a postage stamp in summer—a square of green in all that dry ground.

I didn't really tap into gardening until the early eighties, then the bug bit hard. As I got more into it, I came to understand that you couldn't just plonk things anywhere but had to garden with some sort of rhyme and reason. Then you keep honing it, pulling out things you don't like any more and creating some other scene.

When we designed the garden, we started by excavating the site. Around the house I wanted as much flat ground as possible, so when you walk out off the verandah you don't need one leg longer than the other. That necessitated digging a huge quarry on the side of the hill to make four or five terraces and flat ground for the house. When the excavation was completed, I did the rock wall at the back to keep everything together.

We do have the advantage of plenty of water. The river is one of our boundaries. But you tend to make things weaker if you keep watering them, so if they can survive without it's better. And there are plants that simply aren't suited to our dry summers however much you water. I had about sixty birches when we started and more than half have died.

I find it's quite easy keeping the hedges under control with the petrol hedger. When it's a high hedge you can only do a couple of sweeps and then you have to put it down, but with the lower ones it's at a comfortable height. You can't keep a hedge looking really sharp, really straight and precise, with hand shears.

The privet hedge along the front has a really strong base and you just need to cut all the fine sappy stuff off. With cutting, it gets a very close texture. The pool garden is hedged with laurustinus, which makes a wonderful hardy hedge.

I got rid of the lawn at the entrance and made a diamond-shaped bed using a low hedge filled with 'Goldheart' ivy. The green-on-green effect is very restful and relaxing. The backdrop mirror bush [coprosma] hedge along the driveway is a rich, glossy green. A lot of people think it's really common but we were quite happy to have anything that grew at all when we first came here.

The shaped privet hedges in front of the house need clipping every two weeks when they are growing, the *Lonicera nitida* 'Aurea' less often, and the lawn twice a week with the little push mower. But right through the summer, the lawn is always green. It hasn't got that ragged edge that rotary mowers create.

I don't like a lot of colour. It is nice to have occasional colour, like when the crab apples blossom, but it doesn't last very long and that is enough.

The rose arbour on the rockery is covered with copper roses copied from Jenny Hine's 'Mrs Richard Turnbull' roses. Originally I made the arbour frame to grow real roses over it, but there was too much root competition and whatever I grew would always look straggly. So I made my metal climbing rose instead.

I enjoy building things. I built the shade house by the pool and the wisteria walk and lots of seats. I like doing that sort of thing in the shed on a cold, wet winter's day.

With the rockery wall, I was trying to recreate what you see when you look across the hills to the rock cliffs. The path goes right around the top. You look over the horizontal canopy of prostrate conifers and you can see right down into the garden. I love that, it's like looking into a bowl.

sinking in

DIANNE McCLELLAND'S GARDEN

Dianne McClelland's garden is at Barmera in the Riverland, 240 km east of Adelaide. The 1.2 hectare (3 acre) garden has been developed on ground that was formerly used for fruit farming. The highly alkaline soil is red sand and loam over a limestone ridge, and water is also alkaline. The average rainfall is 150–200 mm, usually occuring in winter although summer downpours are not uncommon. In June and July the diurnal temperature range is frequently –4°C–20°C, with night temperatures to –7°C in drought years. Summer temperatures are constantly high, with weeks of 40°C–42°C days.

An old chaff cutter stands on the corner of a winding gravel path softened by cottagey plants and pots.

WE MOVED UP here from Adelaide in the summer of 1982 and the heat was a real shock. The climate has been a tremendous learning experience.

There wasn't really a garden around here we could look to as a model for this one. I read a lot of books for inspiration. I avidly read anything I thought was pertinent to what I was trying to do. Initially it was a small garden and it has only recently become so big. You know, the more you do, the more you do.

Because it is so hot in summer, I plan most maintenance jobs for the winter. The watering is a constant summer task and it's not automated. We don't like automatic watering systems because you are not aware of how much water you are using and whether it's right or wrong for what you are trying to achieve in the garden.

It is a very low rainfall area but we have an irrigation allocation relating to the time that this place was a fruit block, a grape property. The water is pumped straight out of the Murray River. The drawback is being a small property in the middle of large vineyards, so you have to call and say you want to water, but if everybody else is watering that day it only dribbles out.

Water quality varies a lot, from chalky white to mud to sometimes clear. The salinity's not the problem it was since the salt interception scheme started but there is fairly high alkalinity. Without water the Riverland would be a desert. People have lost sight of that because it looks so green and lush but one day water is going to become very scarce.

The garden is basically flat. There is a ridge of rock running through it roughly north to south. We have got about a foot of reasonable topsoil to work with, then it goes very quickly into extremely poor quality limestone subsoil.

There are virtually only two seasons. You go from winter to summer, which lasts from October to April. I think we have had only two true springs, when there was soaking rain.

During January to March it is not unheard of to have a whole week of forty-five degree temperatures. You can cope with the odd day or two like that but after four or five days of forty-plus weather, plants shut down. It doesn't matter how much water you put on in weather like that.

A lot of people don't realise that certain plants do shut down over summer in this climate. Summer is their dormant period, not winter.

People just assume we should plant in spring because we have got all this warm weather for things to grow in. But spring here can be less than three weeks. Autumn is the best time to plant.

We get extremely strong winds. We lost a belt of fifteen-year-old native trees in the wind. We had weakened them by overwatering, and once they went, other plants that they'd been protecting suffered. Shade and shelter are essential, and I like the garden enclosed to stop the hot wind.

I have tried all sorts of plants that are reputedly tough but they won't survive summer here. They get to the middle of February and then they keel over because they are sick and tired of the heat and wind. Watering doesn't compensate for climate. You can't create an Adelaide Hills garden here. You buy plants labelled 'full sun' but that means southeastern Australian conditions. Here they'll burn to a crisp.

The first thing we did in the garden was pull out the grapevines, which took up the whole front garden. We planted two-thirds of it with plum trees and apricots, leaving a small apricot-drying green at one end. Eventually I pinched bits of that and added a tree for each of the children and gradually the garden was built around those. The plums and apricots came out when we decided to start a nursery.

The garden has gradually got bigger, evolving bit by bit. To me, the layout is paramount, much more important than the plants. I plant things to be useful. But I am not a grand plan person. I sort of linked it up as I did each stage and each area has developed its own style and mood.

In planting, I like that old-fashioned feeling; I love old-fashioned roses especially. I grow a lot of them because I like their shrubbiness. My favourites are 'Duchesse de Brabant' and 'Cornelia', the hybrid musk. A gigantic multiflora rose grows over a fence in the nursery area, with a white banksia on the other side and honeysuckle coming through, so you get a succession of flower and perfume. I also like rugosas. I really like roses that grow well without much pruning, that form a shrubby barrier.

I have learnt it is important to have shelter plants—westringias and oleanders and all those

A sunken path tunnels between jam-packed borders of hardy flowers and tough groundcovering foliage. Staple plants include *Cotoneaster dammeri* (right), purple berberis and variegated periwinkle, with alyssum and pink geraniums. The rampant crimson-purple moss rose 'William Lobb' is pegged to run the length of the border. At the end, a tall conifer screen increases the sense of enclosure.

really tough things. Lots of gardens have small sections of little plants but I have large areas of spreading plants. There are things like plumbago (*P. auriculata*) and variegated periwinkle that take over. They work particularly well in this climate, in this sort of romantic, overgrown style I have established. I don't mind a bit of wildness. Little fussy bits are frustrating.

The trees are the essential element of the garden. They add a huge amount of atmosphere and give that green, cool feeling all through summer. If I made another garden I would quite happily do away with a lot of the planting and simply have lawn and trees. There is an ash with a broad canopy which casts beautiful shade over the lawn near the house where we eat outside in summer.

An archway leads through to a wider lawn, which originally was the apricot-drying green. It is shaded by a huge spreading golden elm, corkscrew willows and a plane tree, all planted for the children about fifteen years ago.

The garden uses lawn as pathways between sections. The garden beds have just gradually evolved and are fairly informal, with bulbs and ferns under the trees where nothing else will grow. I like the cool, green feel of foliage, rather than lots of colour.

From the shaded lawn area, you move into the bright sunshine of the sunken garden, which is formally laid out in a geometric design of pathways. The sunken paths are probably the best idea we have had. The front garden was completely flat and boring. John's lateral thinking went to work and he got the Bobcat out and cut the paths way down, and the garden is framed by them. We love the perspective. You can stand in a corner and you are twelve inches lower than the garden bed, yet you can't see the pathways. It's as if you are in a sea of plants.

The centrepiece that supports the roses was inspired by a visit to Venice, where we saw some ornate metal structures, and John made this twisty blue feature when we came home. He wanted it to be symmetrical and I wanted it to be twisty. I love the blue because it's so fresh. It is almost the colour of the sky. Green would just have disappeared into the garden. It is underplanted with saltbush, so you get the grey and blue which is very effective. But we try not to tell people it's saltbush. I tell them its proper name, *Rhagodia spinescens*, because as

soon as people know it's just saltbush they lose interest! It works very well and it's very tough, which it needs to be here in the hot, glary gravel. The reflected heat is quite intense.

The garden is only metres from the highway but the big castor oil (*Ricinus communis*) and cypress hedges all round make it very secluded. Originally the noise and heat and the wind out there were quite horrendous.

Although it is a formal area, I have trouble keeping to that geometric design and can't resist putting in the extra half a dozen blue salvias or something, so the theme is softened a bit. The white garden wasn't entirely successful and can look very tired and brown very quickly with the heat, so I have added a bit of blue, which is nice and cool.

One of the most effective parts, I think, is the long straight path lined with white agapanthus. It runs for seventy-five metres and you can see from one end to the other.

Other staple plants here are berberis, diosma which I like for that fresh green foliage, and masses of wild verbena. I use a lot of those tough, wily plants like verbena because they do so well in the heat. In a big area they give colour and draw you in to look more closely. Grey foliage plants do extremely well. I have got *Artemisia* 'Powis Castle' and the tall *Teucrium fruticans*, which has a stiff, angular habit and a mauve flower and makes a good backdrop. And the little blue flowering convolvulus (*C. sabatius*) goes beautifully on the northern side of the path sheltering under the agapanthus. That won't survive in the full heat of the summer sun on the southern side.

As a focal point at the end of this long pathway I have placed a weeping mulberry with a seat under it. The drawback of course is the fruit, which the birds love. So the seat underneath is covered with bird droppings or mulberries in fruiting season. It is becoming overgrown now with *Cotoneaster dammeri* and I don't cut it all away because I like the effect of it being a little bit hidden.

I think it is the sense of enclosure I enjoy so much. I like the feeling of being lost in the garden when you wander round all these enclosed areas. And I like the feeling of being in a little oasis, being enveloped, rather than standing on a bald sweep of open lawn and borders.

'yakkas' on a sandhill

RUSSELL'S CAMP ANNIE MOORHOUSE

Russell's Camp is at Padthaway in South Australia's Upper South East, 280 km from Adelaide. The 1 hectare (2 $^1/_2$ acre) garden is on the east facing slope of a small sandhill. The soil is alkaline, non-wetting sand. Average rainfall is 500 mm and falls mainly in winter. Bore water is plentiful but tends to be salty. The garden is virtually frost free and although daytime temperatures in summer can be as high as 43°C, the nights are generally cool.

LEFT: One of the original pink gums has become a marvellous living sculpture in the front lawn. Between its gnarled branches, a seat looks out over the garden.   RIGHT: The creamy spires of yakkas accented by orange-flowered leucospermum draw the eye towards the simple low house. Festooning the verandahs are jasmine and 'Francis E. Lester' roses.

WE HAVE BEEN here about twenty years. We built the house in 1980 and started the garden the following year. First of all we planted the lawn because when we built it was a terribly bare sandhill. That first summer was horrific—we just had to shovel sand off the verandahs. We planted the lawn in the middle of January and somehow it grew, which was quite amazing. We really weren't fussy about where it was as long as it covered as much sand as possible. Later on we cut out bits for garden.

The only trees here were a few pink gums (*Eucalyptus fasciculosa*), one by the tennis court, one in the middle of the lawn which is now a lovely old tree, and a clump down by the front gate. Over the years a few eucalypts have sprung up in the garden and I have left them where they have come up. But everything else here apart from the yakkas (*Xanthorrhoea australis*) we planted.

I didn't have a real plan for the garden, except that I did have in mind the views, because it's such a pretty spot and I didn't want to block them out. I needed shelter from the horrific wind, so I planted quite thickly to start with, shrubby things and larger trees to the west and north. The view to the west is gorgeous because it looks out over the flats, so I have left peepholes for that.

The house is set on a rise, so there are views almost all the way round. We chose the house site because of that but also because it was part of my father's land and it was always his favourite spot. Most of the hills here are very stony and he'd coped with making a garden on stone all his life. He said this sandhill would be easy digging. It is, but he forgot to mention that it would also drain very quickly!

I say I didn't plan the garden, but once you get started you can see the outline of where you want to go, and it carries on from there. My mother, who's a wonderful gardener, came over and we got the hose out and started laying out edges and planting bits and pieces.

I remember in the first year I started to plant, a man from the Department of Agriculture came and said, 'Oh, I feel so sorry for you, you'll never get anything to grow here.' I just wish I could remember his name so I could get him back to have a look.

Many people influenced me in the beginning. My mother's friends would come to the site and say,

'Annie, there is a lot of sky.' So I thought I'd better get rid of some sky. Neville Bonney [the native plant expert and author], who's now with Greening Australia, had a local native nursery and he advised me to start with natives, so at least I would get something established. I knew nothing then. I came home from Neville with three boxes of plants labelled small, medium and large, which was a very sensible way to deal with a new gardener.

I have stuck with native plants ever since because I think they suit the area, and they blend with the pink gums and yakkas. I have learned a lot about them. I find them really interesting now and all through the year there is always something to pick. But I can't resist a few English bulbs and odd exotic plants that will grow here, so I sort of poke those in between—little hooped petticoat daffodils, freesias and anchusas.

I think by doing that, you get a full picture. I also can't resist camellias, so I grow them in huge pots on the verandahs. And I have pots of daphnes, gardenias, azaleas and hellebores. They are all things I can't grow in the garden but they are all quite healthy and happy in their pots, and I get all those flowers and scents I wouldn't normally have. I couldn't live without scented plants.

This is a garden using native plants but I am not recreating natural bushland. I think bush gardens tend to be a bit hot. A lawn around the house just makes the garden so much cooler, and with our hot summers I think you have got to create coolness.

You have got to do what you can with your climate and site. It is no good trying to plant a wonderful English garden when you have terrible water and very hot summers. There is really nothing worse than sick-looking plants. It is better to use the plants that will grow well and have them healthy and tough, even if they are not your favourites.

The winds here are the worst problem, especially the summer northerly. But over the years that has improved because of the shelter. And the soil is now brown instead of white because I have built it up with manure from under the shearing sheds. I now actually get my hands dirty gardening. They used to be quite clean once.

When the garden was very new, I mulched like mad with everything I could find and it has slowly built up a bit of soil, but I still can't water enough in summer because it just goes straight through.

The view looking west of the flat is magnificent, especially during a wet winter. You can see the line of trees along the Marcollat watercourse and the sun shining on it in the evenings is quite beautiful. Almost all the planting here is very low apart from a few stands of trees and I like the views of the yakkas in the paddocks. There are hundreds of them and in November they are gorgeous. They look like white candles sticking up out of the paddock. So that is quite an unusual backdrop and the garden blends into it quite naturally.

Down the eastern side round the tennis court I've put all my daffodils and other bulbs, which have been successful. They used to be all over the garden and kept getting lost under everything else.

It is tough under the pink gum, so I have just planted agapanthus, old-fashioned succulents and haemanthus (blood lilies). It looks good and it's a splash of colour.

I am very pleased I've got lemon-scented gums (*Eucalyptus citriodora*) to grow because Neville told me I would never manage it. The first lot grew like mad and I have since planted a few more out in the paddock which are going well. I can grow them because, being on a rise, I am above the frost line most of the time. Occasionally we get terrible frosts and things will get a bit singed but it is now fairly protected with all the trees.

All the yakkas were in the garden to begin with and I planted round them. I clean them out a bit every now and then. I have made lawn pathways down into the eastern side of the garden, winding between proteas, masses of thriptomene, grevilleas and banksias. Most of the banksia species are easy to grow here.

Roses here are absolutely awful and I was told not to waste my time with them. But I love to have them to pick in spring. Deane Ross [South Australian rose grower and nurseryman] said to me: 'Annie, take no notice, just put them in and don't carry on with all this spraying that people do. They'll look fabulous in the spring and they'll look rotten for the rest of the year, but that doesn't matter, next spring they'll look excellent again.' And he was quite right. They give me huge pleasure in the spring and I don't worry about them for the rest of the year.

I think this is a very Australian garden. It is sort of tough. In most parts of Australia, if a garden is going to look healthy it's got to be tough too. People from overseas think it's very Australian. They love the outlooks and they are mad on the space.

I try to collect unusual and different plants. A friend of my mother's said to me early on, when this was just a house sitting on a terrible bare sandhill, 'Annie, you will never have a beautiful garden but you'll be able to make it interesting.' That has always stayed with me, so I try to collect things that you don't often see in South Australia. I've got lots of Western Australian banksias, a big collection of hakeas which are excellent here, and proteas and leucadendrons from South Africa.

It is never stable, this garden. There is always something dying out, so you tend to get a bit of a new look each year. Planting trees in the paddock is an ongoing project. This was a very bare hill and it's taken me twenty years to sort of sink it into the countryside. The house stuck out like a beacon when we first built it but now you can hardly see it. That has been my theme, not to put a scar on the countryside. I am planting each side of the house with trees going into the paddock. It'll be a good bird corridor.

I adore it here and I don't think I would like to garden anywhere else. I have lived here forever, and I love it. It is probably not the most ideal climate to put a garden into but you cut your coat to fit your cloth.

Annie Moorhouse.

the house is an ornament

MYRABLUAN ANNE BISHOP

Myrabluan is near Merriwa in the Upper Hunter Valley, 320 km northwest of Sydney. The soil is alkaline black clay, heavy in winter and setting like cement in summer. The annual rainfall is 600 mm and spring dominant, although unpredictable. Supplementary water comes from a bore which is fairly hard. Set deep in a valley, the 1.2 hectare (3 acre) garden is in a frost pocket, with recurrent frosts throughout winter of –4°C to –5°C. Summer temperatures reach a high of 40°C.

Vine-clad verandahs and cornerstone trees tie the house to its garden. Low borders planted in soft colours dress the front of the house and define the edge of a flowing lawn.

Weeping willows overhang the secluded pond at the bottom of the garden.

WHEN WE MOVED here, everybody said don't build down low, don't build on the wrong side of the creek, don't build on the heavy black soil. But we kept coming back to this spot because we absolutely loved the yellow box trees (*Eucalyptus melliodora*). One of the advantages of being down low like this is we don't get much wind. When it's windy here, it's blowing a gale everywhere else. I think I belong down here, in the hollows.

Quite often we get cut off by the creek. It is very inconvenient but I love it when it comes down because that is it, we are stuck in our little cubby house.

In summer I am always terrified of bushfires. If a fire came down here, it would sweep along all these trees because we have never cleared any of it.

The garden is too big, really, and it makes its own arrangements in a lot of areas where you wish it wouldn't. In some ways that is nice because nature has a way of getting it right but certain things get away from you. The future of this garden sometimes worries me. It's probably going to end up eating me!

The site is flat but it slopes away down to the creek. Like most country gardens, the fence has been moved out a couple of times. The black clay soil is a nightmare in some ways. It is either wet or rock-hard. But it has tremendous depth, so the trees I have planted have all done very well.

The best thing about the garden is the way it follows the natural contours of the land—it doesn't muck up any of the natural landscape. That, and the trees. I like the way the European trees near the house blend into the Australian trees beyond, the gums and the river oaks (*Casuarina cunninghamiana*). I think trees give a garden interest and mystery.

I was warned at the start that if we had all these yellow box trees around, I would never be able to have a garden. We completely ignored everybody's advice. And it did make gardening, in the sense of digging and planting things like little petunias, very difficult.

We started with the house in the right spot in this paddock and I gradually worked outwards with the garden. I have never had an overall design in mind but I think I've got an instinct for it. It was meant to fit very comfortably with the landscape, with all the surrounding trees, and the peek that you get at the paddocks.

I treat the house as a sort of gigantic garden ornament. I see the garden in relation to the house and the landscape as an extension of the garden. The garden dresses the house. I always think first in terms of shape and I've always tried to fit the garden with the shape of the house and the land.

I wanted a green lawn outside the door because it was quite bare all along the front and if you wanted to go out you had to jump out of the doors. So we planted a bit of lawn and I mowed out to the edge of the bank, making a gentle shape. Then I found everyone was drawn to the curved lawn edge to look over, but there was nothing to see but a shabby old bank. I realised there had to be something there. Mowing banks is a nightmare; so I planted over that ugly bank. And one thing kind of led to another.

Unfortunately with the turning of the first sod and the first watering of the lawn, we started to kill the beautiful gums we had chosen to build beside. They took twenty years to die but when they all came down it was absolutely devastating because really, all the work we'd done in the garden went for nothing. I still had all the trees outside, it was just the central ones.

So the garden has had two phases—before the box trees went, and after when they were replaced by deciduous European trees. By the second phase I had learnt so much more about gardening.

In this garden now you are constantly drawn on to explore. You come in over the ramp and you see the front door but there is no path to it, just lawn to the door. Your eyes are led through the European trees and across the bank, where you see the group of kurrajongs (*Brachychiton populneus*) and apple box trees (*Eucalyptus bridgesiana*). The curve of the lawn makes you want to go to the edge to see what's over it. You follow the little path, gently curving down the bank, to a natural little amphitheatre at the bottom where the pond is. It is really the focus, but you don't see it instantly. When you come to it beyond the willows it's a lovely surprise.

We always wanted to have a pond after I'd heard Beatrice Bligh speak about her garden Pejar Park at Crookwell [New South Wales] which I thought sounded like fairyland. I've since seen it and I think it's beautiful. She realised perfectly what she attempted. Her book *Down to Earth*, about Australian gardening and the difficulties, really had a great influence on me.

When I am asked what makes an Australian garden, I think it's the Australian gardener. Most of us have had to cope with some devastating things happening, and something makes us keep on going.

Anyway, Beatrice Bligh had a lovely pond and I always wanted one. Mine is only a little pond—Tony had very grandiose ideas about damming the whole paddock, but I would have spent the rest of my life on the lawn mower because if the stock aren't there to eat the grass down it becomes a jungle. I think it is just right. It all looks quite natural, slightly wild, and all we had to do was push up the edge a little bit and build the island in the middle.

The pond leaks like a sieve and has to be topped up every fourth night on an automatic system. Every so often when we are out of water, Tony says we have got to let the pond go dry. Well, if he makes me do that I am going to run away because without the pond the garden's nothing! It is the focal point, everything draws you to it. An Australian garden must have water in it because that is kind of bound to your spirit.

I have planted here mostly plants that manage for themselves and that people don't get excited about these days. I like things that are tough and try hard—buttercups, periwinkle and ivy, the silver poplars that went in from cuttings, the may hedge and laurustinus, and the willows. One of the big willows crashed down. I had a plague of bats and they love the willows. There was an enormous branch, and these thousands of bats weighed so much that they broke the branch off. I should have cut the whole tree down but I couldn't bear to. It has become a feature, part of this corner of the garden.

Australian gardeners are taking more account of their environment than they used to. Most of the early settlers were terribly nostalgic for everything they'd left behind and tried to recreate it. I would absolutely love an English country garden but I can't do it here. In England the surrounding countryside is just as green and beautiful as the gardens. Here we create a little false world in our harsh environment, we water it and make it green. I am sure it does hark back to our heritage.

In the drought times, it's really a haven for Tony to come into the garden where it's green. It sort of reassures him that grass can still grow. But I also think we've managed to get both here, the landscape and the haven. In winter when the trees are bare, you can look out at the paddocks, and in summer when the European trees are in full leaf, it's lovely to have this green enclosure, this little sanctuary, separate from the droughts and all the other troubles outside.

I love being in my garden. It is where I am happiest of all. I have told my children I can't live without a garden and that when I am old and silly they are not to put me in a flat or a box in the sky. They say gardening is a search for a lost Eden, so maybe one does have a sort of fundamental need to create a garden. Perhaps everybody does and a lot of people never get a chance.

My nephew, who used to come and stay with me quite a lot, told his grandmother very solemnly when he was about five that when you come to Anne's garden you enter an enchanted place. That was one of the nicest things.

Tony and Anne Bishop with 'Arthur' and 'Edward'.

the gardeners of moree

Moree, 650 km from Sydney on the northwestern plains of New South Wales, has a capricious climate with marked diurnal swings. In winter the temperature can swing from –5°C to the low 20s within a few hours. Spring may last only a few weeks before summer sets in, with prolonged periods of over 40°C days and hot nights. Rainfall is slightly summer dominant but unpredictable, and floods are a constant threat.

COMBADELLO RUTH LEITCH

The 1 hectare (2 1/2 acre) garden of Combadello, 30 km west of Moree, has an even harsher climate, and until the advent of irrigation for cotton farming, had no permanent water supply for gardening. Ruth Leitch has recently left Combadello after gardening there for fifty years.

ROCKDALE EDNA HARDMAN

Rockdale is north of Moree on the south bank of the Gwydir River. Edna Hardman has developed her 2 hectare (5 acre) garden on deep river silt as a series of microclimates in which a wide range of plants can be coaxed to grow, and has incorporated flood-retardant levee banks as a landscaping feature.

BOOLOOROO HUGH LIVINGSTON

The 1 hectare (2 1/2 acre) garden of Boolooroo, northeast of Moree, has belonged to the Livingston family since the 1920s, when the distinctive olive hedges and conifers were planted. Over the past twelve years, Hugh Livingston has worked to strengthen the garden's design and draw it into the landscape, while softening the formal lines for a more contemporary feel.

Viewed across the lagoon, the roof of Combadello gleams in the evening light. Palms create a distinctive silhouette against the sky.

RUTH LEITCH: I COULD NEVER forget the climate here. I came in 1951 and there was a drought and in those days there were no fans. We had electric light but that was by a generator and we didn't have any water and it was forty-seven degrees in the shade every day, and stayed thirty-seven at night. I said to my husband if I had known what it was like, he would never have got me here. But these days with air-conditioners and the water it's quite different.

This was the first house built here a hundred years ago, and it was built up on a clay ridge like all the old homes because of the floods. When there is a flood, it comes up to the bottom of the palms but the house doesn't go under water.

Moree country is very flat but you are not conscious of it because it has quite a lot of vegetation. And I am so lucky to have my own garden going down onto the lagoon, so you have the illusion of a slope. My house is raised and there is a garden off it and then the lawn, and the lagoon is lower down, so to me it is a slope.

I have always loved the outdoors but when I first came to Combadello I wasn't into gardening. I lost my husband early and was running the place and being station-hand with three small children, so I never had time to garden. There was nothing here except the palm trees, some old oleanders and a little piece of lawn.

Whoever planted the Canary Island and cotton palms (*Phoenix canariensis* and *Washingtonia filifera*) had great foresight. Anywhere in the country you'll often see one stuck right next to a house. But here they were planted in a circle of six on the front driveway. Somebody told me I could get $75,000 each for those palms. I said I wouldn't take a million.

Beyond the palms for years it was just all rubbish, briars and emu bushes and not even any trees. It just stood in a paddock. In those days you didn't have any garden. The houses were just stuck out on dirt.

With the cotton farming, now we have more or less permanent water, unless the dam goes dry. But this place, although it is only thirty kilometres west, is nothing like Moree; I can't grow roses or irises or many of the things the gardeners there can grow so well. I think more than the lack of water, it's the soil, which is heavy on top and clay underneath. The roots hit that and can't go any further. It is very hard work to dig, and you have really got to do it when it's dry, and you need plenty of strength. Kick it and you'd break your toe. I lose so much when summer comes. Most things have to be replaced every year or two. Fortunately they don't all go at once, so you just put something else in. But I even lose tough shrubs and trees—spiraeas, buddleias, brooms, the flowering fruit trees. You have to learn to live with it, to work with the elements and grow what you can and enjoy it.

A tough climate like this makes you appreciate more what you get. We have lots of droughts. Our average rainfall is twenty-one inches but you can get seven inches in one night and then you can go weeks and weeks without rain. There is no pattern to it. You might get most of it in the summer, or the other way around. And we get a lot of hot westerly winds, and cold southerlies.

The site has very much determined the type of garden I have made. I like to sit on the verandah looking out to an expanse, looking down to the lagoon. I don't like being closed in. I love the openness of it. People often say to me, why don't you put in more trees, why don't you put willows over there, and I say no, I just love the old native coolabahs (*Eucalyptus microtheca*). It mightn't be attractive to other people but I love the natural landscape around the garden. There is so much beauty in the bush. I have kept the coolabahs, and anything that comes up in my garden stays there.

Moree is not known for its old gum trees, so I am lucky to have what I've got. Nearly all the trees in the garden, like the pink ironbarks (*Eucalyptus sideroxylon* 'Rosea') that do very well here, are ones I have planted. I put in athel trees (*Tamarix aphylla*) to make a screen to the west. And I have beautiful big old pepperinas (*Schinus molle*) around the stables and the meat house.

Even before I got water I started gardening around the house. Then I gradually changed the entrance. There were red and pink oleanders at the front and bougainvilleas that never flowered because the frost hit them, so I took those out and planted more oleanders, and made gravel and paved areas around the palms, and gradually extended the garden.

I've got a big bed for my spring garden in front, and I fill it with pansies and poppies and all sorts of other things, and keep replacing the roses as they die. I start getting the beds ready about March. Once my spring things finish, I put my garden to bed for the summer. By January if I didn't put hay

A mature bottle tree stands at the entrance to Combadello. In the background, century-old palms guard the house.

all over it I would lose most things anyway, even the shrubs and trees.

Verbenas and lantanas grow well here. I have native clematis in the trees in different parts of the garden, jasmines and several honeysuckles, like the two woodbines either side of the front steps. I try to have perfume all year round. There are tea roses, the murraya, and then my daturas and a night-scented cestrum (*C. nocturnum*), whose perfume wafts into the house at night.

I made a dam in what was a natural billabong or lagoon and it only used to fill at times of flood. Now I have permanent water, I can pump from the creek into my lagoon and keep it filled and use it for my garden. I really only get water from September on, when the cotton farmers start irrigating, so my lagoon gets very low. We can't clean it out without pushing the gum trees down, which I'll never do. I like the contrast between the water and the gravel on the driveway and at the back.

From the front garden you follow a path into a little woodland area where there is a fish pond and an iron birdbath surrounded by forget-me-nots and little daisies, and then you come to the lagoon.

There is an old seat there where I often sit with my daughter when she comes home and have a glass of champagne as the sun is setting. There is an island with Louisiana iris, an old swamp gum and a coolabah, and a wonderful pelican statue the children gave me for my seventieth birthday. This is natural bush around here, with lots of weeping wattles and the native clematis, which has the most beautiful perfume. I have gradually planted some more pink ironbarks which are so lovely in a group in the moonlight.

I love the view of the house from the other side of the lagoon. It is sort of nestled back in here. I have kept the roofline view clear, so even at night when you drive in you can see the house, you can see the lagoon, you can see quite a lot of the garden, and in the moonlight the roof is unbelievable. It is painted white, so it really glows.

There is a big jacaranda out the back, and when it's in flower, from the bottom of the garden you can see that beautiful blue behind the white roof. I have quite a few jacarandas scattered around the garden, some of them self-sown. They flower at the same time as the oleanders and the old silky oaks (*Grevillea robusta*).

This is a big garden. I have help once a week to do the lawns and edges and rake the gravel, but I do all the other gardening myself.

Gardening lets you create what you want, your own beauty. All the things in this garden have been done by me and, in the olden days, my station-hand built the little stone walls and built up the beds. You have the companionship of birds and cats and dogs, and when my children were little they'd be riding in the lagoon on their horses while I gardened. I never feel lonely in my garden because you have just got so much around you, so much happening. And even though it is basically a spring garden because I lose just about everything in the summer, I love it.

My gardening friends all live in what I call easy country but I have never known anything else. My mother lived on a hard ridge like this too. Sometimes I wish I could just poke a stick in and grow something like Edna Hardman does, but I know I can't.

The hardest thing is when you get a drought and you haven't got any water and you just know that your plants are going. People say not to bother trying again but you don't even think about that. When you have time you put a few more things in the ground and when they grow it's exciting all over again. The world wouldn't exist if we all gave in, would it?

Ruth Leitch on her wide verandah.

EDNA HARDMAN: I'VE GOT THINGS in my garden that are not supposed to grow here, but I believe that if you really know the requirements of a plant and you create that mini-climate within your own garden, it will grow. There are hellebores in flower as well as clematis, and there is no way in the world they should grow here at Moree.

Moree gardeners are very very lucky, in that we all share. I think that is why there are so many good gardens around here, because of that community spirit. My son says he has never been anywhere else where people go to somebody else's garden bringing a box and their garden fork!

My husband Ron's citrus grove and vegetables help to keep the local hospital and nursing home in produce all year round.

As soon as we moved here we started clearing the briars and box thorns, then drilled for water and put the bore down. It is top quality water with no corrosion or salinity. And we have absolutely wonderful garden loam, river soil. That, with our reliable summer rainfall, makes gardening relatively easy here. But with Moree's winter frosts and hot summers, the frying forties and the southwesterly winds, if we didn't mulch very heavily the garden wouldn't survive.

I don't battle the elements, I work with them. If we get a big windstorm and it blows things around, I always say, 'Nature's pruned today.'

We drew the basis of the garden on graph paper but we have had three fence shifts since then, so it has come out to about five acres. If I was younger, I would have the whole twenty-three acres under garden. I planted trees very densely at first—I called it my nursery planting—and as the garden grew we pulled trees out—twenty-one in one weekend! You couldn't, in this heat, get garden beds established without overhead cover.

Before the house was finished, we had a mini tornado and the flying iron and debris cut all the trees off along the back lawn, so we had to start again. Then in 1984 and the following year, the first garden got completely washed away with floodwater.

We built floodbanks, which I call my landscape banks, because they are part of the landscaping.

We knew sometime in the future we'd get water from the south but we didn't expect what we got in 1988. We had levelled a paddock including the natural waterway, so the water couldn't drain to the south, and it ponded. There was six feet of water for ten days and I thought everything in the bottom third of the garden was gone.

The agapanthus and the daylilies and surprisingly the roses survived and came up again. I have now mass-planted with those tough, hardy things that the flood didn't damage so I won't have that problem again. The agapanthus go all the way round the landscape banks and the top of the bank is edged with hippeastrums. Then there is a rose garden, with 'Meg' trained on swags. This is a great rose-growing area.

I always wanted a water feature in the garden, so on the southern side of our landscape banks we made a big lake with an island. The men wanted it like a funnel but I insisted on undulations so it looked more natural. There are Japanese and Louisiana irises and waterlilies on the lake, and lots of trees are now growing up around it. The *Leptospermum* 'Pink Cascade' is incredible in flower and it doesn't mind going under water. There is desert ash, *Cassia fistula*, which is beautiful, and golden melaleuca, which has made a huge tree.

Now the trees are bigger, I have even managed to grow a mango here. The murraya and laurustinus hedges make a sort of maze, with cool shady pathways where I can grow azaleas and things.

The site is actually perfectly flat but because of the landscape banks and the undulations in the lake area, it doesn't seem to be. There are big areas of open lawn—raised up after the floods—because I love the open space.

In most parts of the garden there is a continual succession of blooms. I don't like a bed to be like in a park where everything flowers today and next week it's empty. I like to use foliage—big lush leaves, or a striking silver plant—as a focal point.

Anything will grow if you create the mini-climate for it. This is just paradise for so many plants. We call it our little bit of heaven.

In a tranquil corner of Rockdale, an ornately carved sundial is surrounded by gazanias.

Transparent sails of shadecloth protect delicate plants around a pond at Rockdale.

At Boolooroo, oil jars mark the intersection of two grass walks bounded by clipped olive hedges.

HUGH LIVINGSTON: UNTIL THE 1980s this was a very traditional garden. My mother came here in 1952 and she added many more trees and maintained it for about forty-five years. She would have done a lot more, except my father liked the way it was, so she really wasn't allowed to. She had to fight to add the trees, I think!

My father died in the early eighties, and around 1987 we decided as a family that it was time to make some changes.

The old garden was very angular and I have continued that fairly strong formality, with strong axes leading out to the paddocks. The aim was to soften all the existing lines and at the same time strengthen the whole thing by defining different areas. We enlarged the borders, which had been pretty mean little borders, and made them bold and sweeping. We extended the garden by planting trees outside the fence to link up with the trees in the paddock. We wanted to soften the whole area and bring it all in together because the garden was very isolated from the rest of the place.

You need to put a reasonable amount of planting around gardens like this so that they don't stick out. That was the idea behind planting a park area on the northern side of the hedges. We have used eucalypts—lemon-scented gums (*E. citriodora*), spotted gums (*E. maculata*) and river red gums (*E. camaldulensis*)—and myalls (*Acacia pendula*).

Some of the things my grandmother planted are still important features—the olive hedges (a non-fruiting variety of *Olea europaea*), the pencil pine (*Cupressus sempervirens*), and the red cedars (*Toona australis*). Olives were quite popular plants around here in the twenties because they are a very tough plant and don't require much water. Originally there was only one olive hedge enclosing the lawn area. I have added more to eventually define other areas. I was tempted to use other plants for hedging but I decided to stick to using olives because they give continuity and do so well here.

Inside the hedges we have planted exotic trees like planes, Chinese elms, taxodiums and liquidambars. We have seen terrific growth with the shaded areas now, because of the good soil and plentiful water. There is a very long growth period here—ten months of the year really—if you choose the right species. We'll plant more shade trees to strengthen the shade areas that are so important in summer.

We have planted the borders with a few simple, tough species: agapanthus, irises, plumbago (*P. auriculata*), teucrium, bog sage (*Salvia uliginosa*), erigeron, golden privet and murraya. If you grow the right things, they don't need much water and looking after. We are really looking for leaf texture and colour more than flowers. I am not really a flower gardener. Growing flowers seems to take up an enormous amount of time and then it's all dead in a few weeks.

I have planted in big masses. I only use one group of each plant, but each group is about four metres long. I think planting looks better on a large scale here. There is still quite a lot of work to be done with the borders, to simplify them further by using more of the things that grow best. And we would like to strengthen all the garden areas and compartments by using hedges and more groups of plants to define particular areas.

What I have learned is to draw on what grows well in your area, to strengthen up with local plants so each part of the garden stands up in its own right, rather than trying to grow too many exotics. We have kept the exotic plants within the hedges and beyond that we attempt to blend what we plant with what's naturally there, or might have been there before. There are a few peppertrees (*Schinus molle*), kurrajongs (*Brachychiton populneus*) which my grandmother planted, and wilgas (*Geijera parviflora*). We were very light on for evergreens because my mother planted mainly deciduous trees. Adding the gums gave the garden an evergreen background, which also makes the deciduous trees look better. I tend to use evergreen shrubs in the borders as well, to hold it all together in winter.

I have removed all the trees from the front of the house except the taxodiums planted by my grandmother. I anguished over taking the trees out for about ten years but it is the best thing we ever did. It let lots of light in, and you now get a nice view of the taxodium.

Taxodiums need lots of water, so it was a very odd choice of my grandmother's to plant them, but I must say I am very glad she did. They have that incredible foliage going from russet to green. There is only about one bad week, when you wonder what's wrong with it, and then it's green again.

At the back of the house there is a gravelled area enclosed by a low murraya hedge with brolga sculptures sitting on a mound of rosemary. I would like to put more sculptures like that around the garden. It is important to me that garden ornaments are simple. We used to have classical urns, but we've replaced them with big old oil jars that work much better. It was a lucky break to get them, because it's hard to find things on the right scale.

I love classical features but they don't tend to look right up here in the flat plains. The flatness is a big challenge. It is very hard when you have no view to focus on, as you have in a hilly situation. You need to add a lot of height to get that vertical emphasis. I think there is more intimacy in a cool-climate landscape, where deciduous trees seem to give a shape and a scale we can't get up here.

That's how we arrived at using lemon-scented gums, which do give you that height and scale very quickly and also have such decorative white bark. They have really been our big triumph. I didn't realise how important they were going to be. We planned just to stick one or two in but we have ended up planting a hundred or more.

We look out through the trees. I have left large areas where you can look straight through to the paddocks. I have also used trees to close the views in some places. Something I want to do is somehow incorporate a view straight down the river from the orchard.

When we began changing the garden, I had a mind's eye view of it but I didn't know that much, I didn't understand the importance of relating it back to the landscape then. Russell Page is the big hero for me. In the early days when we were just starting to make those alterations, I thought I must be able to read something about this, and I was very

lucky because I just happened to fall upon *The Education of a Gardener*. It was the first gardening book I ever read. It all made a lot of sense to me. His ideas are so simple, straightforward and practical. It is very unfussy, and I hate fussiness. The concepts have to be reinterpreted for our climate but they seem to suit. The Italian gardens he talks about all use simple lines and simple plantings, and that made great sense to me.

There have been lots of other influences. Joan Law Smith's *The Garden Within* was particularly good. I got a lot out of that and I still refer to it, and to Edna Walling's books. And I talk a lot to other gardeners I admire.

One of the gardens I admire enormously is Combadello. We have a good, deep alluvial topsoil here but it's a shocking soil there. It is amazing what Ruth Leitch has managed to grow. More than that, though, I admire the way she has used the huge gravel areas that work so well, and the way the garden all links up together.

Gina and Hugh Livingston.

walling out west

KARABINE KERRIE ROBINSON

The 0.4 hectare (1 acre) garden of Karabine is near York, 125 km east of Perth. Summer temperatures are high, with weeks of 40°C–45°C and occasional 47°C days. The average rainfall is only 350 mm and falls mainly in winter. Dam water is highly alkaline (pH 10), and the supply of water in summer is limited. Frosts as low as –8°C are not uncommon, but established trees protect the garden to some extent from their impact as well as providing shelter from the frequent southeasterly gales.

Fieldstone paving in the shape of a Maltese cross surrounds a tall stone jar. Bougainvillea provides a splash of colour, and acanthus and the gnarled pruned trunks of a large tecoma add structure and mystery.

I CAME HERE on Mother's Day in 1985 and I had no interest in the garden whatsoever. It was a totally foreign type of garden to me. I grew up at Quirindi in northern New South Wales and I was used to sweeping lawns and shrubberies and deciduous trees and all the exotic things that you can grow in the eastern states. All the stuff that was here, like oleanders and plumbago (*P. auriculata*), in our eyes was considered fairly cheap and nasty. It was just a jungle. For my first eleven years at Karabine, we lived up in the cottage, which was absolutely derelict when we came, with wild oats up to the windows. But in all those years, I hardly ever set foot in the garden of the main homestead.

So when I inherited a garden that I had nothing in common with, I was in trepidation as to what on earth I would do with it. I decided I would live here for a year and do nothing and get the feel of it. I didn't have time to garden anyway; I had three young boys, a husband and a farm and all five of them were very demanding.

That was the best thing that could have happened for the garden, because I didn't spoil it. I could gradually get to know it and then just slowly over the years the garden totally enveloped me and I fell in love with it. And although I have transformed it, I came to realise that all those trees my mother-in-law originally planted, that I found so foreign and jungle-like, were absolutely right. In summer the old oleanders and tecomas never miss a beat. They are always looking happy and flowering at their best when the rest of the garden is having a sleepy-hollow time.

My mother-in-law was married in 1940 and lived here briefly but then went back to her family during the war when Tony's father was away. She came back as a young bride in 1945. Nothing in the garden would have been watered during those five years because Karabine was considered just an out-camp for shearing. The huge duranta was here, a tecoma and a Geraldton wax (*Chamelaucium* sp.)—they were the only trees. The sheep used to come up to the front verandah. She planted the jacaranda, the oleanders, bougainvilleas and tecomas, and brought the old yellow jasmines from her home garden.

She couldn't cope with the wind that used to howl in, so she did everything she could to block it out. And in doing that she blocked out the views of the surrounding countryside.

This is a very difficult climate; even though there is a lot of shade it still gets intensely hot in summer. I have had many a year when come January the temperatures haven't gone under forty degrees for two months. The prevailing winds come from the southeast and those howling southeasterly gales are the bane of my life.

When you drive in, you wonder what on earth you've come to because I've sewn shadecloth over the whole fence. But I would never have grown anything here otherwise. It keeps the rabbits out, it stops the sheep from doing a lot of lower pruning, and it keeps the spray jet coming over from the paddock. Every second year this paddock is in crops, and I have a husband who says when it has to be sprayed it has to be sprayed, and the garden doesn't really come in for a great deal of consideration. So I have been out there at times literally doing my greenies act, lying on the ground in front of the tractor saying, 'Stop, stop.'

Tony's mellowed over the years but now I've got my sons to contend with. They love the garden, they admire what I've done, but if it comes in the road of farming, no. So I've had to sort of create a garden with four very strong men in the household. It was very much a male-dominated house. We even had boy cats and dogs. At times it would all get too much for me and I would just escape to the garden and lose myself. The garden became my salvation.

When I came, they put me up a new fence, and Tony stipulated that I wasn't to grow *anything* outside it. If he saw me creeping something out over the fence, he'd just put in a mob of sheep. At times I used to think, what a terrible husband, he won't let me do this and he won't let me do that. But as the years have gone by I have come to realise I was lucky I had a very strong husband because if I had gone any further it would have been far more than I can cope with in summer.

Our water problem is terrible. Since I have been here the rainfall has ranged from ten to seventeen inches, usually concentrated in one four-month period. Sometimes you can get rain in March but more often than not it starts in June and it's finished by October. It is easy to get carried away in winter, and plant and plant when everything is looking absolutely magnificent and the rain is falling. But come summer the garden is looking at you and saying please water me, and the tank's empty and

you can't. Remembering those hot days when the plants are crying out for water and you can't water them is really what keeps me within my boundaries.

I have succeeded by being very careful about my choice of plants. I decided to skirt the fences with very hardy, drought-proof plants so I wouldn't have to water there. There were the existing old trees like the tecomas and durantas which always did well on no water, and I filled in with wormwood, echiums, honeysuckles, lots of different jasmines, a couple of very hardy roses like 'Dorothy Perkins', and plumbago. Plumbago is wonderful because it'll cope with dry shade, which I've got a great deal of.

My greatest mentor was Tedye McDiven who lived just down the road at Tipperary Church, a wonderful garden. She opened my eyes to what you could create by gardening with vistas, how you could open the garden up and bring the countryside into it. It has taken me a long time to understand that you need to take the garden into the surrounds, or bring the surrounds into the garden. I have tried to do it by creating vistas and merging the boundary with grey planting so you flow out into the landscape. That idea, and my paving and stonework, have been the basis of the garden.

When I started, there was just bare dirt everywhere, with all these trees taking up huge areas and nothing growing under them. Something deep within me couldn't cope with the bare dirt, so I had to pave. I went and got bricks from all the old buildings they were renovating in York, which is a very historic town. I would go into town with the trusty old Land Rover, load them up, bring them home and spend hours cleaning them, and then I paved little areas at a time.

All the brick areas have a history. The ones down the side of the house came from Holy Trinity Church at Meckering when the tower was reconstructed following the earthquake in 1968, so that I call the Holy Trinity walk. The bricks behind it in my lavender keyhole garden came from the Castle Hotel. There is a chair there and I say to people, come and have a drink at the Castle.

I love working with stone too, and for the paths I broke it up into what I suppose you'd call crazy paving, with bricks along the edge. I wanted a design in the paved walk but I didn't have enough bricks, so I did the outline in bricks and in-filled with stone. A lot of the garden has been created like that, through what's been available.

It is quite eerie how the structure works out. I don't draw a design and when I start I honestly don't know what I am going to do. I know the end picture but not how I am going to achieve it. Once I am with stone, my hands just work. I was too busy to read gardening books to get my theories or my ideas until much later, when a lot of the garden structure was done. But when I started reading and discovered Edna Walling, I found a lot of what she was saying I had already done. There were the paths that you can't see around and the air of mystique because you don't know what's around the corner.

My love of stonework started with the stone house foundations needing repairs. My fingers were itching, I was dying to have a go at fixing those foundations. And after that I knew I had to do a stone wall. First I had to underprune a huge tree. I do a lot of these things when Tony's away, so while he was over east I managed to get a man to help me chainsaw, but he had no intention of helping me cart it away because it was forty-five degrees that day. So I carted and carted and I think my blood actually boiled, it was so hot, but I was possessed with this vision of the stone wall I was going to make. This was February and I knew it had to be completed by seeding time because I wanted to do all the planting around it and I had to do it when it rained. So I had a time limit and I had never done a stone wall in my life.

I started and I got more and more excited. I made two sides and kept filling it up, hoping it would not rain and fill with water. So the panic was on to finish before the rains came. Tony was back by then and immediately knew that I was doing the wall because there was a load of stone outside that nobody could jump over. He thought I was crazy but I managed to finish it in six weeks.

The boys would never help bring in rocks. All their lives they'd pushed rocks and picked rocks out of the paddocks. They absolutely hated it and there was no way in the world they'd bring rocks in for me. So if I wanted rocks I had to go and pick them up myself. The only time I could get the ute was in summer when they were all having their siesta during the day. So I would quietly sneak out and get myself a load of rocks then.

Meadow-like drifts of statice and everlasting daisies link the edge of the garden to its bleached landscape.

Then I discovered we had all this gravel on the place, so I have done gravelled areas to tone in with the rocks and Bryant McDiven from Tipperary lent me his dear old roller.

Though wind protection is so important in this garden, to me the wind whistling or howling through the trees is soothing. It seems to give the garden a soul. And I love the play of light and shade on the foliage. I am working with that a lot more.

I also love the effects of colour. I have used a lot of grey foliage plants to lift and soften other colours, and I think yellow, which lots of people don't like, is a very good element in a garden. I especially like limey yellow euphorbias, yellow gaillardias, and daylilies. You need yellow when you have got a lot of blues and pinks and mauves, which can look very wishy-washy. All the other colours are defined much better once you put yellow through.

You come into the front garden under an arch of pink tecoma, planted with white plumbago and the repeat-flowering 'Autumnalis' rose. All of those perform really well in summer. The perfume of the rose is unbelievable, it drifts through the whole garden.

That first wall I had so much trouble with takes a semicircular shape inside the gate, and leads to another arch covered with jasmine, roses and oleanders.

There's a big Chinese elm giving shade to the area. The Chinese elms have turned out to be the greatest trees. The locust plague didn't worry them and they don't burn in the easterly winds. When I started my first cottage-type garden, the men were too busy to bring me any soil in, so I thought, blow it, there's a paddock out there that has been ploughed up, that will be easy to dig up. If I just go out and get a little bit here and a little bit there in a wheelbarrow, they'll never notice that I have taken their precious soil. So I would dart out and get a wheelbarrow here and a wheelbarrow there. Then when they were working it back, they said, 'I don't know what's happened in this paddock but there are little holes everywhere.'

I've used a cottage garden effect in my underplanting through the garden. The key plants are helichrysums, wormwood and lavender, pelargoniums, erigeron, euphorbia and forget-me-nots, together with the good old species annuals that self-sow. The species are far better than all the hybrids we are getting today because they are very tough and will go without a lot of watering. They are the basis of all my spring colour—larkspurs, cornflowers, Queen Anne's lace, valerian. I let them all die down in summer, mulch over with straw and then they come up with the winter rains.

A stone path leads to a bank of *Artemisia* 'Powis Castle' in front of my first two old roses, 'Souvenir de la Malmaison' and 'Mme Isaac Pereire', both superbly scented. I use artemisia a lot in foreground planting to give some structure in summer when all the annuals have gone and the garden's gone down to just roses and the tough hedges and edges that don't need water.

Under the shade of a big *Eucalyptus sargentii* I have woven in peppermint pelargonium with variegated periwinkles, the old species felicia, violets and a plectranthus with marvellous grey foliage in the centre. It is all wonderfully hardy and shade-loving and I am thrilled with the effect. It can take me six years to get the effect I want, something that works well. I'll trial it for two years and then if it doesn't work, I'll try something else.

Another arch frames a little paved area with a seat made from a huge bit of jarrah, which comes from the Nil Desperandum goldmine Tony's grandfather had up at Burtville, right in the outback northeast of Kalgoorlie. That's a nice piece of family history. The seat looks north over the countryside. On the edge of the garden I've combined wormwood with a bright orange-red geranium, bauhinia, larkspurs, valerian and 'Sidonie' lavender in the foreground, and 'Sarah van Fleet' roses that I struck myself from a cutting. Then there is woodbine (*Lonicera fragrantissima*), with a perfume that unlocks hundreds of memories for me.

You move through the shade of a tamarisk to another sunny area, a little quadrant garden with African box (*Myrsine africana*) lining each quadrant. There is the old gnarled Geraldton wax from the original garden and a little pond with Louisiana iris and acanthus. I call this my window room because it is a window on the world outside. You can be here when it's forty-seven in the shade of this old tecoma and so hot you can see the mirages shimmering off the ground, but you get a breeze under here, and it's another world.

high plains oasis

MYALLA   BARBARA LITCHFIELD

Myalla is at Cooma on the Monaro High Plains, 90 km south of Canberra. The undulating 1.6 hectare (4 acre) garden was first established in the 1860s on a site with deep basalt soil and boasting a reliable supply of spring water. Due to its elevation (1000 metres), the climate is severe. In winter, prolonged periods of below-zero temperatures are the rule. Temperatures of –7°C to –9°C, often falling to –15°C, are common. Frost can occur in all months of the year, and snowfalls of 30–45 cm are especially devastating when trees are in leaf. The summer-dominant rainfall of 600 mm is erratic due to the rainshadow effect of the Snowy Mountains. Summer temperatures vary between 28°C and 32°C with extremes to 37°C.

I GREW UP in the Riverina where the gardens were totally different. I learned about gardening in this climate by looking at other people's gardens and by talking to Judy Pfeiffer, Pam Glasson and Joan Massy, all local women and very good gardeners. I also got inspiration from Edna Walling, Russell Page and Beatrice Bligh.

The garden is protected by the large trees, and my son Jim put in the two metre high stone walls, which made an enormous difference. It is now quite sheltered, except from the west. The courtyard is very sheltered. When we first came here, it was totally open to the south, so we put in a bluestone wall and two great big wooden doors to block that out. The courtyard is paved with basalt stones and now the grass has grown among them, we mow it so the stones still show through.

I have got used to the climate now and I love the way we have separate seasons because I am always looking forward to the next one. The frosts and the lack of rain are the two main difficulties. We haven't had enough rain since 1991 and the late frosts are awfully irritating.

I have lived through quite a few terrible storms. Once in April, you couldn't get up the drive here because of all the branches and things, the pine trees had all crashed. But probably snow is the worst for damaging trees and shrubs.

James' great-grandfather, the first James Litchfield who came out, actually lived at Myalla in 1854. The main house wasn't built then, and there was a little stone cottage down near the pond. It is the saddest thing because it would have been lovely to still have that cottage at the bottom of the garden.

The garden was laid out in the 1860s by a landscape gardener brought over from England by Mr Pratt, the then owner, who was a master at Sydney Grammar School. There are records of trees and all sorts of marvellous things he planted including a privet maze. I have a couple of old photographs that were taken in the 1870s and 1880s showing a tremendous number of gentlemen with lawnmowers, and Aunt Lorna Wilkinson can remember the maze when she was a little girl at the turn of the century. With fewer staff, the garden deteriorated and many of the trees died. All that survived were radiata pines, the elms, a huge deodar and an ash, and of course the privet.

When we first moved to Myalla, Beatrice Bligh was a great help. She designed the driveway to come up past the tennis court and through the elms. Before that, you just drove up to the garage. Right in the front of the house was a round bed that looked terrible and she immediately suggested I do away with it.

A lot of old gardens shut themselves in. One of the things that we did was to open the garden up to the surrounding countryside, which I think is very important. I like being able to look at the sheep across the pond and the horses out in the paddock and the shearing shed in the distance. It's a very pastoral setting.

We spent several years living at Hazeldean [a family property nearby] which is a much more architectural, formal garden and hard work to maintain, whereas Myalla is quite informal. Here if things go a bit wild it doesn't matter. Also, the house here is much more integrated into its garden.

These days in the country, everybody does everything themselves. I am the gardener and James mows the lawns. I do have this old boy who's nearly eighty and comes one day a week. He does a bit of whippersnipping but that is really all. I do most of the heavy work.

When we first moved here in 1968, the privet and elm suckers had got totally out of control. We really just had to go in with the bulldozer. We made some little copses and tried to leave some of the old pine trees and grassed most of it, then put the pond at the bottom.

You have to have a good design and a balance, and fortunately James is good at that, so when we were bulldozing great heaps of privet and shrubs and stuff he did it quite cleverly and got that balance right.

It is very good basalt soil here, very black down at the bottom where the pond is. Trees grow quite well, although not terribly quickly because of the long winters and late frosts.

The pond works very well, when we get enough rain to fill it up! It's my favourite part of the garden in spring when there are thousands of daffodils and the pond is overflowing down to the creek. It's amazing how people who have visited the garden always remember my pond at the bottom of the garden.

Snow-laden elms and pines line the drive to Myalla.

I try to grow things that I know will grow in this climate, although I still try others, like geraniums, which is stupid. I have really come to appreciate things that grow easily—shasta daisies, erigeron, daffodils and Christmas lilies that come up year after year. We've got millions of bluebells, and both autumn and spring crocuses love growing at Myalla. Hellebores and Japanese anemones are brilliant, and peonies too. I don't do anything except give them a bit of manure and compost. My garden doesn't get a lot of pampering. I have put in a wild garden among the elms, which seems to work quite well. Daylilies do very well, aquilegias grow like mad, and comfrey is very pretty in the spring. The buttercups, which I would never give to my worst enemy, also look very pretty when they are in flower. I have got some Scotch roses growing there, and forget-me-nots everywhere.

Myalla is mostly a spring garden but I really look forward to summer and the roses, especially 'Heritage' and other David Austins which thrive here, and the huge 'Lamarque' which threatens to pull the house down. Then autumn and all the colours. And the winter's really not all that terrible.

I am a very keen vegetable gardener. I have got a little greenhouse where I start a lot of things off, which is great. I have just had my first ripe tomato in the middle of January. Because tomatoes are so hard to ripen in our short season, my son Jim claims Cooma as the green chutney capital of the world!

I love getting out into the garden. There are so many millions of things I ought to be doing inside. But I give myself an hour every day. I try to do it late afternoon and it's amazing what you can accomplish. Even if you can't finish the job you get halfway through and then there is not nearly as much left! I enjoy just being outside in the garden, weeding or digging or pruning.

After so many years of drought, my greatest joy is when we have rain and everything's flowering, and there are no weeds.

Barbara and James Litchfield.

dead centre: alice springs

Alice Springs is one of the most challenging environments in the world for gardening. The desert climate brings extremes ranging from ground temperatures of −15°C, with an average of thirty winter frosts, to 46°C in the shade at the peak of summer. In an unkind year, summer may last six months, with days at 38°C plus, while winter's black frosts can kill 9 metre trees. Rainfall is fickle: 60 mm one year, 500 mm the next. Months of drought may be broken by inches falling in just a few hours. Typical soil is a fine, poor-draining and highly alkaline silt. Subartesian water which is high in salt, and the threat of flooding from the Todd River, are additional problems for gardeners.

GEOFF MIERS' GARDEN

Geoff Miers is a horticulture lecturer and gardening writer who has lived in Alice Springs since the 1970s. In his 700 square metre urban garden on the flood plain of the Todd River, he has simulated a dry creek bed as a growing environment for rarely cultivated Centralian plants which he propagates himself.

BRUCE AND MEG SIMMONS' GARDEN

Bruce and Meg Simmons' garden is set on the edge of sand dune country south of the town, with magnificent views of the Macdonnell Ranges. The Simmons have gardened in Alice Springs for twenty-five years and have won several gardening awards, both for their town garden and their present 2 hectare (5 acre) rural property, where native and endemic plants are combined with a very productive permaculture food garden.

Geoff Miers' front garden retains sightlines to an important local landmark, Spencer Hill. Indigenous species (eucalypts, acacias, sennas, saltbush including *Rhagodia spinescens* and *Enchylaena tomentosa*, and native lemon grass *Cymbopogon ambiguus*) are framed by white cedar *Melia azedarach*, a shade tree planted in the 1950s.

GEOFF MIERS: I AM LARGELY a self-taught gardener. I was inspired by old Bill Ford, a swaggie who used to come to Alice Springs once a year and clean up people's gardens. All he ever had was a shovel and a file to sharpen it, and he could turn the most unruly garden into the cleanest and most beautiful.

My garden is a long, narrow block in an older part of town. The house is placed right at the back, so the backyard is only ten metres deep. The garden was designed for the family to enjoy, so that we are not slaves to it. It evolved around the house, and being on a small block, we have developed every square inch of it. We have designed it to work with the elements and to be a comfortable, attractive and very, very low maintenance garden—an hour's work once a month!

The front garden is shaded by a large white cedar (*Melia azedarach*), which was one of the original trees in the garden. Despite the problems of berries dropping on the paving and white cedar moth larvae, it does mean we have a large tree providing a lot of protection for the front, which faces directly north, and it still allows the winter sun to come through. The only other trees are four surviving desert kurrajongs (*Brachychiton gregorii*) along one boundary, and two ghost gums I planted in the middle of the yard so they don't impact on our neighbours. Ghost gums (*Corymbia aparrerinja*) are so evocative of Central Australia. One is local, the other is a southern form, and they will become big trees.

The central feature of the front garden is a large dry creek bed, which serves as a flood mitigation area, because we are in a potential flood zone, and also for water harvesting. We are on the flood plain of the Todd River, which is just a few hundred metres away. In the 1988 floods, the Todd actually came down the street and flooded some of the houses. I had mine sandbagged, but the front yard was completely under water.

The garden is designed so that when you get a heavy downfall of rain, water flows either onto the tiny lawn or into the creek bed, which fills up and allows the water to be slowly absorbed through the garden.

We have also mounded up garden beds to combat the very poor soil. There's about 75 millimetres of topsoil, then you hit a thin layer of shale, and below that it's very heavy, poor draining clay, whereas a lot of the plants of Central Australia like free draining soils. Soil dug out of the creek bed formed the basis of the mounded beds, and I also brought in fresh soils, compost and manure and other soil conditioners to build it up.

You enter the garden along a winding pathway that leads up to a curved bridge. Under the bridge is a meandering dry creek as you would find occurring here naturally, with river pebbles at the upper reaches grading into fine creek sand. It is lined with local red rock and sandstone, and on one side I have made undulating beds of Central Australian plants.

Wildflowers come up through the sand and I leave them to seed and just pop up right through the garden and over the nature strip. We have about fifteen different varieties of Central Australian wildflowers and a couple of local grasses, including the lovely scented oil grass (*Cymbopogon ambiguus*).

I have difficulty growing eremophilas but there are a number of them here. *Eremophila bignoniiflora* is a magnificent large shrub nearly nine feet tall and less than two years old. It looks quite exotic, it's always very green and has beautiful white speckled native fuchsia-type flowers. *Eremophila christophori* is one of my most fantastic plants. It tolerates the soil conditions and its lilac-blue flowers last from late winter right through until February, over six months of the year. It loves being pruned, so you can clip it into a hedge form or any shape you want.

A wonderful little plant that never stops flowering is *Justicia kempeana*. It has beautiful little purple flowers and quadruples in size just weeks after planting. It's best treated as an annual or pruned back severely. The local parakeelya (*Calandrinia balonensis*) came up out of some mulga mulch I introduced into the garden. You could say it is Central Australia's version of portulaca.

The two mallee gums, Webster's mallee and the round-leaf mallee (*Eucalyptus websteriana* and *E. orbifolia*), are both unique to Central Australia. Behind is a very quick-growing pendulous *Acacia jennerae* and the introduced *Acacia iteaphylla*, the willow-leaf wattle from the Flinders Ranges, which is a good screening plant.

We propagate almost all our own plants, and I've got about eighty Central Australian plants for foreground planting.

The front garden is as much as possible local native plants and I have tried to create a microclimate consistent with that environment. So there are areas of red sand, areas of mulch with mulga leaf litter, rocks and logs through the garden.

At the back I have made a different sort of microclimate. It's a cool, shady retreat with a tropical theme. Because it's a very small area, I was able to completely replace the soil to grow different kinds of plants.

There is a small lily and fish pond with a sandstone waterfall and split sandstone paving around the pool. It is designed to be a nice relaxing setting when you are sitting on the back patio and it's planted with a range of exotic, Australian and Central Australian plants: native rosemary, small grevilleas, hardenbergia, westringia and melaleuca, complemented by the coral bush (*Russelia equisetiformis*) and a feijoa in the corner. On one side of the waterfall is a small caustic vine (*Sarcostemma australe*), which grows in the hills here. It is a quite magnificent plant for rockeries or hanging baskets.

There is grey-leaved *Eremophila glabra* 'Kalbarri Carpet', which is from inland Australia. Most eremophilas don't like wet feet, yet that 'Kalbarri Carpet' is hanging over into the pond itself and seems to thrives on the pond spillage.

The average rainfall here is 250 mm but it's very unreliable. We are totally subject to influences from elsewhere. If there are cyclones during the summer monsoon season to the north and they have a real big wet, we can get the offshoots of those cyclones with heavy downpours of several inches in twenty-four hours. Equally, during the winter when the south gets its wetter months, Alice Springs can get the benefit of that too. But if there is no heavy wet season north, and no turbulent weather south, we could have no rain at all.

The summer heat is a great problem. In January and February you can get ten days in a row up in the forties. The soil also makes gardening difficult. Alkaline soil is common in inland Australia and it's a particular problem for gardeners coming to Alice Springs from other regions.

I think the key to gardening here is firstly to recognise the climate, respect it and work with it, rather than trying to work against it. The second thing is to try and create particular microclimates and environments. The water is subartesian bore water, and it has a fairly high mineral and salt content. That raises the salinity levels and also increases the soil pH, so you need to adopt certain techniques to cope with it. One thing I advise people in Alice to do two or three times a year is to actually flood their gardens for an extended period, to move the build-up of salts and minerals back into the subsoil and away from the plants. And when it rains, to go and put the watering system on, because the rain can actually move the salts and minerals back towards the plants and sometimes kill them.

People used to start out by saying, 'I've got a problem with dust, so let's cover the area with lawn and we'll worry about putting trees and shrubs and garden beds in later.' Now they'll put in maybe a small lawn, or no lawn at all. That is a big change.

There is also the use of local resources and materials, which gives character and definition to our gardens. We have the most wonderful colours of sandstone here, for instance, which are unique to this area. So it is used for garden features and crushed sandstone is used as mulch.

This is an oasis in a vast desert. But with knowledge and understanding, the diversity of plants you can grow here is absolutely enormous.

Geoff Miers.

BRUCE SIMMONS: I WAS INTRODUCED to gardening at an early age and it has all translated into the things I have done since we came up here. Meg was a very reluctant gardener but she has become more and more interested. She joined the Society for Growing Australian Plants and does all the propagation and plant identification.

The block here is five acres and we garden about a third of it. It was very degraded but we didn't have to clear much. Our previous house ran east–west which is a good orientation for Alice Springs, so we did the same thing here. It is about a kilometre from the Todd River and there is flooding up from the river. It is the end of a sandhill and there is a three-metre slope from the top to the bottom, which has flooded several times. To be safe and to make the most of our view of the Macdonnell Ranges to the north, we built an earth slab to raise the house slightly. In doing that we also created a bump on a stump as it were, so we then had to blend the bump into the surroundings.

We drilled for water and found it at seventy metres, having gone through sand and clay but no rock. The soil pH is neutral but once you start watering with bore water it becomes alkaline unless you mulch heavily. The two essentials here are mulching and water harvesting. Because of the slope, really heavy rain runs straight off. So I try to create bumps and swales to hold it. It's all designed to have areas of water catchment.

We have a lot of drip irrigation but you can't have the bore going all the time, so I've got to try to work out how to utilise the water and distribute it over this big area and multitude of plants.

At the bottom of the garden I have made a creek bed to try to stop the flow of water and also for visual effect—the river bed against the red sand. You step up the bank to the vegie garden. There is a beautiful mulga tree specimen there, *Acacia aneura*, a witchetty bush (*Acacia kempeana*), mulberries and a little duck pond. We have planted a windbreak to protect the vegie garden and fruit trees against the hot winds from the west.

It was the sand that attracted us to the site because our previous block was clay, and to dig a hole to plant something meant crowbars and soaking the hole for two days. Here you can just stick the spade in and go.

We wanted a garden that would complement the house and fit into the bush surroundings. In planning the garden we had to take decisions about what I call feral plants. I am a romantic idealist but once I got out here and saw how dominant buffel grass is and how much there was on the property, I decided to eradicate it.

They are big clumps of grass, and you need plenty of muscle to dig them out, so I gave up golf and took up swinging a mattock. I created a huge weed heap. It took about six months to get rid of the grass and I also got down on my knees and weeded out the wild hops, bush turnips and various other plants. That for me was the highlight—creating the canvas for whatever might reseed or regenerate.

We use no herbicides here, it's either mulch, fork, chooks or other strategies based on permaculture.

In planting the garden, we have used Australian natives around the house, then further afield we have stuck to local plants. This particular area doesn't have a very wide range of naturally occurring species. The dominant ones are acacias: *Acacia kempeana*, *A. murrayana* (the colony wattle) and ironwoods (*A. estrophiolata*). There are also hakeas. We have propagated lots of whitewoods (*Atalaya hemiglauca*) and we have brought in river red gums (*Eucalyptus camaldulensis*) and grey mallees (*E. gammophylla*) from neighbouring areas.

Meg thought the outdoor living area was extremely hot, so on her suggestion we added exotics for the greenery, including wisteria, weeping mulberry, bougainvillea, jacarandas and a fiddlewood, which has a cooling, softening effect around the house. I would have liked a fully native garden but I am happy with the way it has evolved.

Meg has propagated her favourite Central Australian eremophilas, *E. christophori* and *E. polyclada*—bright green shrubs that are constantly flowering.

We try to keep the foreground planting low so we have a clear view from the house towards the Macdonnell Ranges. We planted a ghost gum to one side for shade, which frames the view without blocking it. We have a lot of welcome 'volunteers' that have joined us in the garden—acacias, a cassia, a lot of ruby saltbush which has just come up between the self-sown marigolds and evening primroses, and various little native paper daisies and wahlenbergias. And popping up through the herb garden is Sturt's Desert Pea (*Swainsona formosa*),

At sunrise, the most spectacular and serene features of the Simmons' garden are highlighted in the expansive desert sky and the sinuous curves of the swimming pool. The natural acacia shrubland with its understorey of native grasses has been enriched by the inclusion of the inland tea tree *Melaleuca glomerata* and various local sennas.

which is Meg's pride and joy. Once you have a few light showers of rain, this reddish sand is the perfect environment for seeds to come up.

We have brought in rocks as landscaping features and for stepping stones and pathways. The reddish colour blends in well with the pavers and the colour of the sand.

An essential part of the design is to protect the east and west walls with a wide verandah and then shade the verandah with creepers. Otherwise the heat in the house would be really unpleasant. The west facing verandah is a favourite place to watch the birds in the mornings. It is shaded by a fruiting grapevine and a huge *Grevillea* 'Robyn Gordon', which is somewhat out of place, but the birds love it.

One area of the slope is planted with local species. This has been divided into sections and will gradually have a more and more enclosed feel. On one side I am making a no-dig garden built up with lots of manure and straw and hopefully there'll be minimal evaporation.

We have been very successful with our vegetables. As summer draws on, though, everything becomes very harsh. Vegie gardening in the open is almost impossible then, so we usually abandon it over the real heat of summer.

On the southern side, which is the entrance to the house, the intention is to have a reasonably wide green belt, without having tall trees too close to the house. The house is almost hidden now by planting and in five years the shelter belt has created very good protection.

We have built a natural-looking ornamental pool with clumps of reeds and eremophilas around it, and surrounding groups of mulga and *Melaleuca glomerata*, which is the local inland tea tree. There is spearwood creeper (*Pandorea pandorana*), growing

through the bushes and shrubs which is a mass of beautiful white tubular flowers in July. Meg's quandongs (*Santalum acuminatum*) are a great success. They grow naturally south of here, down towards Uluru.

There are a lot of plants packed together closely, and I think it's really nice to have the shaded area even though it's not particularly accessible. You can get on your hands and knees, which I don't mind, and go and sit under there in the leaf litter. And our bedroom opens onto the garden. The whole area just looks green and cool and inviting, with the pond at the centre. You can sit on the rocks and it is like a naturally occurring scene. My lovingly crafted creek beds here have disappeared and a lot of little paths have grown over, but that is part of the garden's evolving.

OVERLEAF: Poached egg daisies *Myriocephalus stuartii* are a distinctive example of the many wildflowers that naturalise in the red sand of Alice Springs gardens.

Bruce and Meg Simmons with one of the bearded dragons that live in the garden.

return of the native

THE INTERNATIONAL TREND TOWARDS NATURAL GARDENS USING NATIVE PLANTS
HAS GENERATED A NEW WAVE OF INTEREST IN AUSTRALIAN NATIVE GARDENS.

The tradition of Australian plant gardens is well established. One of its earliest
proponents was the late Gordon Ford, who championed the appropriate use of
native plants in gardens throughout his fifty-year career. The timeless quality of
his work derives from a mastery of form grounded in classic landscaping principles,
and is nowhere better seen than in his own Melbourne garden.

Paul Thompson is a landscape architect in full command of his medium and
materials. The suburban garden of CARRAMAR stands on one-time bushland
immortalised by the painters of the Heidelberg School, and was designed in
close collaboration with its owners. Paul's extensive plant knowledge has enabled
him to make precise choices for the garden's different soils and aspects. The
ostensibly natural scene of the back garden was contrived with considerable skill
and sophistication.

THE SORN is a small, strongly-designed garden composed of Tasmanian plants.
Lindsay Campbell has carefully studied soil and aspect to make effective groupings
of alpine, lowland and rainforest plants. Native grasses link the garden's different
areas, while the repeated planting of Tasmanian snow gums gives a unifying canopy.

WYEMANDO celebrates Western Australian wildflowers. The Harper sisters' garden
proves that for richness of colour, native flora are the equal of any exotics.
The Harpers' aim was to cover the ground, and in spring luminous reds and pinks,
dazzling yellows and pure primary blues create a brilliant, close-woven tapestry.
Nan Harper's pleasure in native plants is as strong in her eighties as when she
first thrilled to the sight of black kangaroo paws growing in her father's garden.

A site varied by gentle slopes, a creek and a framework of mature gums made
an interesting setting for the diverse collection of native plants at DRYANDRA.
Thelma Vandepeer sees plants with a floral artist's eye. Her plant groupings are
skilfully arranged to vary heights, textures, forms and colours, and by using plants
from different regions and climates she is able to extend the flowering season
through the year.

Merv Hodge's Queensland garden is dominated by a magnificent overhanging
sandstone outcrop, where he has encouraged flannel flowers to naturalise in
sheets. Merv Hodge has pioneered new methods of grafting native plants, and
many of the grevilleas in his fine collection are the result of his own work.

HORSE ISLAND is a garden landscaped in grand formal style, but using only
native plants. Framed by a neoclassical colonnade, clipped westringia hedges
and a strong line of blueberry ashes in the middle ground define the garden's
sweeping lawns and native parkland, and frame vistas of estuarine lakes beyond.

Sculptor Peter Adams' natural garden on a wild and beautiful stretch of
Tasmanian coastline is ordered by a clifftop path. At intervals along the path,
stone and timber bench sculptures provide stopping points that direct the eye
to chosen vistas. Planting of endemic coastal trees extends and reinforces the
existing landscape. For Peter Adams, the essence of gardening, like walking in
the landscape, is spiritual.

OVERLEAF: 'Galaxy', a Tasmanian myrtle and granite bench sculpture, nestles in an alcove of casuarinas at Windgrove.

in the great tradition

FÜLLING GORDON FORD

Gordon Ford, who died in 1999 aged eighty, was an elder statesman of Australian landscape design. A month before he died, he spoke for this book about his own garden, Fülling, in the artist's community of Eltham, northeast of Melbourne. Gordon spent fifty years developing the 0.7 hectare ($1^3/_4$ acre) garden, which illustrates many of his natural landscaping principles and philosophies.

Built out of earth excavated from the site as it was landscaped, the cottage at Fülling achieves a rare unity with its garden.

I BECAME INTERESTED in landscape gardening in the early 1950s through the architect Alistair Knox's wife, Margot, who knew Ellis Stones. Ellis wanted someone to work with him, and I spent a couple of years with him and then I started on my own. I found my forté in about four hours with Ellis. I realised I'd be good at free form shapes, rather than sticking to geometry.

The way I express myself in landscape, I feel as if I am working like a three-dimensional painter. Of course the fourth dimension comes into it very strongly in landscape, but I have always had a three-dimensional way of looking at things. It is a sculptural problem really, landscape. But I have tried to work a bit like a representational painter too.

This is a fairly wild garden in a way. The size can allow a fair bit of flexibility as far as plants are concerned. The Adams garden followed the same principles. It's in the same manner, just more ordered.

When I bought this land, I immediately started planting out the boundaries while we did the house—it was a homogeneous thing. We had to dig out to get the excavation done, and that made it great for our mossy boulder outcrops against the banks (my little bit of Rocky, as we called Ellis).

Edna Walling's influence was very strong, you can see that in the cottagey environments of the house. We've got a third of an acre of native garden down in the southwest corner. That was a progression with time. Just as Edna progressed from exotics into more native mixtures, so did we.

My father was a Presbyterian minister and I grew up in country towns in the middle of New South Wales and Victoria, so I was really a country boy. Mother loved flower gardens, so she probably instilled in me, unconsciously, the feel for gardening. She used to do a bit of representational painting too.

By the time we had completed the heavy boundary planting and the house, I'd had a fair bit of experience in simulating natural rock outcrops, so that is how all the rockwork took shape.

I wanted a homogeneous feeling of inside and outside, to combine shelters and externals rather than separate them. The ground and floor levels are about the same, so you get an immediate flow between inside and outside. Frank Lloyd Wright did this so well in modern architecture and learned it from the Japanese I think.

The planting around the house is basically exotic, with a few natives mixed in. I've got one of the most primitive trees in Australia, the ironbark (*Eucalyptus sideroxylon*), and next to it is a silver birch. But it works if you know how to place plants, and how to use groundcover. The bridging material between natives and exotics is reedy plants and ferns because they are universal. They are marvellous if you want to tie the two together. I am not a purist. I am not a fanatic on native plants, although I do love them and was one of the pioneers of the bush garden. This isn't a bush garden because I haven't all natives. I call it a natural style garden.

There are two sorts of bush garden. You can have a designed bush garden, or you can have a plantsman's garden where you collect plants like stamps and the emphasis is on the horticulture rather than the design. Sometimes, just by accident or good fortune, a plantsman's garden or a bush garden can be quite a good landscape garden because there is a marvellous textural relationship between the native plants.

I haven't actually got many plant specimens here. It is not a horticultural display. We are not flower gardeners depending on a spring display. The composition relies on textures. I have tried to get the feeling of the bush by using a lot of the same species, and by putting through the wallaby tracks, the sort you get in the bush. And it is not just visual, it's the sounds and scents. An Australian garden should have the aroma and the bird life of the bush.

I learned a lot about the use of native plants from Ernest Lord. I used to go to his night school, with suitcases full of specimen plants. He was a classic example of someone who was a fantastic horticulturist and botanist but couldn't lay out a garden. He didn't have the vision of it.

I think unfortunately there are many people coming into landscape architecture who don't know how to place plants. I think this is where a bit of art comes into it. Ellis Stones' great maxim was: 'When in doubt, plant a spiraea.' Well, he was absolutely right. If you have a grassed area and you want a shrub to hang nicely over it instead of being upright, you plant a spiraea, because that is exactly what it does. You can do the same thing with a grevillea because it has the same pattern, whereas you wouldn't plant a hakea against what we call a

Shafts of light catch water glistening over mossy rocks in the shady heart of the garden.

void of the grass. That has been my obsession, the juxtaposition of mass and void. Alistair Knox used to joke and call me 'Gordon void and his massy boulders'. It is basically a painter's concern.

Geoffrey Jellicoe, the English landscape architect and writer, thought the greatest contribution the English made to the art world was their eighteenth-century landscape, and he was probably right. Another English landscape architect, Christopher Tunnard, who wrote *Gardens in the Modern Landscape* in the 1930s, says the same thing, and that garden design is an artform.

We have never been able to put our finger on what the Australian garden is. I think I agree with George Seddon [author of a number of influential books on the Australian landscape] that there isn't one. We developed it to a certain degree in the sixties and seventies, though it was poorly executed. We are too locked into the old world. There has been so much bad design of Australian plant gardens—wattles under eaves, or grabbing a few grevilleas and the odd sleeper, and calling it a native garden. Well, that had to go.

That bush garden down in the corner is definitely an Australian statement. But I would still say it's very much influenced by the free form design of eighteenth-century English landscaping—Capability Brown on a smaller scale. And when I plant a huge driveway on a property, I won't have an avenue. I'll use asymmetrical planting like Brown used to do. I might be using red box (*Eucalyptus polyanthemos*) but I'll still use it in a free form manner.

So it is very derivative really but it's an inevitable derivative I think. The Australian bush garden could never have come out of the Italian formality, or the French follow-on formality. It had to come out of free form English eighteenth-century landscape, out of that free form natural way of doing things which seems to suit the Australian temperament as well as our plants. It is more casual.

Before we started on the bush garden in the 1960s, we hardly used any native plants at all. We used all exotics because that is what was available. And before the Second World War there was hardly anything—lemon-scented gum (*Eucalyptus citriodora*), silky oak (*Grevillea robusta*) and *Grevillea rosmarinifolia*, and that was about it. Now it is a massive industry.

I have often said that if every Australian plant dropped dead overnight I could still design this style of garden, because design is what I am really about. And there were gardens I designed in the early years that were entirely non-Australian.

In shaping the site, we were terribly fortunate to have a gently undulating piece of land which we could cut into, and then we could heal the cut up with mossy boulders to simulate natural rock outcrops. If we'd had a flat piece of ground we'd have had to make arbitrary shapes, moundings and things. The rocks were brought in. The rock here is sedimentary. I have always disliked sedimentary rock used as field rock. It's great in walls and houses, but it has been under the ground for so long and is raw, and doesn't look right to me. Whereas the boulders we use are volcanic rock which has been out of the ground for millions of years, and has got this marvellous texture that works in very well with Australian plants.

You can use them against banks, or you can use them as grouping stones—we call them outriders of the outcrops—just placed like bits of sculpture in the garden. It was fairly ad hoc what we did here because it took place over a long period. It is quite amazing to me when I look at that hundred-foot mahogany gum (*Eucalyptus botryoides*) out there, and I think how I bought it for sixpence from the Forests Commission.

We didn't do the waterfall and ponds, which are now the centrepoint of the garden, until about twenty years ago. Since then, water has become much more important in my design. It is the multiple effect, the tranquillity, the light coming off it, and the cascade movement.

Japanese gardens have influenced me a lot, especially with the rock work, like where I have put the stepping stones across the water there. The Japanese are wonderful at using rock, though they are a bit more formal than we are. I am sure Ellis Stones, from whom I learned the principles of placing rocks, was influenced too—not trying to imitate the Japanese, but just using the aesthetic.

I don't use rock just for the sake of using rock. If I think it is required by the *genius loci* I'll use it but lots of times I don't use it at all. I didn't want to be a water feature specialist, and I didn't necessarily want to be a rock specialist, though I have turned out to be in the end.

master of his medium

CARRAMAR PAUL THOMPSON

In 1988, Colin and Liana Joyce bought a new house on a 0.4 hectare (1 acre) subdivision in the Melbourne suburb of Templestowe. Their dream was for a native garden that would recreate the setting of scenic bushland characterising the area before development. But as a result of extensive clearing and building work, the site was degraded and drainage was a serious problem. The Joyces' introduction to landscape designer Paul Thompson through the Society for Growing Australian Plants turned out to be a meeting of true minds. The development of Carramar has been very much a three-way process, with owners and designer consulting closely over each stage.

Run-off water is collected in the naturalistic pool at the bottom of the garden. Groves of gum trees grade into a reserve on the lower boundary.

WHEN THE JOYCES rang me and said, 'We've got this place, and we've got a bit of a drainage problem and we really want to put it back the way it was,' I practically jumped through the phone.

We started on the journey in June 1989. The basic form was there by September and over the years there have been many amendments. I always tell people, three years and the intent is apparent, five years and you are starting to live within the intent, ten years and it's the beginning of the maturation and you are actually living within the garden. After twenty years, it will feel mature but it won't be the total climax of the garden—it's beginning to change into something else. What happens beyond that depends on what you did in those preceding years.

One of the things I told Colin and Liana initially was that I didn't want to modify things too much, I wanted to deal with the land as it was. With some exceptions, that is pretty well the way it's been. First we dealt with the drainage, making a subtle version of a flood retarding basin to slow down the flow and increase the moisture percolation into the ground. It's an age-old fundamental principle which is not used enough in gardens today. Excess water is directed down the creek bed to feed the dams.

We wanted to nurture the site rather than dominate it. It has been a question of finding plant material that is appropriate to the soil rather than changing the soil to suit the plants. One technique I employ here is to use an exceedingly robust plant which if it was in good conditions is far too big but in rotten conditions it is dwarfed. In this particular space, lots of the plants are at the limit of their tolerance. In better conditions they would be extremely vigorous.

Along the driveway the character is fine, visually neutral, non-demanding, and you come through a sort of a tunnel of fine foliage which says: I am going to get to something splendid somewhere along the way. On the lower side is a grove of she-oaks (*Casuarina glauca*) and native grasses. Closer to the front door there is a bit of what I call 'instant oomph' where you have things that are a little bit seasonally showy, sort of saluting as you come in, saying: I've arrived. *Eucalyptus eximia* from the bloodwood group of eucalypts flowers terminally; it's just absolutely covered, and it's a ball. Here, too, is *Acacia rotundifolia* that is just vivid yellow like a waterfall in late winter. Other one-off specimens out the front include *Angophora bakeri*.

Near the house are two beautiful trees: the red cedar (*Toona australis*) for its wonderful foliage colour and the white cedar (*Melia azedarach*), a deciduous Australian native tree that goes gold in autumn, gets berries on it in winter, in spring the little mauve-purple flowers have a wonderful lilac smell at night, and in summer there is the shade canopy. It has a dark polished trunk which in time will contrast with the nearby leopard wood (*Flindersia maculosa*) as it develops its marvellous spotted trunk. These are planted in shale and one of the reasons that they are selected here is if they were in good soil they would grow that much bigger and I don't particularly want them to, so again, it's using plants to the limits of their tolerance.

The approach we have taken with *Acacia hakeoides*, on the opposite side of the forecourt, illustrates another way in which understanding a particular plant can help in its cultivation. Naturally, it grows in very tough environments and it's a small shrub, but actually what's going to happen here is it's going to end up being a small tree. If you chopped it off at the socks, it would sucker, and you can actually stimulate suckering by scratching its roots. Another striking plant here is *Dodonea sinuolata*, a hop bush from the Grampians [in Victoria] that tones well with the bricks. The colour of the hops varies according to the coldness of its position—the colder the conditions, the brighter the hops.

Clematis microphylla and *C. aristata* interweave, and *Aphanopetalum resinosum*, an exceedingly robust rainforest plant, clambers over the carport.

On the east side along the path are native orchids and an interesting Victorian plant that is not widely cultivated, *Geitonoplesium cymosum*. I like its foliage. Generally I am more interested in form, and flowers are a bonus. Form is with you all the time, and if you can produce an interesting place with that alone, you have done well. And then you have this extra thing called flowers and then you have these black berries which bring birds and lizards.

Beyond the fern area is another very robust Grampians plant *Thomasia macrocarpa* ssp. *dacyphyllum*, one of those plants that grows in shade and poor soils. In time these will form a backdrop for phebaliums.

The zierias here are wonderful plants. Only a couple of species are in cultivation—there is a huge suite of them in New South Wales which has such a big flora that has not been exploited. Once again, they are in that group of plants that is very happy in harsh environments, the same as *Pomaderris racemosa*, which would make a good sort of formal clipped specimen. Also here are *Elaeocarpus reticulatus*, which, growing on clay, will be exceedingly slow, and correas.

It is only in recent times that you have been able to get *Acacia implexa*. It is long-lived, and as an old plant the trunks are gorgeous. It is widespread in its natural habitat from southern Victoria to the Murray River and up into New South Wales. The birds love the seeds, so you get all the little parrots and bronze-wing pigeons. I am always interested in where plants come from because that gives me an idea as to their tolerances. If you can't find a plant to suit a particular place, you just need to do a bit more research.

We introduced different sorts of plants along the western side to screen off the neighbours. *Melaleuca huegelii*, often grown as a cut flower, is very effective. It is a tough Western Australian plant, one of many plants that found favour with growers in the fifties and sixties and then didn't get a guernsey at all. It ought be a street tree.

The lower area of the garden has quite a different mood, with groves of *Eucalyptus mannifera* ssp. *maculosa*, she-oaks and naturalistic ponds where the shallows have been pebbled so that they appear as beaches when the water level falls. Among the groves are stone chairs and tables. Beyond where the ponds overflow, subaquatic plants like *Bracteantha subundulata* find their homes.

The bottom region will end up being like a woodland. The grass is gradually being suppressed and this will end up being a moss garden with perhaps some tussocks, a garden of shade patterns on the ground—a completely different mood.

You can divide the success of a garden into three components. The first thing is a good idea. The second is a well-implemented idea. And the third is a well cared for idea. I was responsible for the first two and that ongoing thing is for Colin and Liana. In any garden, maintenance is more successful when there is understanding. When you have people who don't have a relationship with the garden at all, it rarely works.

I see myself as a catalyst for change rather than somebody imposing a vision. And that is a big difference. It took me a long time to realise that. Carramar is sort of 'our garden' but it is very much their garden. We all have our own adventures here.

hardy in two gardens

THE SORN   LINDSAY CAMPBELL

Horticulturist and garden designer Lindsay Campbell pioneers the use of Tasmanian plants in his garden at Gardners Bay, 50 km south of Hobart. Situated on the edge of *Eucalyptus obliqua* forest at an elevation of 400 metres, the 50 × 40 metre garden faces west with views of the Hartz Mountains. Vegetation is predominantly wet sclerophyll and annual rainfall is 900 mm. Summer temperatures are generally mild (low to mid-20s), while winter brings light frosts and sporadic snowfalls. Lindsay's emphasis on good design and cultivation highlights the gardenworthy qualities of some very rare plants.

Clumps of flowering grasses—here, *Poa labillardieri*—are a feature of the garden in summer.

I GREW UP in Sydney and became interested in native plants through bushwalking. We travelled for a while and ended up spending a couple of months working on Wilkinson's jam fruit farm in Essex, England. The owner had a manor house and the gardener was away, so I got a job working in the gardens. It was really feudal—maintaining the croquet lawns and going in at the servants' entrance for my hot lunch. But I found I really liked gardening, so I applied while I was still in England to study horticulture back in Sydney.

My first job was with Willoughby Council, working in a memorial rose garden with lots of annuals, alongside an old gardener who was about to retire. It was a fantastic grounding in basic horticulture. I have always remembered what a visiting professor at Burnley Horticultural College in Melbourne, where I studied afterwards, said: 'The trouble with most new gardeners going through the education system is that they are not prepared to weed winter grass for ten years.'

Some people want to get straight into their own business designing gardens. For me that is the culmination of all your skills. I always had it in the back of my mind that design was what I was aiming for. But I was happy to work towards it in jobs like the rose garden, then in nurseries, then the Scottish Hospital garden in Sydney, which had fantastic rainforest plants.

Even when we were travelling we were thinking about where we'd like to settle eventually. We loved the environment in Tasmania, where you can be isolated yet really close to the city. We found this 100-acre block on the edge of stringybark forest (*Eucalyptus obliqua*) and I worked in the Royal Tasmanian Botanical Gardens and set up a landscaping business.

Although it is a large block, I have deliberately chosen to keep the garden small. The cool climate and different soils—mudstone on the lower level and sandstone on the bank above the house—means I have been able to grow a range of plants from alpine, lowland and rainforest areas.

My great interest is in native plants, and I have included in the garden some very rare ones, but for me the most important thing in the end is not whether you have used native or exotic plants or a combination, but the way the garden affects people. A student told me recently that someone had asked them to design a garden without any Australian plants. This is a fairly common attitude. Does that mean you can use plants from Ecuador, Fiji—every country in the world but Australia? You can't imagine someone in England saying to a designer: 'Use plants from anywhere in the world but I don't want you to use any from Australia.'

There is great ignorance about the way Australian plants can be used in a garden. People still think of the fast-growing dry sclerophyll plants that were popular in seventies planting, such as grevilleas, hakeas and acacias. There has not really been much progress from that idea.

There has been quite a lot of overseas interest in this garden, and I have been told it's because I am using native plants from a garden point of view, an ornamental point of view. I am growing these plants as a gardener, and that means people can see how they might be used in other gardens.

The great misunderstanding about Australian plants in gardens is that people think they have got to be used to look like the bush, that you let them grow untouched. But they don't seem to understand what they are looking at in the bush. The places we relate to most strongly have had thousands of years' work on them by wind, snow, caustic salt winds, fire and animals. Natural elements have created the spectacular images we relate to as humans. The Japanese have understood that. They have realised that to recreate the essence of that natural feel needs incredible control. Some of their great gardens appear far more naturalistic than ours, yet they have taken more work than the gardens of Versailles.

For me there is no incongruity in the idea that to get a natural feel requires a lot of contrivance. And what's exciting to me is that whereas many exotic plants have been under 400 years of culture, the plants I am using are only just coming into cultivation. I am always finding new plants in the bush, and it is like pioneering. You are exploring and adding good plants to the gardening world.

There is a brachyglottis here, for example— *Brachyglottis brunonis*—which is only found on Mount Wellington and Mount Direction in the wild, and I think it is only grown in one other

A deck at tree-canopy level enjoys distant views of the Hartz Mountains.

garden. So you could write on the label 'hardy in two gardens'.

I am following the same horticultural and design principles as a gardener of exotic plants. I work with native plants because the ecological thing is important to me—I like to think I can help save rare species—and also because I want to show people how good Tasmanian plants can be in the garden. But if I couldn't use those plants, I would be quite happy making a garden of the same style using other plants sympathetic to the site. In fact, plants from parts of South America would be more suited to this particular site up in the hills than native plants growing just a couple of kilometres away down by the Channel. So you can't be simplistic.

I follow the Thomas Church idea that sense of place or sympathy for the site is the prime thing to have, and obviously the local plants are going to suit that best. But if I only used plants that grow on this site, I'd be fairly limited. A student asked me why I didn't just use plants from the area. I explained that the dominant tree species, *Eucalyptus obliqua*, was far too large for a garden. I have selected all the trees here to be on a human scale, which a lot of forest trees aren't.

You don't have to limit yourself to local plants to fit into your environment but you do have to take account of it, and I think where we really fall down, especially in public planting, is failing to connect with our landscapes. In Hobart, for instance, everywhere you go you see the river or the mountain. There is such a strong link to the natural world, yet the plants we use are in total contrast to the environment. What's interesting is that in the initial list of plants for the Botanical Gardens in the 1820s, about a third were Tasmanian plants. And in old gardens you'll still find hedges of Tasmanian shrubs. I don't think there was a division between native and exotic plants. This happened in the fifties and sixties as the native plant movement grew.

The prime reason for me to create a garden is to have somewhere nice to live. I love what the Mexican architect Luis Barragán said about the house being the heart of the home and the garden the soul. The garden needs to be a haven, and that drives my thoughts on design more than anything. As Barragán says, the most important design element is serenity. I can understand if people want excitement and drama in their gardens but if I am designing for them I try to keep the excitement to a limited area. It equates with disharmony and dislocation, which isn't what I want out of a garden.

I was forming my ideas when I started the garden. I knew I wanted to use Tasmanian plants and I made some drawings, but it wasn't for eight years that I tried to tie it all in to an overall plan. So most of the garden as it is now is only ten years old.

I have planted Tasmanian snow gums (*Eucalyptus coccifera*) as an open forest drive approaching the garden and throughout as the main canopy tree. I'll keep them clear so they spread out, rather than growing up. I am taking out shrubs under the trees and just planting dianella and diplarrhena under the eucalypts, mainly as a fire precaution, to get wind flow over the house. There is groundcover, and trees to filter out embers while not providing much for fire to take hold. This keeps the garden open and lets the light through, and the repetition of the gums and grasses helps it flow from one area to the next.

The rock and gravel area between the driveway and lawn is planted with Tasmanian grasses, and there is another area of grasses suited to wet conditions—restio, carex and button grass (*Gymnoschoenus sphaerocephalus*), with mountain spice (*Ozothamnus ledifolius*), the prostrate spreading *Leptospermum rupestre* and native boronia (*Boronia citriodora*) to give different textures.

There is one small area of lawn with gravel paths going right round so you can walk along what are almost like herbaceous borders, with lots of colour and scent and texture. There is stackhousia, boronia, hibbertia, spyridium and lasiopetalum, which has wonderful leaf texture. Grasses are mixed through here too. *Danthonia carphoides* makes a semi-formal edging and there are bold clumps of tussock grass (*Poa labillardieri*). The way the grassy plants now link all the different garden areas is one of the things I am most pleased about.

On the sandstone bank above the house there are plants from the east coast, including the very rare *Phebalium daviesii*, a shrub with cream and yellow flowers, which was only rediscovered in 1990. In the shady sheltered areas along the sides of the house there are rainforest plants—King William and Huon pines (*Athrotaxis selaginoides* and *Lagarostrobus franklinii*), leatherwoods (*Eucryphia* spp.), richeas, myrtle beech (*Nothofagus cunninghamii*) and native laurel (*Anopterus glandulosus*).

The design of the garden has stayed more or less the same, though I have fiddled around the edges. The biggest change was extending the verandah, which now gives you a different perspective on the garden because you are up among the branches and this really connects the garden to the house.

I wanted to base the skeleton of the garden on just a few plants to give it unity. I re-evaluated what I was trying to achieve with the feel of the garden twelve years ago and I decided I really loved the open forest effect of the Central Highlands. So I concentrated on that grassy, lomatia-type texture and bolstered it with snow gums throughout. Now that we have the structure of the garden, I can play around with the finetuning.

What I like in gardens and want to aim at in my own designs is a sense of timelessness. A garden should be functional, attractive and graceful, not quirky. The most important thing is how good it is to look at and be in.

Many people in landscaping are starting to go for Tofer Delaney [the American garden designer] sort of gardens, which I don't think are gardens at all, but ingenious pieces of art. I am after something much simpler and subtler and what really pleases me is that people relate to the garden whether they are native buffs or not, because of the structure.

The internationalisation of horticulture worries me, with the emphasis on plants that will grow anywhere, like gleditsias, plane trees and birches. Every garden should be unique because every gardener and every site is unique. When you think about it, all the great gardening traditions and trends—Islamic gardens, Italian renaissance, Japanese gardens, the English landscape movement, James van Sweden in America—have drawn on native plants and the site environment.

I really don't think there is an Australian garden style. The native grasslands trend is interesting but it has come mainly from Germany and America. There is a style I would like to see called Australian, which is the sculpture garden at the National Gallery. It is a simple, repetitive landscape and it's really relaxed and informal— like Australian culture—yet it has formal elements. I like a contrast of structure and nature, so there is a natural feeling to the planting but some formality and control. The good Australian gardens I have seen have that.

Lindsay Campbell.

winds from africa

WYEMANDO NAN HARPER

Wyemando is at Darlington in the Darling Ranges 25 km east of Perth. The 0.2 hectare ($^1/_2$ acre) garden is on a west facing terraced hillside, and the soil is loam mixed with heavy clay. The average rainfall is 840 mm, occuring predominantly in winter, and the garden is essentially frost free. Early in the garden's development, the strong easterlies were a challenge but shelter plantings have to a large degree overcome this. The sea breezes which mitigate Perth's summer temperatures do not reach as far inland as Darlington so summer daytime temperatures tend to be hotter, although nights are generally cooler. Nan Harper and her sister Sue began the garden twenty-five years ago.

Western Australian wildflowers create a tapestry of singing colour around a bird feeder. Tall kangaroo paws echo the brilliant red of melaleucas, while lechenaultias and *Verticordia chrysantha* add splashes of primary blue and yellow. In the foreground are the arching sprays of hypocalymmas.

MY FATHER WAS very, very keen on native plants and gardening and he always knew the botanical names of everything. I remember black kangaroo paws being grown. I always loved growing things. My earliest memory of gardening—and I must have been very tiny—is staying with my grandmother in Perth and going to the markets very early in the morning to get the best plants, then going home to breakfast and planting them all.

The name Wyemando comes from a big freshwater lake at Windemurra, up north in the Murchison where my father had interests. He liked the name and he liked the property, so he called the Guildford property Wyemando and we brought the name up here.

We have always loved the hills here. We used to come for picnics as children, so when we sold our home in Guildford we bought this block at once.

When we came here twenty-five years ago, you could see clearly through to Perth. The first thing we did was to put in a line of calothamnus (*C. quadrifidus*) as a backdrop and windbreak because there was nothing between us and the winds from Africa across the ocean. We now have big trees around us and are set in the hill so we are protected from the easterlies. But we still get frightening winds off the ocean in winter.

I worked out the garden on paper. I had to work out the different levels to follow the contours and I had decided to use all native plants. There was a great big brick wall each side of the drive and right across the back, like a prison exercise yard. So I had that taken down and rock walls made. The rock outcrop, which used to be hidden by the ugly brick wall, makes a lovely backdrop. The only plants here were shasta daisies, stands of bamboo and in every crack in the rock a piece of prickly pear. It was terrible.

What we did right from the start was to try to cover the ground. We put everything down we could and really planted densely.

The garden has changed a lot over the years and some early things like the melaleucas have grown absolutely colossal. The whole trouble with the garden is you eventually get a bit too much shade because things grow very quickly. *Melaleuca hypericifolia* is a beautiful bush but is now getting too tall, and I never thought the eremophilas would get to that size. We have lots of eremophilas. I am very keen on those and I am experimenting with them up here because they grow inland. Those grey foliage things are very hard to propagate but I am getting on quite well with them. They are such beautiful plants and look as if they ought to be sheltering under an English oak.

The native *Banksia lemanniana* is also very large. It has a hanging-down habit and orangey new growth and it's one of the few that will grow in our heavy soil. Underneath we have planted a darwinia with a little greeny pink flower.

The lower part of the garden is quite steep and has become Sue's area. It was the last area to be done, about five years ago. We had to bring in a lot of soil because it was sand. We put in a flowering gum (*E. calophylla* Rosea) where a big marri (*Corymbia calophylla*) blew over. It is a lovely red. There is a beautiful *Hakea victoriae* which has a red-flowered creeper twining through. *Hypocalymma angustifolium* is a wonderful tough little plant. It looks very delicate and goes down to dead sticks but after the rain all the little buds come up. I am also very fond of the little blue sowerbaea.

One of the best sights is all the kangaroo paw (*Anigozanthos* spp.) hybrids in flower. There are some wonderful colours in the new varieties, including a very pretty delicate pink. Pink kangaroo paws have a personal history for us. Many years ago we were picking flowers on a friend's block and Sue found this pink kangaroo paw. We took a piece and grew it in our nursery at Guildford and I think all these hybrids have come from that.

We started the nursery when we were looking after our mother. She was always supportive of our efforts. In the early days when we collected seed and cuttings she would come with us, and loved the trips up to the Dandaragan area and Lake Grace. I had grown things all my life and when the Tree Society started, I used to grow masses of eucalypts and things and give them away, and people said why didn't I sell them. So we moved the chooks out of our backyard and made it a native nursery. We had a marvellous Italian gardener, Charlie Di Marco, who still comes up here. He is one of the family practically. I think he regards it as his garden as well.

In those days, a native nursery was very unusual. I still remember sitting outside our shed with kennedia seeds on hot sand on a piece of tin. The

Kangaroo paws (*Anigozanthos* spp.) have an enduring significance for the Harpers.

seeds got too hot and they were hopping all over the place! We learnt then to do them in boiling water. It was very much trial and error in those days, both getting the seeds and propagating them.

One thing we have in the garden with an interesting history is the little pink *Pimelea ferruginea*. We had a cottage at Busselton and it was growing beautifully all over the rocks, so I took cuttings and planted it out in our heavy clay soil at Wyemando Guildford and it grew into the most beautiful bush. That was really my great start. People said you couldn't grow them because they grew in sand, or they just wouldn't take. So that gave me the most tremendous fillip.

We grow a number of grevilleas. There is the prostrate *Grevillea synaphea*, *G. endlicheriana* which grows through the rock crevices and is very hardy and indigenous to this area, and others that are now appearing naturally, such as *G. bipinnatifida*, *G. saccata* and *G. thelemanniana*.

One of the nicest little things is *Dampiera lavandulacea*, which has gone right up the bank. We have also planted native clematis to cover the bank. *Kunzea sericea* is spectacular, covered in big pink flowers, and the guichenotias are absolutely gorgeous and flower for ages. There is native hibiscus, *Alyogyne huegelii*, which has been marvellous, and the little red running postman, *Kennedia prostrata*. We also have *Kennedia nigricans*, the black coral pea.

So much is now self-seeding. It is quite extraordinary—when we came there was nothing and then suddenly these things have brought themselves up here. You get areas just covered in blue orchids. A beautiful *Stylidium bulbiferum* makes little clumps everywhere and the parrot bush, *Dryandra sessilis*, also comes up by itself.

We have quite a few dryandras. The little *Dryandra praemorsa*, which grows on the verge at the front, has a large yellow flower and is absolutely marvellous in this heavy soil.

Hakea orthorrhyncha is quite beautiful in flower. It is shaped like a bird's bill. I don't do anything for these—they have to sink or swim up here. But imagine coming from the desert sand to here. When we first came up, we had to use a crowbar to dig!

The Rottnest Island daisy has the most glorious blue flower and it flowers right on into the summer. Hoveas in one corner make a nice windbreak.

I always know when the hoveas are out because everybody sneezes and they have such a strong honey perfume.

Melaleuca elliptica is another favourite. It is such a rugged thing with brilliant red flowers and it's always full of lizards and insects. Things have to be rugged and really strong here, with the winds straight from South Africa and the very hot summers. The thryptomenes are wonderful. You don't even know they are there, then they come out after the rain.

The yellow hypocalymma is another marvellous thing. It flowers practically all the time and has a good rich green foliage too. *Thomasia macrocarpa* with its big mauve flowers also has an attractive large leaf.

I have always been very keen on the foliage of plants. I think that in a native garden it's one of the greatest attractions. I'll always remember Charlie Gardner, the Government Botanist, saying that people in Europe would be absolutely astounded at the beauty of the native plant colours—the gold tones in the dryandras and banksias and things. He was the botanist of the Wildflower Society which started in the late 1950s and he took us on the Society's first excursion to Dandaragan, near Moora.

We have always wanted to get more people interested in using our world-renowned Western Australian wildflowers and also let them see you can have a beautiful garden with little maintenance and very little water. They have all gone mad on these cottage gardens. When you talk about a native garden, most people see a gum tree and a kangaroo paw. We wanted to share the knowledge we have to show that you can have a really beautiful garden using different native plants. You see plumbagos and petunias in the supermarket and everyone buys them—the whole world's going to be covered in plumbago and petunias.

In any garden you lose things but it is especially so with native plants because they have been under cultivation for such a short time. Roses have been cultivated for hundreds of years. But things like that pimelea, I was one of the first to grow those, forty years ago.

We still make trips to the bush to look at the flowers. It was always our great joy, going for picnics in the bush when we were children, and that is still what we love.

diverse artistry

DRYANDRA THELMA VANDEPEER

The 0.2 hectare ($1/2$ acre) garden of Dryandra is at Tea Tree Gully, a northeastern suburb of Adelaide in the foothills of the Mount Lofty Ranges. The undulating contours of the site enabled the establishment of a number of microclimates for Thelma Vandepeer's thirty-year-old garden, with its large collection of plants drawn from all over Australia. Average rainfall is 660 mm and summer temperatures are frequently in the 40s.

WE DELIBERATELY CHOSE a block with trees and started on the garden in 1969. There were big South Australian blue gums (*Eucalyptus leucoxylon* ssp. *leucoxylon*), the golden wattle (*Acacia pycnantha*), and prickly Moses (*Acacia paradoxa*), as well as two of the xanthorrhoea species (*X. semiplana* and *X. quandrangulata*) that are local to the area.

I grew up in the country at Coonawarra [wine growing region in the southeast of South Australia], on that famous strip of terra rosa limestone soil, and both my parents were great gardeners. As children my sister and I used to go and pick little bunches of flowers in the scrub. There were some beautiful things, and I would like to go back now and identify them all. I love plants of all sorts but my interest really lies in Australian flora.

We decided to concentrate on natives here because it's a very light sandy soil and with the big trees and the slope of the land, the maintenance of lawn and exotic plants would have been very high in terms of mowing, watering and fertilising.

We didn't know an awful lot at the start. We joined the Society for Growing Australian Plants and started learning and the more we learned the more we wanted to find out. We had success with one or two things, then went on to try more and more plants.

The site here is an unusual shape because it encompasses a small winter-flowing creek. It slopes in all directions because of the creek banks. There are areas of full sun and fairly shaded areas, and we've got steep and very gentle slopes.

The soil is quite deep and neutral to slightly acid but there is not a lot of body in it. Ideally we would like slightly heavier soil but I build it up with mulches and it does suit a wide range of plants.

There were quite a lot of indigenous plants on the property and we left them except the prickly Moses, which was taking over the creek area. The creek is a natural feature and we didn't really have to do much landscaping because we could design around that and the natural slopes. We brought in a similar soil type to level out the steeper areas.

The layout of paths through the garden really just evolved. We made a path up to the front door and various other things naturally determined where paths and tracks went. We built the railway sleeper steps down the creek because it was just a narrow walkway on a fairly steep slope.

I have made plenty of mistakes with plants and I learned as I went how they grow in these particular conditions. If they haven't grown well, or have been in the wrong place, or they get too big, I move them or take them out. And if something does well and looks attractive, I put more of those in. I am a collector of plants but not a one-of-everything collector. I've got a dozen of some things, others I've put in spots where I think that particular style of plant is needed.

I try to have things flowering most of the year, even in the height of summer. Winter is a good time for many Australian plants but summer is quite difficult. There are summer-flowering eucalypts and banksias. I am putting more banksias in to get extended flowering. Correas are good, and some grevilleas, then thryptomenes for late autumn. I am still learning an awful lot and that is part of the fun.

With this soil and the big trees and the lie of the land, I have to water most things to get them really well established. If you make a dish behind the plant, it very soon fills up with mulch and silt and then the water just merrily runs straight past the roots of the plant: 'See you later, mate. I'm going to the bottom of the creek'. So we put in drippers. Once the plants are established, I water by hand just when they need it.

We aim for a low water use garden, although because I am a collector and don't just grow plants selected for this area and soil, I need to water some plants more often. For instance, plants that are native to wet areas, or plants from the New South Wales and Queensland coast that like summer moisture, obviously need extra watering because of our dry summers and hot winds.

Some of the grevilleas, particularly the Northern Territory and Queensland ones like *G. refracta* and *G. banksii*, need that summer humidity around their branches and leaves. I grow lots of grevilleas, probably about sixty different species, and also quite a few dryandras which of course gave the garden its name. They are all from Western Australia, with a similar climate, but my soil doesn't suit a lot of them. They are plants I really love, so I keep trying with them.

In this cheerful bed, the golden flowers and striking foliage of *Beaufortia squarrosa* (yellow-flowered form) are combined with orange *Grevillea juncifolia* (left) and bright red *Grevillea* 'Long John'.

Near the back door is a big, shady South Australian blue gum, one of the trees that was here when we came. Along the creek bank I have planted correas, grevilleas, thryptomenes and eriostemons. Round the top of the bank there is a little thomasia, which is only a few inches high, but spreads nearly a metre, and the dodonaeas, whose fruit lasts a long time and gives a lot of colour to the garden.

We have used fallen limbs and logs to edge the different areas, and rocks dug up on the property or brought in from our land at Houghton. They are mainly there to protect the roots of plants from the hot sun.

I have tried to make the planting look natural. Obviously plants aren't growing with their natural neighbours but I have tried to mix heights, colours, leaf shapes, sizes and textures, as they are in the wild. So there are big trees grown with little things and the colours are mixed through. There are no patches of all pink or all blue in the garden. But I have noticed that at one time of the year, the garden will have a yellow look with all the acacias and other yellow-flowering plants, and at another time the pinks and mauves will predominate.

There is a Geraldton wax hybrid 'Revelation' (a hybrid of *Chamelaucium uncinatum* and *C. megapetalum*). I have trouble growing megapetalum itself but this hybrid seems very happy in the garden. It isn't a big grower but it has clusters of large flowers on slender branches that are pink in the bud, then white, and fade to a darker pinky red. I have planted four in a group because they are so light and delicate. 'Blondie' is another from the same cross, with almost pure white flowers. It's a good idea to put several plants together to bush them up if they don't have that natural habit. It gives a better effect.

Another pretty shrub with a strong perfume that flowers for weeks and weeks is *Scholtzia oligandra* from Western Australia. It is an excellent filler, a bit like a thryptomene in its usefulness. We have a pale one and a real lolly pink one. *Isopogon dawsonii* is a gorgeous eastern states plant, with creamy yellow flowers on long, straight stems. It is ideal for floral art, beautiful in bud and has interesting seed pods too. The foliage is soft, whereas a lot of isopogons are prickly. I also love *Thomasia grandiflora*. It is

only a small plant, so again I have put in a group, and it's something that does well in this soil.

One of my favourite areas is where a little path leads off the driveway up to the gums. There is a South Australian *Acacia sclerophylla*, which is low-growing with a spreading trunk and it is very, very hardy. Nearby is a lasiopetalum species with small white flowers, which reaches to about a metre. I like looking up the path to the eucalypts in the background, with trunks going in all directions. There is *Eucalyptus caesia*, *E. salubris* with a stark, shiny fluted trunk, some Western Australian gums that the birds like to nest in, and a clump of lemon-scented gums closer to the house, with the South Australian blue gums in the background. I love the different colours, shapes and textures of the trunks.

In the foreground are little plants. Sprawling *Thryptomene saxicola* with white flowers grows next to the little *Darwinia oldfieldii*, and next to the driveway is a dark red *Dodonaea sinuolata*, which keeps its fruit for ages. In the background is a birdseed hakea (*Hakea orthorryncha*), which is absolutely brilliant in flower—in the late afternoon with the sun on it, it looks like it's on fire. Near that is a huge pink-flowered melaleuca, and *Kunzea jucunda*, a very attractive small shrub with bright pink flowers, another very good filler.

I look out for unusual plants, like the rare *Grevillea flexuosa* from Western Australia. It has yellow flowers in a rod shape but the best thing is its foliage. I also love the foliage of *Dryandra drummondii*, which an Irish floral art man who visited thought was a fern. *Dryandra polycephala* also has the most wonderful prickly foliage.

I have collected a few interesting ornaments for the garden, like the old engine carrier by the creek that makes a handy seat and is also useful to stand on for pruning. The two 'totem poles' we got at a clearance sale up at Saddleworth in the mid-north of South Australia. They are actually augers for flourmills—poles of wood with lugs sticking out in a spiral.

We travel a lot to see plants in their natural areas. They often look quite different in the wild and it helps you to see why you might be struggling to grow something.

Augers from an old flourmill make unusual totem poles, echoing the trunks of surrounding eucalypts and adding vertical interest to low-growing shrubs.

a crop of flannel flowers

MERV HODGE'S GARDEN

Merv Hodge's 1 hectare ($2^1/_2$ acre) garden is at Logan Reserve, 40 km south of Brisbane. The twenty-year-old garden is established around a sandstone ridge which divides the property into east and west slopes. The soil over the sandstone is shallow gravelly clay, and as most of the garden is watered only by rainfall (averaging 1000 mm but very erratic), plants have been carefully selected to suit the conditions.

Sheets of flannel flowers interspersed with grass trees colonise the dramatic outcrop. In the background, the scarlet flowers of doryanthes are etched against the sky.

THE ROCK OUTCROPS here just blew my mind—that was why we bought this place. They are so imposing and spectacular, and tongue orchids (*Dendrobium linguiforme*) grow naturally in the crevices. The elevation meant good drainage but I was so overwhelmed by the rocks themselves that I forgot to see what the soil type was like. It is frustrating to work with because it dries out very quickly and if you dig a hole you are almost sure to find a lump of sandstone. There are big rock shelves just a foot or so down. On the western slope you can see the tops of huge boulders just protruding from the ground but on the eastern side they are all bare.

I couldn't grow anything on the rocks at first. It wasn't until we eventually removed the wattles and the soap bush (*Alphitonia excelsa*) that things started to grow there and the flannel flowers (*Actinotus helianthi*) started to thrive. Now there are seedlings coming up everywhere. I put one or two plants into different garden beds and next season you find dozens coming up.

It is a tribute to the native plants that while they don't look good all the time, during the long dry periods they do survive.

Because of the impoverished soil and the lack of water I've had to be very selective about plants. We have a few native rainforest plants but they have to be the toughest—those that will also grow as street trees in Brisbane, such as *Stenocarpus sinuatus* (the firewheel tree), *Xanthostemon chrysanthus* (the golden penda), *Grevillea baileyana* and *Ficus platypoda*.

Growing native plants has been a passion of mine since 1960, when I went along to my first meeting of the Society for Growing Australian Plants. I had to almost have my arm twisted to go, then I suddenly found I was interested. I persevered with the long botanical names, which frightened me at first, but they stick after you use them enough.

I developed new methods of grafting Australian plants and became even more passionate about that side of it. I like grafting all sorts of plants. Some natives can be very frustrating. The family I like best is the proteaceae, which covers grevilleas, banksias, hakeas and waratahs, but unfortunately they are probably more trouble to propagate than any other family of plants.

There is nothing much written on grafting native plants. I would probably be at the forefront of it. I was introduced to it by Harvey Shaw, a retired farmer, about twenty years ago. He had a passion for grafting and he'd been playing with grafting native plants for probably thirty years before I knew him. He'd grafted eucalypts and banksias and he used a method called 'approach grafting'. I learned a great deal from him.

The reason some plants need to be grafted is that we are trying to grow them in conditions that may be quite foreign to them—desert plants for instance—so they need a pretty strong root system to keep them going. By grafting them we can grow many more plants we'd love to grow and the strong root system will look after them and cope with conditions like poorly drained soils and diseases.

Silky oak (*Grevillea robusta*) is generally used as the root stock for grevillea standards because it gets that nice straight trunk so you can get the height. Some grevilleas aren't compatible with it and then I use alternative root stocks. I also graft eremophilas, which are a desert plant, using prostanthera root stock. There is a lot to learn still about grafting native plants. The more we get to know about it, the more we realise we don't know. You have constantly got to be trying new things out.

There are over 20,000 species of native plants, so when people say they don't like native plants it is really like saying they don't like plants! I think it is because they don't understand them. Some native plants may look rather untidy and some of them are very difficult to grow, but there are plenty more that are easy and very attractive plants.

I use very little fertiliser. Plants are selected because of the type of soil they normally grow in and if they don't do well I don't persevere with them unless they are really special and I think they might go with a bit of extra care. For instance, we have had waratahs up to around six foot high, then lost them in the hot dry weather, but I have planted more and I keep an eye on them and water them if they seem to need it, because I would just like to keep them going. The waratah is a plant that if you'd asked me ten years ago whether I could grow that here, I'd have said, 'Don't be ridiculous.'

Generally, the trick is to select plants suitable to your soil type and climate so they'll be healthy whatever the weather throws at them. I am not saying they couldn't be grown better. One of the worst things ever said about native plants I think, was that they are plants for a no-maintenance garden.

A no-maintenance garden is a neglected garden. Native plants respond to good horticultural practices like any other plant, especially with pruning. Some people growing native plants like to leave them as they grow naturally but I think what they have to realise is that in nature plants are growing under very different conditions.

Grevilleas are my first love. There are other individual plants I probably like as much but I come back to grevilleas as a genus. There has been tremendous progress in developing cultivars. Some of them are fantastic, especially some of the new hybrid grevilleas. I have raised some myself: 'Superb' and 'Coconut Ice' are hybrids between *Grevillea bipinnatifida* and *G. banksii*, and 'Forest Bright' and 'Strawberry Blonde' are the result of crossing *G. venusta* and *G. longistyla*. The original plants of 'Superb' and 'Forest Bright' are still here in the garden.

You can get a fair life-span out of grevilleas if conditions are reasonable, especially drainage. 'Superb' is twenty years old. When I saw the first flower on it, I couldn't believe my eyes. I showed a friend of mine and said, 'What do you think of this, it's a new hybrid of mine.' He took one look and said, 'That is too hot to handle.' Well, it came out with a whimper, and was slowly released onto the market, but over the years it has proved to be very popular and reliable—it is regarded now by some people as the best-flowering grevillea in Australia.

The other cultivar that is of historical interest in the garden is 'Moonlight'. I have the original here and it's probably about fifteen years old. It was given to me by a friend as *Grevillea whiteana* and when it flowered, I realised it was a hybrid and we worked out it was *G. banksii* crossed with *G. whiteana*.

I have grafted onto silky oak a *Grevillea formosa*, which came from Kakadu National Park originally. It has been popular around Darwin and some of the north Queensland towns for some years. It grows to around half a metre high, with a three-metre spread. I have grafted it as a high standard, so it gets a pendulous sort of growth. The foliage is beautiful and the flower is bright yellow and very spectacular.

Some of the low-growing grevilleas are beautiful plants. *Grevillea nudiflora* gets to about a foot high and throws long runners out with nothing but flowers on them. The prostrate *Grevillea* 'Royal Mantle' can cover big areas, but is flat on the ground.

The garden has gone through a number of phases over the years. I did tend to resist putting things into garden beds and just dotted things here and there all over the garden, but the maintenance was too great and it didn't look good. So now we keep a reasonable area of grass for easy access around a series of big beds. There is a handful of exotics here and there that I like, such as proteas and leucadendrons from Africa and a couple of New Caledonian grevilleas. Being so interested in grevilleas, I couldn't leave those out!

I think it is essential in a large garden not to have too many plants that need a lot of attention, plants that are growing away from where they should be grown. I try to minimise that by choosing suitable plants or root stocks for the conditions. But I am also guilty of trying things I know I shouldn't and sometimes it works. You have to keep pushing the barriers. In some cases I have been known to try as many as fifty plants before giving up. It is a weakness of mine, having one more try!

The way the garden has evolved is that I have always wanted to grow certain plants and I begin with that but I am also thinking about landscaping. I try to put a plant where it will survive but also where it's going to fit in with the plants around it. I try to work out whether it's going to swamp those plants and whether it's eventually going to have enough space.

A lot of people put plants into their garden without any thought as to how big they are going to grow, particularly the spread. Plants with a three-metre spread placed a metre apart will inevitably lead to a mess. There is an idea that you can close-plant natives for instant landscape because some of them are going to die anyway. I don't think that is good gardening. It is better to give the plants space and if it looks bare, fill in with either smaller plants or temporary plants, things you know are going to run their course in about a year or two.

Even with all the room I have got here I'll still wander round with a plant under my arm like a dog when he wonders where he is going to bury his bone! Rarely do I dig a plant out to put another one in. But some plants can be extremely slow and you sometimes wonder if you have picked the right spot for them. For instance, I have a palm that is

Doryanthes spears contrast with a ferny cushion of *Grevillea formosa*, the Mount Brockman grevillea, which is native to Kakadu National Park.

fifteen years old and even the flannel flowers were swamping it, but it is coming good now.

There are a lot of native plants you could regard as cottage garden plants and I reckon they have a real place in a garden. Hibbertias, darwinias, kangaroo paws, some of the little eriostemons and grevilleas, and flannel flowers are becoming a mainstay around the garden—they are coming up everywhere. In fact a friend of mine once referred to my place as a cottage garden.

A garden needs to be well balanced and I think you have got to have the whole range of plants from annuals to groundcover to small shrubs, large shrubs and trees. Some plants have a reputation for being difficult but often it's a matter of getting to know the plant and what its requirements are, sun or shade or good drainage or extra watering.

The northern side of the garden is a very hard area because it is very close to the rock shelf. So plants have to be really tough to take it there. I have kept it to fairly low-growing plants, such as a number of prostrate grevilleas that can cover around three metres each. The little flannel flowers have certainly worked in very well. We find the little seedlings coming up all over the place now, moving into the rock crevices and garden beds.

There are also naturally occurring plants on the rocks, like the lomandras (*longifolia* and *multiflora*), which need regular cutting back. The slow-growing grevillea here is a prostrate form of *Grevillea banksii* called 'Ruby Red', which is very much at home in these conditions, and there is a grafted *G. formosa*.

Up near the top of the rocks there are mainly the tropical plants. At the bottom of the slope, you get frosts. Plants like *Grevillea formosa* and *G. dryandri*

won't survive down there. But at the top the heat collected by the rocks means it is warm enough overnight for plants like that to survive.

I've got around 160 species of grevilleas in the garden and a lot of different hybrids. At one stage there were over 200 species but I have let some go because they just weren't worth growing.

The range of foliage on grevilleas is just unbelievable, with different textures and shades of green and gold. Some you wouldn't recognise. There is one like a tiny kangaroo paw, *Grevillea bronwynae*, and the Northern Territory *G. goodii*, which is a spectacular green and red and doesn't look like a grevillea at all.

Gardening is a wonderful passion, I think I would wither up and die if I couldn't garden. There is always something new. It doesn't matter how much you get on top of something, there is always another challenge around the corner.

Merv Hodge.

a garden for the republic

HORSE ISLAND CHRISTINA KENNEDY

Horse Island is a 80 hectare (200 acre) private island off the New South Wales coastal town of Bodalla, 330 km south of Sydney. The design of the house was inspired by early colonial neoclassical buildings. The 8 hectare (20 acre) garden begun in 1991 is also very much in the classical tradition, freshly interpreted through the medium of Australian plants.

In the East Rill Garden a large formal basin with fountain draws the eye down the rill to views of the distant headland. A low screen of prostrate *Melaleuca hypericifolia* defines the edge of the lawn. The bronze turtle and wallaby sculptures are by Sylvio Apponyi.

GARDENING FORCED ITSELF on me when
I realised I had to put something between the
cottage and the wonderful surrounds. Wherever you
looked was a beautiful vista of the lake and the
bush. I realised that what you put between them
was a garden, and I had to get thinking about what
I was going to do.

Horse Island is an estuarine island in the Tuross
Lakes, sitting right between Tuross Heads. It is quite
protected from the sea, although the sea isn't far
away. It has all sorts of landforms. We have
rainforest, paddocks which were probably once
fertile areas for growing potatoes, hills and flatland,
and beaches around the edge. But the dominant
visual force is the water all around, and all the
beautiful mangroves and gums stretching away,
and, beyond the water, the other islands.

When we came here, the island had had many
years of cattle grazing. All the young casuarinas
(*C. glauca*) and mangroves had been chewed down,
so we had a lot of old forest but no new trees. For
the first couple of years we left everything, which
allowed some regrowth. It is wonderful how it all
comes back. I have reseeded the casuarinas where it
was bare, and replanted them around the foreshores.
In the cleared flatland, where we have cattle grazing,
I have fenced off the few stands of mature trees and
planted young trees around them.

Quite a large part of the island has black soil but
it's sandy in many parts and there are also areas of
clay. We had to work up the soil in each area to suit
the needs of the plants I wanted to put there.

We started the cottage in 1991. I remember sitting
on the back steps looking northwards, and there
was nothing much, except disturbed ground where
the house had been built, and bush in the distance.
I really had a clean slate. I wanted to do something
to marry the house to the beautiful surrounds, and
be sympathetic to both.

I drew a design on paper because by this stage
I had learnt how to scale things. Then an artist
friend, Robbie Mayo, who has a beautiful garden,
Whitley at Sutton Forest [in the Southern Highlands
of New South Wales], sat with me on the same steps
one day and said, 'Why don't you make a native
garden?' And everything clicked into place.

It was a good idea for various reasons. It gave me
a parameter for learning, so I could confine what
I needed to know to native plants. Also native

plants would be sympathetic in colour. They didn't
have the exotic force of plants like roses. I felt it
would be a great blend with the environment.

I began around the cottage, not knowing very
much, so I went to the gardening books. I planned
the shapes on paper, then I had to plan the planting
from books, and then I had to find the plants. This
didn't really work because I would find plants in
books and they wouldn't be available. So it became a
kind of hotch-potch of what I had fixed in my head,
and what I found in nurseries.

The project grew when my husband Trevor
decided he wanted a study, and I didn't want to
disturb the way the cottage sat in the landscape,
so he pushed me into building another house!
Once again I had to marry this house to the outside
but it was a lot easier because I'd kind of had my
baptism of earth at the other place. I had started
to find my way around the native plants world,
and I enjoyed the business of conceptualising and
realising my dream.

The major work of laying out and planting the
garden beds was finished in 1996 but I have done
a lot of additional planting and replanting as I find
out what works, where and how it works. The
waratahs (*Telopea speciosissima*), for instance, work
only on the sloping bank. And I had a really big
hedge of *Westringia brevifolia* but odd ones kept
pegging out, so I replaced the lot with a variegated
westringia that had already proven itself in another
area. In terms of longevity, I am prepared for certain
things to die and to have to be replaced but we put
a lot of work into trying to maintain the life of the
plants by using the cultivation methods that you
would use with exotic plants—giving them the
amount of water and the type of fertiliser they need,
and being very tough with pruning.

You can train an Australian native plant to look
like a very luxurious plant if it doesn't have to
struggle for survival. And some may say, well why
bother, because that is not the natural way it likes
to grow, but exotics were all native somewhere
originally, and that was probably not the way they
wanted to grow either. I prefer to use Australian if
we can. That is the way I am feeling right now.
This is the garden for the Republic.

The south coast is the sort of country that looks
like it needs a drop of water every night. It likes to
be green and lush. But Horse Island always looks

green, even where we don't water during the worst droughts. We are blessed with good natural moisture. But we are trying to reduce watering by mulching heavily and by appropriate planting. Once they are established, the gardens here hardly ever get watered.

I probably got a latent gardening gene from my mother. She is a great gardener, and has always been deadly keen. Still, she is also keen on bridge and croquet and I haven't taken them up, although I did build her a croquet lawn out here.

I have been strongly influenced by the grand vision I have seen in some large country gardens. That taught me that you can do it all on a big scale and make it look wonderful. You don't have to restrict yourself to domestic size.

I have been very conscious of creating vistas from the house. Every window and verandah looks at something wonderful. But I feel everything out there is so beautiful anyway. I didn't create the distant landscape, I only created the windows to it.

One person asked why, with all these wonderful vistas, we didn't have a glass wall. But by framing views you get more impact. It is lovely to have a feeling of enclosure, and to go from inside to a surprise outside.

I see the garden as my own expression. My sister has spent her life painting, and we have a great history of artists in the family. I always thought I was most unartistic but I now see this as perhaps my own palette—a shape palette rather than a paint palette. There is a bit of colour planning that goes into it too but of foliage more than flowers. Generally though, colours seem to do their own thing just from the fact that plants are clever.

With the scale of this garden, you have to be more interested in shape. You have to go for an impact en masse, and you have got to be able to live with the plants all year. That is one of my objections to, say, azaleas. They are the scrappiest things for eleven months of the year, and then for one month they are absolutely sensational. I try to do the reverse here and have things sensational for eleven months of the year and for the other month, super sensational! So around the garden there are occasional wonderful splashes of colour at different times of the year.

The planting I am most excited about, for its potential, is the waratahs. The kangaroo paws are

what excites everybody else. At different times of the year, particular plants are good as their foliage changes colour. The *Myporum parvifolium* (purple form), which is the groundcover around the croquet lawn, is absolutely magnificent. At one time it is covered in white flowers, at another it has a whole purple sheen, then it's bright green. It is a wonderful plant.

The main grass here is kikuyu, which was very well established when we came. It was probably planted by my great-great-grandfather, who first settled this area. It stays really green right through the year. We have five golf greens, and it has actually become a fantastic garden link. It all became one garden, enclosed at both ends by post-and-rail fences to keep out the emus, cattle, kangaroos and all the other creatures gardens don't like. And golf is a way that people get around the garden. The mown fairways make a pathway between the cottage and the house gardens that brings them together.

It is a strongly formal garden, a formal landscape, but using native plants. I was surprised to find that the concept of using Australian plants in a formal garden was so unusual. I am a bit obsessive, and I decided it was only going to be Australian plants.

To keep the garden's formality, its shape and look, you have to keep it all looking pretty neat, so there is always someone mowing and snipping.

I am inspired by the classic elements in large gardens, the sense of scale you get with huge lakes, the relationship of the buildings to the gardens, the vistas and the surprises around the corner. I find all that very inspiring, and I try to do little bits of it here.

The north facing area is where I envisaged we'd spend most of our time. We are protected from the nor'easter because of the L-shape of the house. The croquet lawn has to be maintained well and looks nice in this position where we spend so much time. We sit on the verandahs and look out across an immaculate lawn to a ring of garden beds with massed patersonia, the native iris. They are going to seed, which excites me because I can propagate a whole lot more. Seven blueberry ash (*Elaeocarpus cyaneus*) make a very forceful, solid green vertical line, and I keep them trimmed really closely to give a very formal shape.

Beside the house there are lemon trees in pots. That is my Italian inspiration. We always need

Mounds of *Agonis flexuosa* and *Melaleuca incana* soften the austere classical lines of the pavilion, sited at the highest point of the garden for dramatic long views of the lakes.

lemons, so I've got a lot of pots around the house. There are three native frangipani (*Hymenosporum flavum*), growing tall and straight in among the eriostemon (*E. myoporoides*) that lead down to the barbecue area. A path leads west past a native orchid garden sheltered by tree ferns and a long hedge of *Melaleuca hypericifolia*. I have extended the hedge and made some wide bendy beds filled with various small plantings such as croweas and prostrate *Micromyrtus*.

There are a number of garden sculptures. My favourite is on the edge of the croquet lawn—a big piece of honey-coloured granite with a snake carved out of the upper surface and polished. It is by Sylvio Apponyi, an Adelaide sculptor who has done various Australian bush animals around the garden.

Framing the view north from the cottage—where I first sat wondering what on earth I could do to join the house to the gum trees and the water and beyond—there is an archway of old stone blocks covered by the native creeper *Pandorea* 'Golden Bells', and in front of that, right in the centre of a circle, is a beautiful hanging 'Royal Mantle' grevillea. There is a mixture of plants here— brachyscomes, Christmas bells (*Blandfordia nobilis*), prostrate grevilleas, and a grove of tall lilly pilly (*Syzygium australe*) which fruits prolifically. Round the other side of the cottage there is a low garden in front of the stone verandah of brachyscomes, chrysocoma and leptospermum, with lots of native violets and correas.

Everything here is a bit rampant but it's happy. There is a massive eriostemon and also some flourishing native geraniums we found down on the seashore.

My one 'sin' is a small bed of agapanthus. In a country garden you have to have agapanthus, and the plants actually come from my ancestors' house near Bodalla, so I thought that was quite legal in my all-native garden!

There is a track you can take along the foreshore from the cottage to the house. It leads to the boronia garden, from where you get nice glimpses of the half-circle verandah on the west side of the house.

There are some shrubs from Albany in Western Australia and semi-tropical trees like the tree waratah, some southern sassafras (*Atherosperma moschatum*) and Davidson's plums (*Davidsonia pruriens* var. *pruriens*).

I have planted terrestrial orchids beside a little stone seat for my mother, which looks down across the bay. The boys who help me in the garden helped me build it and when it was finished they said, 'This is Mrs Miller's chair, and she can look out to sea just like Mrs Macquarie did.'

One of my favourite spots is the western verandah which looks down the reach of the lake. You look through a fringe of tree ferns, past a stretch of lawn and the forest red gums (*Eucalyptus tereticornis*) and a very fine film of casuarinas, to the water. In the evening when the sun is setting and the hills are lit up in the distance, there is a magnificent view. The most important thing of all in this garden is the light. In the early morning and particularly in the evening, it is just extraordinary.

Christina Kennedy in front of her clipped westringia hedge.

healing the soul

WINDGROVE PETER ADAMS

In 1991, American sculptor Peter Adams bought 42 hectares (105 acres) of coastal heathland at Nubeena, on southeast Tasmania's Tasman Peninsula. The natural garden of Windgrove aims to re-establish and enhance a landscape severely degraded by overgrazing. From the 'home grove' of casuarinas where Peter lives in a converted bus, he has made a 1.5 km path along the headland overlooking Storm Bay. His bench sculptures for dialogue and meditation are placed at stations on the way.

Sculpted by nature, the she-oak logs and beach stone on this Huon pine bench relate directly to the vista of Roaring Beach, glimpsed across the deck through an airy screen of casuarinas.

GARDENS ARE A place of healing. I believe that walking in the landscape, or visiting or making a garden, are healing to one's soul. A garden is the meeting place between soul and spirit, where we get a sense of who we are. That's why we need more gardens, especially in cities.

I feel this is a very special place and I want to set up a trust so it goes into the hands of like-minded people when I leave. The reactions of people who visit here are extraordinary. Obviously you could go to more beautiful places, like the Freycinet Peninsula, for instance. This is former sheep country after all. But whether it's the path I've created with my artwork along it, which opens up people's hearts and imaginations to experience it, or the fact that it's right next to Roaring Beach, or multiple factors working together, there is something here that excites people.

I grew up in Detroit. When I was a kid, I remember always wanting to plant a garden. I would take over part of the yard and sometimes I'd put in a flower garden, sometimes a vegetable garden. As well I would go every summer to northern Michigan which was a wilderness experience. There, like here, I didn't have to plant anything, I just had to walk among the trees and the plants and lichen.

I have been in Tasmania fifteen years and what's kept me here is that there is a primordial feeling to the landscape, a sense of deep time where I feel everyone's been here thousands of years.

Before this I had quite a conventional garden, five acres in Kingston just outside Hobart, and I spent a lot of time with it. There was a dam with waterfalls trickling down and I grew all kinds of exotic plants mixed with natives. It all burnt down in a bushfire. So that was five or six years all gone—zip. That was more devastating to me than losing the things in the house because it was alive.

In 1991 I bought this forty hectare property and I decided I didn't want to build again. So I got the bus. I probably wouldn't have bought this piece of land if it hadn't been next to the ocean. There's a real co-joining of forces here, a play between the constantly changing water and the slower change of the trees and the landscape. And I like the contrast, where some days are calm and others are wild.

The land was originally cleared for sheep and had become very degraded. When I first came, there wasn't anything growing here except grasses. All the native vegetation is now coming back. I've had the plants informally inventoried and we found about thirty-five native species just on a quick walk— obviously it could be much more. I put in two dams and became part of Land for Wildlife. I'm not going to develop it or do any agriculture.

What I've tried to do is allow the land to come back in as natural a way as possible. I've extended what's here by planting thousands of trees—callitris, hakeas, banksias, and casuarinas, my favourite. *Allocasuarina verticillata* is the she-oak native to this area and I love its droopy, soft fullness.

What I do is intentionally create vistas by the placement of the benches. You can highlight certain areas and focus a person's attention in a certain direction just as you do in conventional landscaping. I have chosen the places where you'll stop, sit and meditate or talk to the person with you. And you'll take particular images and memories away with you.

The sculptures I create are functional. You can sit on a bench and become part of it while you sit there. It's animated in that sense. The sculptures act to jog the memory. When you are sitting on them, you are reminded you are part of the landscape because they have this sensual organic shape.

I've placed them along the coastal path—I like the Catholic notion of Stations of the Cross—and I plan to have fourteen benches eventually along the pathway so you go on a minor pilgrimage, sit, reflect and talk at each.

By setting my sculptures along the path I'm actually drawing people into the landscape. It can be hard for people to do. They can be quite fearful. There are snakes, ants, fierce sun. But it is also beautiful and can add meaning to our lives, and that's what I want people to see.

The path starts from the little natural grove where the bus is and leads first to the children's grove, a formal ring of South Esk pines (*Callitris oblonga*) which I planted for the children of my friends.

I've gradually widened the pathways to allow people to talk as they walk. It gets narrower as you get into the trees in some parts. There is a little area I cleared of gorse, where I've placed a summer deck, which is probably the nicest view of the coastal heath-type garden.

I have planted native hops and hakeas along the path. There's a *Hakea megadenia* which has soft foliage and a nice colour.

Native currants (*Leucopogon parviflorus*) have established themselves everywhere now the sheep are gone, and you get these wonderful fresh, bright green patches among the grey when you look down to the foothills. They have a fragrant white flower and a little white edible berry. The foothills have no real structure to them. It is kind of nice. They just carry down to the beach.

There are the most beautiful wildflowers which come up through the open areas, where the flat rock is almost like paving stones. I like it when the trigger plants come out.

What I'm getting along the path now is thick walls of banksias and other shrubs. I am cutting it to get a bit of a tunnel sometimes and training the plant walls by chopping them back, so it's almost like a hedged walk. I've placed a bench inside the tunnel and it's like an alcove. It's completely protected from wind and warms up beautifully.

Along the way, because of the effect of the wind, you find stunted versions of forest trees such as remnant blackwoods (*Acacia melanoxylon*). Originally there were blackwood forests to the edge of the cliff, then they were cut down and the she-oaks took over. I'd like to have seen it 200 years ago. And there is a cheesewood (*Pittosporum bicolor*), which is so trim and upright, it's almost like a formal standard.

On the two big hills behind the cliff I have planted big circles of she-oaks. The larger one has 300 trees. It has made an aesthetic impact on the landscape because the rings make a dark defining pattern from a distance.

But the reason I've done it is to create a space within each circle, which I keep mown, for native grasses to grow back. Once that would have been dealt with by fire.

If I didn't do anything, the sags, native currants, banksias and trees would move in one after another and the native grasses would get crowded out. So I thought it would be nice to have a couple of places dedicated just to grasses. Along the wide stretch of open path along the cliff at the bottom of the hill, I have planted a boulevard of she-oaks and South Esk pines.

Then you come to a place which for me has the quality of a Japanese setting. It's on the headland jutting out to sea, facing Wedge Island. The bench here is a sassafras spiral placed on an east-west axis and the salt spray has blackened the wood and I imagine preserves it too.

The long path I have made takes you through several different types of terrain. There is a little gully which collects enough rainfall that you start to get wet sclerophyll vegetation, like the native olives (*Notolaea ligustrina*) and cheesewoods, scribbly bark gums that are bent almost horizontal, and different sorts of grasses and ferns.

I think traditionally there is a barrier mentality to gardening with the landscape in Australia because when the first settlers arrived it was so foreign. It's like in Peter Carey's book *Oscar and Lucinda*, where the man with the Bible carries the Western notion of white spirituality through the landscape and sees nothing, even though all around him are countless worlds and stories. It was the mindset he brought to Australia, and for the most part we are still in that mindset, which is why we clear-fell forests. We still don't see the importance of landscape.

I would like to think it is changing and that the trend towards natural gardening and blending into the landscape will remain part of future gardening— the idea that we don't have to conquer anything, or impose our will on the landscape, we can use what's there. That doesn't mean we have to replicate the natural environment. It's nice to put a human aesthetic in. That's why I made the pathway and put in my own sculptures. But we've got to be more loosely organised, add more mystery to our gardens, make them less formal and planned, allow things to develop more organically. It's a question of simplicity and sympathy in design.

Most people live in cities and I believe they will need to garden in future, to keep sane. There is a real possibility that gardens will be our churches of the future, with a liturgy found in flowers.

OVERLEAF: The undulating form of 'Forest', a weathered Huon pine and myrtle bench sculpture on the edge of the cliff, echoes the movement of the sea. The sculptures are placed at stations along the coastal path.

acknowledgements

Compiling a book on gardens right across Australia was a mammoth task and we were fortunate in enjoying the help and generosity of a large number of people.

Our greatest thanks go to the gardeners and their families who so kindly gave up their time and who have become the subject of the book: Peter Adams, Tony and Anne Bishop, Lindsay and Christine Campbell, Owen and Sally Croft, Guy Cunningham, Murray and Gillian Elliott, Gwen Ford and the late Gordon Ford, Pat and Sonya Gaffney, Forbes and Joanna Gordon, Bob Griffin and Sandra Russell, Ron and Edna Hardman, Nan and Sue Harper, Peter and Clare Heibloem, Noel and Jenny Hine, Merv and Olwyn Hodge, Mark and Cate Hohnen, Dennis and Patrice Hundscheidt, Barbara Jennings, Colin and Liana Joyce, Trevor and Christina Kennedy, David and Jill Kepert, Margot Knox, Ruth Leitch, James and Barbara Litchfield, Hugh and Gina Livingston, William and Robyn Martin, John and Dianne McClelland, Michael and Karen McCoy, Geoff and Kaye Miers, Annie Moorhouse, Fairie Nielsen, Robert and Jane O'Halloran, Phillip O'Malley and Aldo Muia, Gunther and Gitta Rembel, Dennis and Yvonne Richardson, Tony and Kerrie Robinson, Saxon and Penny Rudduck, Stephen Ryan and Craig Lidgerwood, Bruce and Meg Simmons, Michael and June Stafford, Andrew and Minnie Thomas, Paul Thompson, Malcolm and Thelma Vandepeer, Jeanne Villani, James and Luki Weatherly, and Graham Wilson.

Tamie Fraser, the president of Australia's Open Garden Scheme, and the Board of Directors have been consistently supportive of this project and have made the Scheme's network and resources available to us.

Our colleagues past and present on the staff of the Scheme around Australia have been imaginative, helpful and patient in providing original lists of gardens and in undertaking early research. Without their knowledge, this book would not have happened. We would like to thank Mary Klestadt, Merilyn Kuchel, Kate Main, Jan Davis and Nicole Paine, Kellie Penfold, Noela Shepherd, Beth Stokes, Lynne Walker and Barb Wickes. We are particularly grateful to Jenny Large at the Scheme's National Office for her many kindnesses.

We would like to thank the following people: Di Cox, Liz Gow, David and Janet Hopkins, Andrew and Carolyn Quixley, Sandra and Philip Redman and Valerest Yencken.

From the outset, we realised that the quality of the information would depend as much on the interviewers as on their subjects, and to the following enlightened and persistent interviewers who above all were very good listeners we owe a deep debt of gratitude: Shelley Dark, Trisha Dixon, Merilyn Kuchel, Lainie Lawson, Fiona Ogilvie and Noela Shepherd.

Our grateful thanks to Dr Roger Spencer of the Royal Botanic Gardens Melbourne who steered us through the complexities of botanical nomenclature.

In a book such as this, the images are all important and we have been very fortunate in having at our disposal the talents of several masters of the lens: Leigh Clapp, Trisha Dixon, Mike Gillam, John Hay, Merv Hodge, Geoff Lea, Alex Makeyev, Annie Mayo, Michael McCoy, David Sandison, Marg Thornell and Gerry Whitmont.

By the sort of good fortune that has characterised this project, we were introduced to Margedd Heliosz, who brought dedication and good humour to the task of transcribing the mountain of taped material.

Our publisher and editors Sue Hines, Foong Ling Kong and Neil Conning have been a great pleasure to work with, and we hope that this book will repay their faith, indulgence and patience.

A special thanks to Sue Harrison, whose out-of-hours 'courier service' saved many trips to and from Allen & Unwin's offices.

In our designer Ruth Grüner, we have been fortunate in having someone who responded sympathetically to both the text and pictures.

picture credits

LEIGH CLAPP: pages *viii*, 82–3, 104, 106, 133, 135, 136–37, 171, 172, 174

TRISHA DIXON: pages *i*, *ii*, 5, 8, 9, 10, 12, 32, 59, 60, 62, 152–53, 176, 178, 179, 181, 182–83, 184, 186, 194, 196, 210, 213, 243, 246, 247

MIKE GILLAM: pages 198, 200, 202, 203, 204–5

JOHN HAY: pages 16, 17, 19, 37, 38, 41, 116–17, 138, 140–41, 155, 156, 158, 216–17

MERV HODGE: pages 236, 240

GEOFF LEA: pages *vi*, 2–3, 26, 29, 30, 44–5, 52, 56, 57, 208–9, 220, 222, 225, 249, 252–53, 260

MICHAEL MCCOY: pages 64–5

ALEX MAKEYEV: pages 47, 49, 50–1, 76, 78, 128, 130, 131, 161, 162, 166, 167, 169, 232, 234

ANNIE MAYO: pages 21, 22, 34, 35, 118, 121, 123, 124, 188, 190

DAVID SANDISON: pages 85, 87, 88, 90, 93, 95, 96, 98, 100, 101, 110–11, 146, 149, 241

MARG THORNELL: pages 70, 73, 74

GERRY WHITMONT: pages 227, 228

conversion table

Many gardeners continue to express measurements in imperial rather than metric terms. This is particularly the case with rainfall and property size, the latter possibly due to the traditional Australian town block of a quarter acre. Here is a simple conversion table.

length and area

1 inch = 25 millimetres

1 foot = 0.3 metres

1 yard = 0.9 metres

1 mile = 1.6 kilometres

1 acre = 0.4 hectares

temperature

°C	°F
–10	14
–5	23
0	32
5	41
10	50
15	59
20	68
25	77
30	86
35	95
40	104
45	113

We have not included climate zones as it became clear from our research that this would be more misleading than helpful.

index

Acacia
   aneura 201
   cognata 'Green Mist' 62
   estrophiolata 201
   hakeoides 218
   implexa 219
   iteaphylla 199
   jennerae 199
   kempeana 201
   melanoxylon 251
   murrayana 201
   paradoxa 233
   pendula 185
   pycnantha 233
   rotundifolia 218
   sclerophylla 235
Acer japonicum 'Aconitifolium' 70
Achillea
   'Hoffnung' 65
   'Terracotta' 41, 65
Actinotus helianthi 238
Adams, Peter 207, 248
Aeonium arboreum 36
Agave attenuata 86
Agonis flexuosa 'Nana' 34, 126, 246
Airlie Beach 145
Alba 84–8
Alice Springs 151, 197–205
Allamanda carthartica 92
Allocasuarina verticillata 39, 250
Alocasia x *amazonica* 113
Aloe barbadensis 86
Alphitonia excelsa 238
Alyogyne huegelii 230
Ananas sp. 86
Angophora bakeri 218
Anigozanthos spp. 229
Anopterus glandulosus 224
Aphanopetalum resinosum 218
Apponyi, Sylvio 242, 247
Araucaria
   bidwillii 36, 107
   cunninghamii 88
Archontophoenix alexandrae 134
Arecastrum romanzoffianum 86, 98, 107, 134
Artemisia
   ludoviciana 65
   'Powis Castle' 157, 164, 192
Arts and Crafts Movement 39
Arundo donax 40
Ashfield 1, 25–30
Atalaya hemiglauca 201

Atherosperma moschatum 247
Athrotaxis selaginoides 224
Austin, David 22, 48, 49, 196
Australian Plant Society *see* Society for Growing Australian Plants

Bacchus Marsh 154
Bambusa balcooa 107
Banksia lemanniana 229
Bannockburn 154
Barmera 160
Barragán, Luis 224
Barry Humphries' Treasury of Australian Kitsch 34
Bayview 105
Beaufortia squarrosa 233
Beaumontia grandiflora 92
Berberis thunbergii
   'Atropurpurea Nana' 59
Bicknell, Alex 19
Bishop, Anne 170
Blandfordia nobilis 247
Blayney 58
Bligh, Beatrice 173, 174, 195
Bodnant 125
Bonney, Neville 168
Boolooroo 151, 175, 185–86
Boronia citriodora 224
Bossiaea aquifolium 125
Brachychiton sp. 148
   acerifolius 113
   gregorii 199
   populneus 173, 185
Brachyglottis brunonis 223
Bracteantha subundulata 219
Braidwood 4
Brinkhurst 115, 122–26
Brown, Capability 214
Buchan, John 54
Buddleia
   alternifolia 27
   crispa 40
   salviifolia 40
Burnie 53
Burleigh Waters 84
Bussell, Alfred and Ellen 33

Caesalpinia ferrea 113
Calandrinia balonensis 199
Callistemon 'White Anzac' *iv*
Callitris oblonga 250
Calothamnus quadrifidus 229
Campbell, Lindsay 207, 221

Carey, Peter 251
Carramar 207, 215–19
Cassia fistula 180
Casuarina
   cunninghamiana 173
   glauca 218, 244
Centaurea montana 'Alba' 29
Centranthus ruber 5
Ceratopetalum apetalum 105
Ceratostigma willmottianum 13
Cestrum nocturnum 179
Chambers, Carrick 66
Chamelaucium sp. 189
   megapetalum 235
   uncinatum 235
Chatto, Beth 61, 62, 74
Cherry Tree 1, 20–4
Church, Thomas 68, 224
Cinnamomum camphora 144
Cistus salviifolius 126
Clark, Alister 157
Clayfield 88
Clematis
   aristata 218
   microphylla 218
climate zones 97
colour, use of 22, 24, 33, 48, 64, 74, 79, 112, 130, 135, 147, 192
Combadello 151, 174, 175, 177–79, 186
Convention in Trade of Endangered Species 103
Convolvulus sabatius 164
Cooma 192
Cooramilla 43, 58–62
Cordyline kaspar 37
Cormus kousa var. *chinensis* 53
Corymbia
   aparrerinja 199
   calophylla 122, 229
Cotoneaster dammeri 163, 164
Cottee, Barbara 62
Croft, Sally 11
Culzean 54
Cunningham, Guy 145
Cuphea 'Mad Hatter' 113
Cupressus
   sempervirens 185
   torulosa 43
Cyclamen hederifolium 13
Cymbopogon ambiguus 198, 199
Cyperus alternifolius 70

Dahlia 'Clarion' 64

Dalvui 39
Dampiera lavandulacea 230
Danthonia carphoides 224
Darlington 226
Darwinia oldfieldii 235
Davidia involucrata 56
Davidsonia pruriens var.
    pruriens 113, 247
Delaney, Tofer 225
Dendrobium linguiforme 238
Di Marco, Charlie 229
Diospyros kaki 125
Dodonea sinuolata 218, 235
Domaine Du Castellet 115, 145–49
Donges, Brian 108
Doryanthes
    excelsa 40
    palmeri 40
Down to Earth 173
Dracaena marginata 'Tricolor' 86
Dryandra 207, 231–35
Dryandra
    drummondii 235
    polycephala 235
    praemorsa 230
    sessilis 230
Duneira 71
Dural 132
Duranta repens 'Sheena's Gold' 112

Echium pininana 40
Education of a Gardener, The 24, 186
Elaeagnus angustifolia 27, 157
Elaeocarpus
    cyaneus 245
    reticulatus 219
Elliott, Gillian 81, 89
Eltham 211
Enchylaena tomentosa 198
Englishwoman's Garden, The 54
Ensete ventricosum sp. 138
Eremophila
    bignoniiflora 199
    christophori 199
    glabra 'Kalbarri Carpet' 200
Eriostemon myoporoides 247
Eucalyptus
    botryoides 214
    bridgesiana 173
    caesia 235
    calophylla Rosea 229
    camaldulensis 185, 201
    christophori 201
    citriodora 169, 185, 214
    coccifera 224
    eximia 218
    fasciculosa 168
    gammophylla 201
    haemastoma 134
    leucoxylon ssp. *leucoxylon* 233
    maculata 112, 185
    mannifera ssp. *maculosa* 219
    marginata 122

    melliodora 173
    microtheca 177
    obliqua 71, 221, 223, 224
    orbifolia 199
    polyanthemos 214
    polyclada 201
    salubris 235
    sargentii 192
    sideroxylon 212
    sideroxylon 'Rosea' 177
    tereticornis 247
    viminalis 39, 57
    websteriana 199
Eucharis x grandiflora 86
Eucryphia spp. 224
Eudlo Cycads 99–103
Eupatorium maculatum 'Gateway' 64
Euphorbia
    characias ssp. *wulfenii* 126
    cyparissias 27
    rigida 27

Ficus
    microcarpa var. *hillii* 147
    platypoda 238
Flindersia maculosa 218
foliage, use of 40, 74, 112, 130
Ford, Bill 199
Ford, Gordon 139, 144, 207, 211
Fox, Lindsay and Paula 66
Frederiksen, Harry 55
Fremantle 119
Fülling 211–14

Gaffney, Pat 115, 119–21
Gaillardia 'Mandarin' 64
Galbraith, Jean 66
garden design 39, 40, 57, 67–8, 72, 88,
    98, 107, 120, 125, 129–30, 134,
    144, 157, 212, 214, 224
Garden Within, The 186
Gardens in the Modern Landscape 214
Gardner, Charlie 230
Gardners Bay 221
Geijera parviflora 185
Geitonoplesium cymosum 218
Geranium pratense 28
Gibson, Peter 59
Glasson, Pam 195
Gordon, Charlotte 6
Gordon, Hugh 4, 6
Gordon, Joanna 1, 4
Great Dixter 30, 66
Great Southern District 20
Grevillea
    baileyana 238
    banksii 233, 239, 241
    bipinnatifida 230, 239
    bronwynae 241
    dryandri 241
    endlicheriana 230
    flexuosa 235
    'Forest Bright' 239

    formosa 239, 240, 241
    goodii 241
    juncifolia 233
    longistyla 239
    'Long John' 233
    'Moonlight' 239
    nudiflora 239
    refracta 233
    robusta 179, 214, 238
    'Robyn Gordon' 203
    rosmarinifolia 214
    'Royal Mantle' 239, 247
    'Ruby Red' 241
    saccata 230
    'Strawberry Blonde' 239
    'Superb' 239
    synaphea 230
    thelemanniana 230
    venusta 239
    whiteana 239
Griffin, Bob 43, 58
Guilfoyle, William 1, 36, 39–41
Gymnoschoenus sphaerocephalus 224

Hadlington, Phil 107–8
Hakea
    megadenia 251
    orthorryncha 230, 235
    victoriae 228
Hamilton Island 109, 112
Hardman, Edna 175, 180
Harper, Nan 207, 226
Hascombe 66
Hedges, The 154, 159
Hedychium coronarium 91
Heibloem, Peter 81, 99
Heliconias psittacorum 147
Helleborus foetidus 'Wester Flisk' 70
Hestercombe 125
Hibiscus
    cannabinum 40
    syriacus 77
Hidcote 28, 125
Hine, Jenny 154, 157, 159
Hodge, Merv 207, 237
Hohnen, Cate 31
Horse Island 207, 242–47
Hosta
    fortunei var. *albopicta* 27
    sieboldiana 27
Hundscheidt, Dennis 81, 94–8
Hylocereus undatus 91
Hymenosporum flavum 247
Hyophorbe
    lagenicaulis 86
    verschaffeltii 88
Hypocalymma angustifolium 229

Illalangi Villa 81, 109–13
International Cordyline Society 97
Ipomoea horsfalliae 92
Isopogon dawsonii 235
Irvine, Susan 49

Jasminum mesnyi 14
Jellicoe, Geoffrey 214
Jennings, Barbara 1, 25
Jenolen 151, 154, 157
Joyce, Colin and Liana 215
Justicia
      brandegeana 106
      kempeana 199

Karabine 151, 187–92
Kennedia
      nigricans 230
      prostrata 230
Kennedy, Christina 242
Kepert, Jill 122
Kiftsgate 28
Kniphofia 'Maid of Orleans' 65
Knox, Alistair 139, 142–44, 212, 214
Knox, Margot 115, 139, 212
Kolreuteria paniculata 24
Kunzea
      jucunda 235
      sericea 230

Lagarostrobus franklinii 224
Lambe, David 27
Lees-Milne, Alvilde 54
Leitch, Ruth 175, 177, 186
Lepidozamia hopei 102
Leptospermum
      'Pink Cascade' 180
      'Rubrum' iv
      rupestre 224
Leucopogon parviflorus 251
Limonium perezii 157
Litchfield, Barbara 193
Litchfield, James 195
Livingston, Hugh 175, 185
Livistona chinensis 113
Lloyd, Christopher 66, 67, 68, 74
Logan Reserve 237
Lomandra
      longifolia 241
      multiflora 241
Lonicera
      fragrantissima 192
      nitida 'Aurea' 159
Lord, Ernest 212
Luma apiculata 33
Lutyens, Edwin 125
Lysimachia clethroides 60

Macarthur, Mary 6
Macdonnell Ranges 201
Mackay, Jock and Janette 6
McClelland, Dianne 151, 160
McCoy, Michael 43, 63–8
McDiven, Bryant 192
McDiven, Tedye 191
McLaren Vale 75
McVinney, Hamish 71
Magnolia
      campbellii 55

      grandiflora 48
Malus toringoides 157
Manar 1, 4–8
Mandevilla sanderi 86, 88
Margaret River 31
Marsh, Eliza 13
Marsh, Matthew 13
Martin, William 1, 36
Marx, Roberto Burle 98
Massy, Joan 195
Mayo, Robbie 244
Melaleuca
      elliptica 229
      glomerata 202, 203
      huegelii 219
      hypericifolia 229, 242, 247
      incana 246
      'Robin Redbreast' iv
Melia azedarach 198, 199, 218
Melianthus major 27
Merriwa 170
Mespilus germanica 157
Micromyrtus 247
Miers, Geoff 151, 196, 199
Miscanthus sinensis 'Gracillimus' 64
Mona 6
Moorhouse, Annie 151, 165
Moree 151, 175–86
Mortlake 15
Mosaic Garden 115, 138–44
Mount Macedon 63, 69, 71
Mount Noorat 36, 37
Mount Wilson 55
Murraya paniculata 147
Myalla 151, 193–96
Myporum parvifolium 245
Myrabluan 151, 170–74
Myriocephalus stuartii 203
Myrsine africana 192

Nielsen, Fairie 43, 53
Nepeta 'Six Hills Giant' 64
Norwood 127
Nothofagus cunninghamii 224
Notolaea ligustrina 251
Nubeena 248

Oasis Gardens 81, 97
Oscar and Lucinda 251
O'Halloran, Jane 1, 20
O'Halloran, Lottie 23
Olea europaea 185
Olearia paniculata 40
O'Malley, Phillip 81, 84
Onopordum acanthium 70
Ozothamnus ledifolius 224

Padthaway 164
Page, Russell 24, 186, 195
Palm and Cycad Association
      of Australia 97
Pandanus tectorius 147
Pandorea

'Golden Bells' 247
      pandorana 203
Parramatta 6
Pejar Park 173
Perovskia 'Blue Spire' 157
Pfeiffer, Andrew 115, 134, 135
Pfeiffer, Judy 195
Phebalium daviesii 224
Phillyrea latifolia 8
Phoenix canariensis 177
Phormium
      cookianum 40
      tenax 40, 129, 130
Pigeon Hill 43, 53–7
Pimelea ferruginea 230
Pistachio chinensis 24
Pittosporum bicolor 251
Plectranthus argentatus 125
Pleiogynium solandri 148
Plumbago auriculata 120, 164, 185, 189
Poa labillardieri 221, 224
Podocarpus elatus 86
Pomaderris racemosa 219
Populus simonii 120, 157
Powis Castle (Wales) 67
Prunus 'Elvins' 126
Pyrostegia venusta 149
Pyrus
      nivalis 157
      pyrifolia 157
      salicifolia 'Pendula' 8
      ussuriensis 8, 126, 129

rainforest 105, 108
Rembel, Gitta 132
Reverie 115, 132–37
Rhagodia spinescens 164, 198
Rhododendron ponticum 54
Rhoeo 'Hawaiian Dwarf' 86
Richardson, Dennis 43, 75–9
Ricinus communis 34, 164
Rippon Lea 66
Robinia pseudoacacia 'Frisia' 22
Robinson, Kerrie 151, 187
Rockdale 151, 175, 180–83
rocks, use of 144, 191, 213, 214
Roleystone 122
Rosa, rose
      'Albertine' 7, 22
      'Ambridge Rose' 47
      'Autumn Delight' 49
      'Autumnalis' 192
      'Bishop Darlington' 49
      'Blossomtime' 49
      'Bonica' 47
      'Bredon' 47
      'Bridal Pink' 125
      'Canary Bird' 23, 48
      'Canterbury' 8
      'Carabella' 157
      'Céline Forestier' 22
      'Clair Matin' 49
      'Claret Cup' 157

'Comte de Chambord' 24
'Constance Spry' 49
'Cornelia' 48, 163
'Courier' 157
'Dark Lady' 48
'Dorothy Perkins' 191
'Duchesse d'Angoulême' 24
'Duchesse de Brabant' 163
foetida 'Persiana' 48
forrestiana 49
'Francis E. Lester' 166
'Frau Dagmar Hastrup' 49
'French Lace' 47
glauca 49
'Glenara' 157
'Golden Vision' 157
'Gay Vista' 157
'Gruss an Aachen' 48
'Heritage' 196
'Iceberg' 8, 33, 126, 129
'Kathleen Harrop' 49, 126
'La Ville de Bruxelles' 24
'Lady Huntingfield' 157
'Lamarque' 48, 196
'Leander' 49
'Little White Pet' 157
'Lorraine Lee' 34
'Meg' 49, 180
'Milkmaid' 157
'Mme Alfred Carrière' 49
'Mme Isaac Pereire' 192
moyesii 'Geranium' 49
'Mrs Richard Turnbull' 157, 159
'Nozomi' 49
'Old Blush' 13
'Ophelia' 49
'Penelope' 48
'Pinkie' 47, 49
'Pristine' 47
'Ringlet' 157
'Sarah van Fleet' 192
'Seduction' 47
'Sombreuil' 49
'Souvenir de la Malmaison' 192
spinosissima 'Single Cherry' 49
'Tarrawarra' 157
'Temora' 47
'The Countryman' 47
'Traverser' 157
'William Lobb' 163
xanthina f. *spontanea* 48
'Yellow Button' 22
'Yellow Charles Austin' 126
'Zéphirine Drouhin' 49
Ross, Deane 169
Royal Botanic Gardens
   Melbourne 36, 39
Rudduck, Penny 115, 127–31
Russelia equisetiformis 200
Russell's Camp 165–69
Ryan, Stephen 43, 69

Sackville-West, Vita 92

Salisbury Court 1, 11–14
Salix x. erythroflexuosa 70
Salvia
   azurea 64
   'Cyclamen' 79
   uliginosa 185
Santalum acuminatum 203
Sandy Bay 24
Sansevieria trifasciata 130
Sarcostemma australe 200
Scabiosa 'Butterfly Blue' 59
Schefflera
   actinophylla 147
   arboricola 'Jacqueline' 112
Schinus molle 177, 185
Scholtzia oligandra 235
Seager, Tony 107
Seddon, George 214
Sedum
   'Autumn Joy' 64
   spectabile 19
Senecio serpens 22, 24
Shaw, Harvey 238
Simmons, Bruce 197, 201–3
Sissinghurst 28, 67, 125
Sisyrinchium striatum 13, 23, 126
Smith, Joan Law 186
Smith, Roy 91
Society for Growing Australian
   Plants 201, 215, 233, 238
Sophora toromiro 72
Sorn, The 207, 221–25
South African Cycad Society 102
Stafford, June 151, 154, 157, 159
Stenocarpus sinuatus 238
Stirling 46
Strelitzia nicolai 23, 138
Stylidium bulbiferum 229
Stones, Ellis 115, 139, 143–44, 212
Strong, Roy 129
Sunnybank 94, 97
Swainsona formosa 203
Syzygium australe 113, 247

Tamarix aphylla 177
Tan Jung Sari 89–93
Tea Tree Gully 231
Telekia speciosa 60
Telopea speciosissima 244
Templestowe 215
Teucrium
   betonicum 40
   fruticans 164
Thirty Nine Steps, The 54
Thomas, Minnie 43, 46–9
Thomasia
   grandiflora 235
   macrocarpa 230
   macrocarpa ssp.
      dacyphyllum 218
Thompson, Paul 207, 215
Thomson, Colin 31, 33
Thryptomene saxicola 235

Thunbergia grandiflora 'Alba' 92
Thymophylla sp. 113
Toona australis 185, 218
Trachelospermum jasminoides 92, 130
Tropical Garden Design 88
Tugurium 43, 69–74
Tulbaghia violacea 86
Tunnard, Christopher 214

Uralla 11

Valder, Peter 55
van Sweden, James 225
Vandepeer, Thelma 207, 231
Verbena bonariensis 64
Verey, Rosemary 54
Verticordia chrysantha 227
Viburnum
   macrocephelum f. *macrocephelum*
      'Sterile' 72
   opulus 8
Vigna caracalla 76, 77
Villani, Jeanne 105
Vineyard, The 6

Wallcliffe House 1, 31–5
Walling, Edna 18, 39, 144, 151, 186,
   191, 195, 212
Washingtonia filifera 177
water and garden design 120, 134,
   173–74
Waterfall Cottage 81, 104–8
Weatherly, Luki 15
Weatherly, Patricia 18
Westringia brevifolia 244
Whitley 244
Wigandia 1, 36–41
Wigandia caracasana 40
Wijaya, Made (Michael White) 88
Wildflower Society 230
Wilson, Graham 109
Windgrove 248–51
Woodburn 54
Woodend 63
woodland-style gardens 39
Woolongoon 1, 15–19
Wright, Frank Lloyd 212
Wyemando 207, 226–30

Xanthorrhoea sp. 113
   australis 168
   preissii 126
   quadrangulata 233
   semiplana 233
Xanthostemon chrysanthus 238

York 187

Zephryanthes
   candida 86, 90
   grandiflora 86

Peter Adams on his sassafras spiral log.